Battle of the Odon

Battle of the Odon

GEORGES BERNAGE
Translated by Heather Williams

Pen & Sword
MILITARY

First published by Editions Heimdal in 2008 as *La Bataille de l'Odon*

First published in Great Britain in 2017 by
Pen & Sword Military
An imprint of
Pen & Sword Books Ltd
47 Church Street
Barnsley
South Yorkshire
S70 2AS

ISBN 978 1 47385 761 2

Typeset by Aura Technology and Software Services, India
Printed and bound in China
By Imago Publishing Ltd.

Pen & Sword Books Ltd incorporates the Imprints of Pen & Sword Books Archaeology, Atlas, Aviation, Battleground, Discovery, Family History, History, Maritime, Military, Naval, Politics, Railways, Select, Transport, True Crime, Fiction, Frontline Books, Leo Cooper, Praetorian Press, Seaforth Publishing, Wharncliffe and White Owl.

For a complete list of Pen & Sword titles please contact
PEN & SWORD BOOKS LIMITED
47 Church Street, Barnsley, South Yorkshire, S70 2AS, England
E-mail: enquiries@pen-and-sword.co.uk
Website: www.pen-and-sword.co.uk

Contents

Foreword

Author's note

The Battle of Normandy is one of the most famous campaigns in the Second World War, with the infamous D-Day landings, popularised by such films as *The Longest Day*, perhaps the most vivid in the general public's mind. While certainly not an historical document, the film has certainly made the events of this decisive day familiar to many. As well as 6 June 1944, there also exists a collective memory regarding the dramatic events surrounding the 'Falaise Pocket'. However, the fighting that took place between 6 June and the end of the campaign was so difficult and intense, that at one point the American command believed the Allies would never escape from the *bocage* [farmland criss-crossed by dense hedgerows, trees and sunken roads, which is typically associated with the Normandy landscape]. Operation Epsom is emblematic of those first weeks, when the belief was that anything was possible and that victory could still be achieved swiftly.

In the days following the invasion, the Allies were in a race: their aim being to bring in more men and equipment than the Germans could supply reinforcements, not to mention the fact that the enemy were hampered by the incessant harassment of the allied invasion. The Americans quickly seized the Cotentin Peninsula, which constituted a large bridge-head, although at the same time, the British Second Army did not meet with similar success. By the evening of 6 June it had been halted in front of its primary objective, the city of Caen, and it would be another month before the city was finally taken. However, it is true that the US First Army had mainly come up against static infantry divisions, which were often of inferior quality, while in the British sector, two panzer divisions began to counter attack on 7 June: the 21. Panzer-Division and in particular the 12. SS-Panzer-Division 'Hitlerjugend', were elite fighting units that would soon demonstrate their outstanding military capabilities.

These two panzer divisions were quickly joined by another elite division, the Panzer-Lehr-Division, as well as the 2. Panzer-Division, which would arrive in the American sector. They were followed by a battalion of Tiger tanks, the s.SS-Panzer-Abteilung 101, which accidentally ended up blocking the British offensive at Villers-Bocage on 13 June. Montgomery was determined to re-launch the failed offensive and resolved to reach and then cross the Orne river and take Caen from the south. Decoded German messages revealed that reinforcements were due to arrive, including the II. SS-Panzerkorps, meaning that the Allies had to act quickly, and so Operation Epsom was born.

Three infantry divisions, an armoured division and two armoured brigades were sent to the left flank of the *Hitlerjugend* Division. The balance of power appeared to be crushingly in favour of the British and a swift victory seemed at hand. However, the soldiers of the *Hiterjugend* fought with an astonishing determination and the British soon fell behind: clearly, lessons from the earlier Blitzkrieg had not been learned. The offensive had been led by infantrymen carrying bayonets and guns, supported by tanks, just as they had been in 1918. General Roberts' armoured division had to wait a day and a half before it was able to join in, which allowed the Germans to fall back to Hill 112 and halt the offensive, as well as allowing reinforcements to arrive. It was no longer simply an army corps (which involved around 80,000 men or even 100,000 if you include the 49th Division) against a German regiment, and now that the enemy had aligned its forces, the battle turned into a stalemate. Most of the units would fall back, in part, but Hill 112 would remain fiercely disputed until the end of the Battle of Normandy, after the Germans finally decided to withdraw.

Although the offensive was clearly a failure, it was later presented as being merely a feint: Montgomery had allegedly set a trap for the Germans whereby their panzers were drawn to the area around Caen, thus allowing the Americans an easier advance towards the west of Saint-Lô. Although this was undeniably a lie, it was true that General Montgomery was a proud man and it was this constant desire to 'beat' his American allies in Europe that led to other failures. The first of these was the offensive at Villers-Bocage on 13 June, followed by Operation Epsom. Caen would eventually fall on 7 July, but only after considerable help from the Canadians. Operation Goodwood was another of Montgomery's failures, resulting in the loss of half of his tanks without any successful breakthrough, later followed by Operation Market Garden on 17 September, which ended in a humiliating retreat.

With Operation Epsom, Montgomery wanted a quick victory that involved crossing the Orne and capturing Caen. However, on 29 June his disappointment must have been as great as that of General O'Connor [who was tasked with leading Operation Epsom] when he was forced to stop the offensive. The operation was not expected to fail, even though the terrain was unfavourable and the road network leading from north to south was inadequate (the main axis led from east to west), but progress had remained too slow, especially in such a narrow perimeter.

The area is now haunted by history and the local names resonate in French minds like the names of other famous battles in history: Fontenay, Tessel, Rauray, Saint-Manvieu, Cheux, Le Haut du Bosq, Brettevillette, Grainville, Colleville, Tourville, Mouen, Mondrainville, Tourmauville, Gavrus, Baron, Esquay and, of course, Hill 112. The terrain can be traversed easily and the distances between the various locations are short. I have visited the area often over the last thirty years, along with veterans who have shown me the places where they fought. What is striking is the density of the areas where action took place: something seemed to have happened every hundred metres, which the following pages will demonstrate. Once you have read this book, you can visit these places where history took place, and they will never leave you. At each junction, each hedge corner, you will discover the actors of this story, never forgetting, of course, that civilians also often found themselves caught up in the battle. Indeed, their losses were equal to those in the military: 20,000 civilians in Normandy lost their lives, which although a little less than those of the American soldiers, is certainly more than those in the British Army. The reconstructed houses serve as a reminder of the extent of the destruction. The village of Cheux, for example, was at the heart of the battle and fifteen of its inhabitants lost their lives.

This photo was taken on 28 June 1944 by Major Stewart and shows Churchill tanks from 7th RTR engaged in a counter-attack between Rauray and Le Haut du Bosq, after the *Kampfgruppe* Weidinger had arrived to reinforce this sector. This mass of tanks in the middle of wheat fields should not mask the fact that General Montgomery was already losing the speed race he had envisaged. (IWM B 6114)

The account of the battle given here is very detailed, thanks to the testimonies of many veterans from both sides, but also those of civilians. The testimony of Hans Siegel, whose exceptional account is spread continuously over twenty-four hours, and has been used by almost all historians of this campaign, is included here in full. On the other hand, there will always be murky areas that will never be made fully clear, due either to the lack of testimony from survivors, or the fact that there were not many survivors to begin with. Thirty years ago, when I first began to take an interest in this campaign, several thoughts came to my mind. The first was that the operation name made it sound like a horse race (which it certainly was not). The second was that how could the Odon valley, which is very deep and wooded, be such an idyllic location while at the same time be described as the 'Valley of Death', after what had taken place at Hill 112? I also read the incredible reports by Major Stewart describing the attack on Saint-Manvieu by the 6th Royal Scots Fusiliers. The photographs and film of these events also form the origin of a collection of albums, each containing thousands of photographs.

It was at this time, during the anniversary season (June and July), that I would stay near Bayeux and its memorial museum and regularly meet with veterans, including key players in the battle. At that time there was an abundance of available eye-witness accounts, as more and more veterans retired and were keen to talk to one another, often returning to the battlefield every year. Many of them still had bits of shell and shrapnel in their bodies; souvenirs to remind them of the past. One man told me that the shrapnel he'd been struck by on Hill 112 still attracted him, like a magnet, to the place where so many of his fellow soldiers had lost their lives. This influx of veterans, which was almost wave-like as they were often in groups, did not always allow for any historical background work. However, their testimonies have given us an abundance of material that allows us to present a day-to-day narrative with an often astonishing precision. These places are haunted not only by the memories of the missing, but also by those who survived, who now in their turn, are disappearing too. These six days of the Battle of the Odon remain a memorable page in the story of the Battle of Normandy and deserve to be rediscovered and take their place in the nation's collective memory. A second narrative devoted to the fighting on Hill 112 follows this work, and continues the story of the Battle of the Odon.

Georges Bernage,
Historian and Editor
Damigny, 20 March 2008

Did Montgomery keep the panzers around Caen?

We know that Operation Epson was expected to succeed in breaking through the German front line and capturing Caen and the area beyond: there were no further obstacles behind the *Hitlerjugend* Division should the line be breached. To their great surprise, the breakthrough was so slow that it allowed the Germans to recover easily. The historiography favourable towards General Montgomery provided an explanation for this breakdown of the 'operation that couldn't fail': it was actually a feint to keep the panzers around Caen. We will see later that this was not his intention, but was it nevertheless a happy consequence?

After Operation Epsom, at the beginning of July the state of the military forces appeared to confirm this view. Around Caen, from west to east, three panzer divisions were in line: the 12. SS-Panzer-Division *Hitlerjugend*, the 21. Panzer-Division, and elements from 1. SS-Panzer-Division '*Leibstandarte*' (which was in the process of joining the front line), as well as two battalions of Tiger tanks: the s.SS-Panzer-Abteilung 101, and s.Panzer-Abteilung 503. The units had just been joined by II.SS-Panzerkorps, with two new panzer divisions: the 9. SS-Panzer-Division '*Hohenstaufen*' and the 10. SS-Panzer-Division '*Frundsberg*', as well as another heavy battalion, the s.SS-Panzer-Abteilung 102. This new armoured corps was intended to provide a counter-attack, and not for the role it would eventually end up playing near Hill 112. The commander of Panzergruppe West, General Leo Geyr von Schweppenburg, only wanted to use these armoured units for limited operations in order to preserve its attacking force, and as of 30 June, he wanted to remove the panzer divisions from the Caen front, but there were no infantry divisions to facilitate this at the time. What's more, by that evening the Panzer-Lehr-Division, which was facing the British Second Army, was relieved by the newly-arrived 276. Infanterie-Division in order to move towards the American front line.

Facing the British were therefore: four panzer divisions, three battalions of Tiger tanks and a further panzer division (1st SS Panzer Division), which was heading towards the front.

Facing the First US Army from 1 July (from west to east) were: the 2. SS-Panzer-Division '*Das Reich*', the 17. SS-Panzergrenadier-Division '*Götz von Berlichingen*',

Another photograph by Major Stewart, also taken on 28 June, shows a Churchill tank from 7th RTR (note the tactical number 99 at the back) supporting an infantry counter-attack near Rauray. Operation Epsom was particularly well-documented by British military photographers, testifying to the importance it had for Montgomery. (IWM B 6123)

the 5. Fallschirmjäger-Division, and the Panzer-Lehr-Division, which arrived as reinforcements. It was these powerful forces that held the narrow strip of land at the base of the Cotentin peninsula. The area around Saint-Lô was also held by an elite unit; the soldiers of the 3. Fallschirmjäger-Division, who were reinforced by a brigade of assault guns. On the left flank, in the area around Caumont, the Americans faced the 2. Panzer-Division. This all added up to three armoured divisions, a 'panzergrenadier' division and two parachute divisions with an armoured brigade in support. There were consequently five elite German divisions in the US sector and five (or six) facing the British. The gap between was small, especially as at that time the Americans preferred to keep their armoured divisions in reserve, while the British were quick to engage their armoured support. The fact that the Americans had such formidable opponents is reflected in the amount of casualties suffered, which was greater than that of the British. Montgomery had never intended and was unable to keep the panzers around Caen in order to relieve the Americans, so this is nothing but a myth. It must also not be forgotten that the Americans did not break through the front line against these elite troops, but rather pulverised it under a carpet of bombs using a division of worn-out panzers.

Normandy in mourning: the Battle of Normandy's civilian victims
The euphoria of the Liberation and the achievements of the Allied soldiers meant that for a long time, the heavy losses suffered by the people of Normandy remained in the shadows. The victims mostly died during the allied bombing raids,

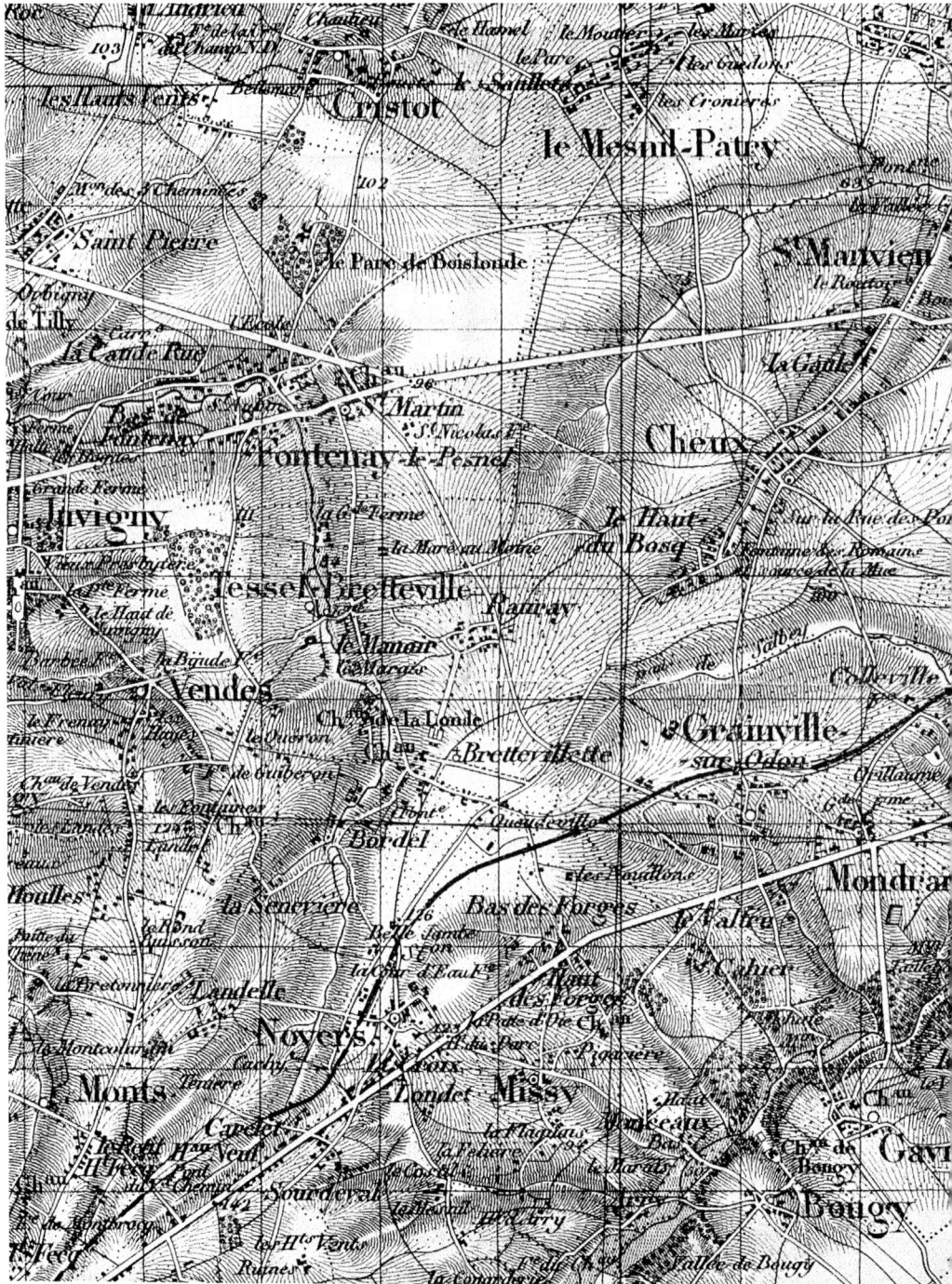

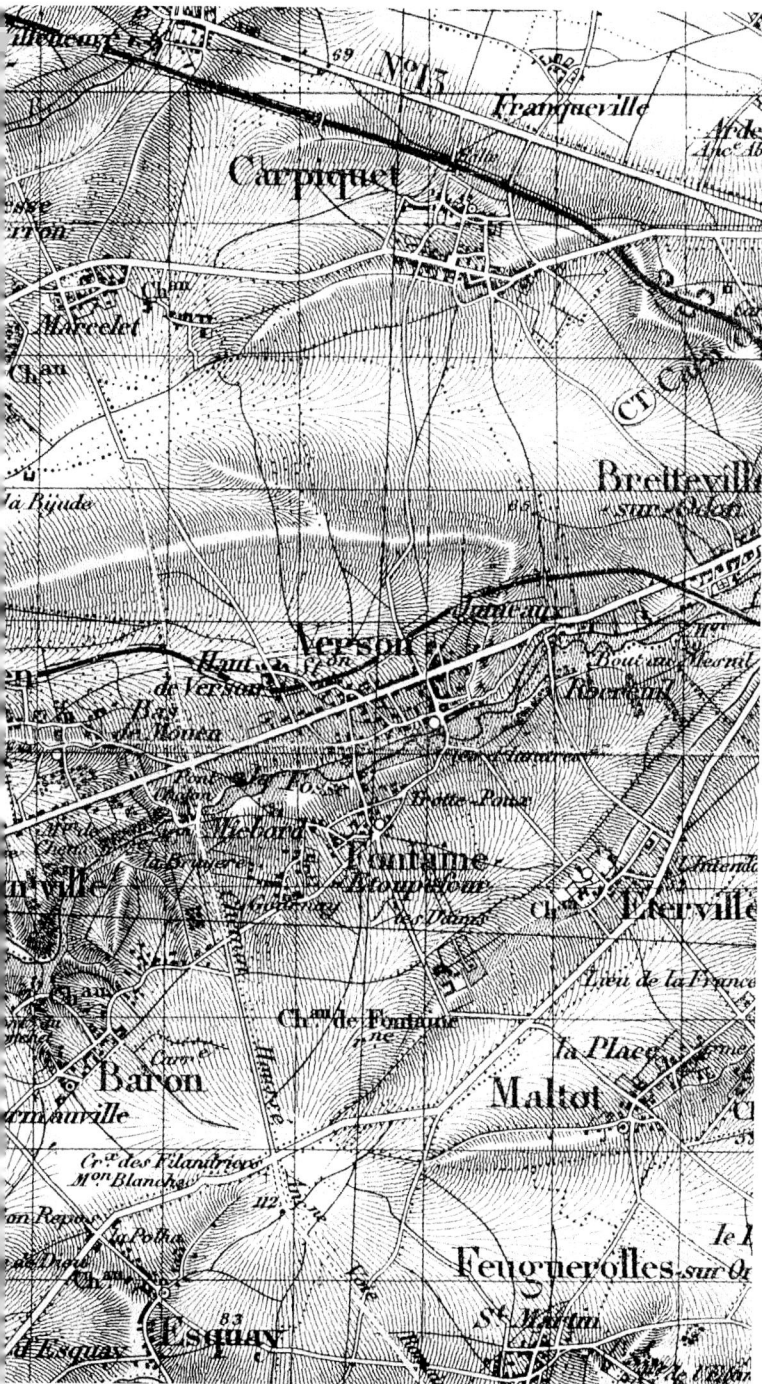

This reproduction of part of a pre-war map shows the area involved in Operations Martlet and Epsom. Note that all the main roads run west-east, converging towards Caen, to the east (right). The operational area of 49th Division is seen to the west: Fontenay and its crossroads, Tessel, Rauray, Brettevillette. To the north and south of the Fontenay/Carpiquet road the terrain is open, covered with wheat fields and includes the villages of Saint-Manvieu and Cheux, which will be hard-fought over. Afterwards is the small obstacle of the Salbey river and the railway (now replaced by the A84 road). After this was a new area of *bocage* followed by the enclosed Odon valley and more wheat fields, as well as Hill 112, northeast of Esquay. Extracts from this map are used in various places throughout the book, as well as the staff map used by the British Army, which has a more modern design that shows contours, rather than the hatchings as used here. (Paich.)

which were intended to block the road junctions and slow down the arrival of the German troops. Two of the deadliest bombing raids took place on 6 and 7 June 1944, at Caen and Saint-Lô and their effectiveness has since been called into question. Lisieux, Pont-l'Evêque, Coutances, Flers, Condé-sur-Noireau, Vire and Argentan were also hit, while in the following days, Valognes, Avranches, Falaise, Vimoutiers and l'Aigle were bombed in their turn, followed later by Aunay-sur-Odon, Evrecy and Villers-Bocage. Afterwards, the civilians were confronted with the battle itself, which would often hit without warning, including machine gun and artillery fire. By September, the Battle of Normandy was over, yet La Havre was still surrounded and bombed in order to put pressure on the German command. This was an unnecessary and particularly deadly bombardment, resulting in around 2,000 deaths and seriously traumatising the population of the town for a long time to come.

The loss of life in the various *départements* is extraordinary: 19,650 deaths in total, including 8,100 in Calvados, 4,850 in la Seine-Maritime, 3,700 in la Manche, 2,100 in the Orne and 900 in the Eure. These figures are much higher than those for the British and Canadian (16,000), and only slightly less than the heavy losses suffered by the Americans (21,000). The civilian casualties are therefore equivalent to those of an army on campaign, made particularly so due to the heavy aerial bombardments. The understandable pain suffered by the population was often expressed by a certain reserve when it came to the Liberation and there are even reports of hostile behaviour from some Saint-Lô residents towards their 'liberators'. Military cemeteries should not make us forget the civilian victims, who are listed on many municipal monuments, and this particular page in history has now been 'rediscovered', particularly since the fiftieth anniversary of the D-Day landings.

Part One

The Scottish Corridor

On 26 June 1944, General Montgomery launched his great offensive, which was designed to break through the German front lines, between the recently-captured Tilly-sur-Seulles and Carpiquet. His aim was to use the Falaise road and take Caen (one of the main objectives on D-Day) from the south. The resources committed to the offensive were extensive, especially considering the enemy only numbered a few hundred infantrymen who were supported by an hundred or so panzers. Yet the German defence was skilful and ferocious, and the Odon river, which joins with the Orne river at Caen, would prove to be a more significant obstacle than expected. The breach in the line formed a kind of 'cul-de-sac'; a narrow corridor opened up by the Scottish infantrymen from 15th Division, and this corner, embedded in the German front line, was to become known as the 'Scottish Corridor'. We will now follow this advance through a land marked by history…

1

In the Face of the Storm

They must be pushed back into the sea!

By 17 June 1944, the Allied bridgehead in Normandy remained narrow and a race was now on: the Allies had to bring reinforcements to re-ignite their attack, but were handicapped by the narrowness of the bridgehead. The Germans, who according to Rommel should have pushed the Allies back into the sea on D-Day, also needed reinforcements. However, the Allies now had control of the air and were thus able to slow down any panzer divisions on their way to the front, meaning they were only able to travel for a few hours every night - at a time of year when the nights are at their shortest.

Further west, at the bridgehead of Utah Beach, the Americans were cutting into the Cotentin Peninsula, before returning to the important deep water port of Cherbourg. Meanwhile, Montgomery had stalled in front of Caen, one of the D-Day objectives, and persisted in launching fake attacks from the west in order to finally capture the city of William the Conqueror. On 11 June, 7th Armoured Division managed to take the Germans by surprise and break through their front lines as far as Villers-Bocage, which they reached on 13 June. Once there, the Tigers from SS-Panzer-Abteilung 101, led by SS-Obersturmführer Michael Wittmann, put a stop to the advance and dashed Montgomery's hopes of breaking through to the south of Caen. Apart from a few quickly-aborted attempts to break through the lines, such as those on 11 June around Mesnil-Patry, where SS-Obersturmführer Siegel pushed back an attack by the Canadian tanks of the First Hussars (who lost thirty-seven tanks in the process), the front was stabilised once more.

In the British sector, the German front was predominantly held by panzer divisions, who were supposed to have been kept in reserve for any potential counter-attacks. In the Calvados area, however, the German 716. Infanterie-Division had been crushed on 6 June, and the 352. Infanterie-Division had suffered greatly. The front was held by elite divisions from the Orne to the Vire rivers, including (from east to west) 21. Panzer-Division, 12. SS-Panzer-Division, the Panzer-Lehr-Division and 2. Panzer-Division, not to mention General Meindl's paratroopers. These units were relatively counterproductive in their positions on the front line, and should be used instead to help re-launch the offensive.

On 17 June Adolf Hitler held a conference in his underground command post at Margival, near Soissons, which had been built in 1940 for Operation Sea Lion; Nazi Germany's planned invasion of the UK. At the meeting were Generaloberst Alfred Jodl (Chief of the Wehrmacht Command Staff), marshals von Rundstedt and Rommel, together with their chiefs of staff, generals Blumentritt and Speidel, as well as other officers from the Wehrmacht Command Staff and German Army Command in the West. According to the report by Major von Ekespare, Rommel described the current situation facing the Allies and the German forces, pointing out the heavy losses to the infantry and the delay in bringing in reinforcements due to the Allied air superiority, as well as highlighting the lack of support from the Luftwaffe. In light of the situation, he requested that the front line pulled back towards Cherbourg, which Hitler accepted as there was no longer any way to prevent the peninsular from being blocked off. Cherbourg would fall ten days later, on 27 June, but the now-devastated great port would remain unusable for many weeks.

Hitler pointed out that the situation would only change if they could interrupt the enemy's supply routes, or by neutralizing the Allied naval forces, and consequently ordered the Navy and Luftwaffe to plant new mines between Le Havre and the east coast of the Cotentin Peninsular. Hitler believed that the 15th Army were better-positioned in the Pas-de-Calais, rather than in Normandy, but acknowledged that there were not enough forces available in the event of a second invasion. He also knew that their defensive lines in the Netherlands were too weak and that an invasion in Brittany was also possible. Operation Fortitude [the Allied strategy to deceive the German High Command in the build-up to the 1944 invasion] had worked perfectly: Hitler had overestimated the number of Allied divisions (estimated at around sixty) that were still available in England, and believed that the presence of the V1 ramps in the north would force the Allies to invade around the Pas-de-Calais, right where the 15th Army were positioned. They also knew that they needed to prevent the Allies from extending their advance east of Saint-Lô, and then 'sweeping east or west, depending on the situation'. At the end of the conference the leaders ate a meal together, after which the Fuhrer took his leave around 3 pm.

Following two studies on the war in the west, the German High Command reported its findings on 20 June, a day after they had been communicated by Marshal Rommel:

1. The Fuhrer's intention is for a concentrated attack by the 1., 2., 9., 10. SS, 2. Panzer and Panzer-Lehr-Division to be carried out in order to destroy the US forces in the Balleroy sector (American II Corps), which is why the infantry divisions must successfully relieve the 2. Panzer and Panzer-Lehr-Division.
2. Before this, the enemy's position east of the Orne must be destroyed by strong defensive means, so that the ground forces participating in this operation are available for the main attack.[1]

The following day, 21 June, Rommel laid out the plan of attack, which was to be carried out by Panzergruppe West. On the right flank (the Caen sector, in the east) were: the I SS-Panzerkorps, including the 12. SS-Panzer-Division, the 1. SS-Panzer-Division and the Panzer-Lehr-Division. At the centre (around Villers-Bocage): the XXXXVII Panzerkorps, including the 2. Panzer-Division, and the 276. and 277. Infantry Divisions. On the left flank (towards Balleroy and the forest of Cerisy): II SS-Panzerkorps, including 2., 9. and 10. SS-Panzer-Divisions. Unfortunately, the attack could not be launched for another ten or fourteen days (between 1 and 5 July), as the units were yet to take up their positions and the ammunition had to be distributed. Rommel's report added: 'As the Fuhrer stated, the attack to the

---

1   KTB Pz.-AOK 5, 63181/4. Telegraph from German Army High Command in the West to panzer divisions, 20.6.44.

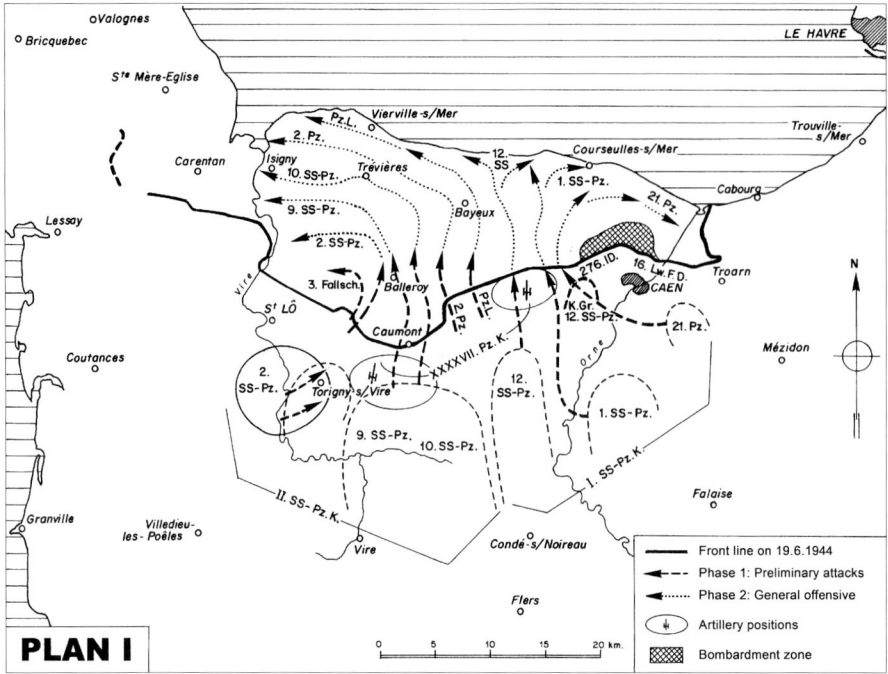

Two versions of the counter-attack plan proposed by *Heeresgruppe B*. In the first case, a high concentration of artillery would hold the Allies north of Caen, while the panzer divisions would pull back towards the sea. In the second case, all forces would advance towards the sea before turning towards the American sector. (Heimdal plans from the archives)

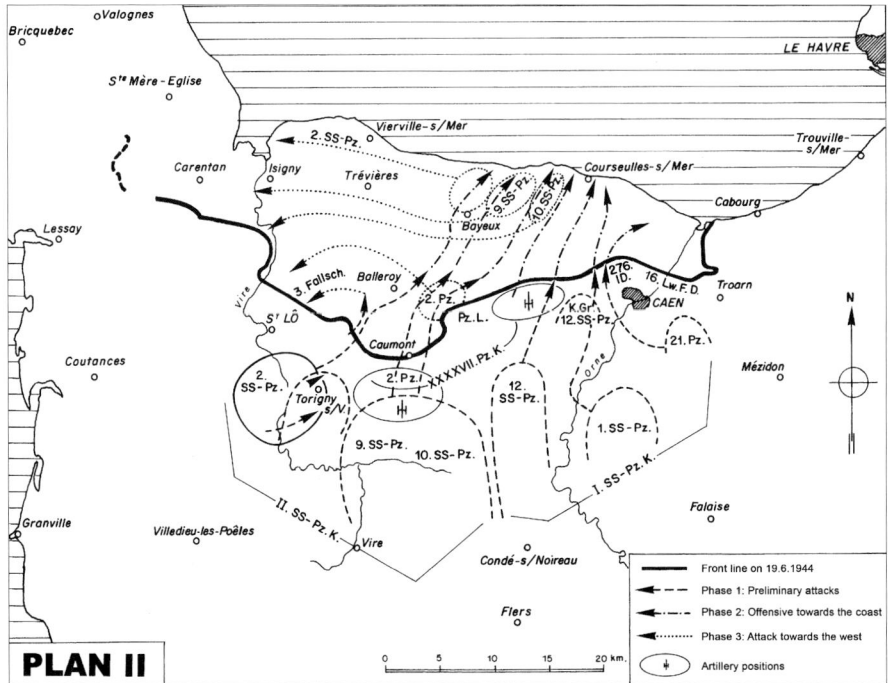

east of the Orne depends on the precondition that the naval artillery is eliminated. Without this measure taking place, as I persuaded myself yesterday, any attack is doomed to failure.' Rommel considered it essential to engage the 16. Luftwaffen-Felddivision and 21. Panzer-Division east of the Orne, as the Infanterie-Division had already lost most of its combat capabilities.

Hitler clearly considered the power of the Allied naval artillery, capable of crushing any concentration of German troops, to be the most serious threat; an analysis that would prove to be particularly accurate. As long as the naval artillery remained active, any counter-attack plans would remain purely theoretical. In addition, only three armoured divisions (plus the 21st, eats of the Orne) were readily available, with the other four not able to reach the front until the beginning of July. The II SS-Panzerkorps was brought back from the Eastern Front as soon as possible, and the last convoy from the 9. SS-Panzer-Division 'Hohenstaufen' had left the Lemberg sector while the bulk of the division had arrived at Epinal (wheeled vehicles) and Dreux (tracked vehicles) on 17 June, the day of the conference at Margival. But although the German railways had got them this far, the hardest part now remained: the drive to Normandy along the French roads and the division's tracked vehicles would not arrive at Sées (south of Falaise) until 26 June.

The Germans had not been able to eliminate the Allied naval threat and were losing the reinforcement race against them. Only the elements could help, which is exactly what happened. A violent storm (for the time of year) hit from 19-22 June, interrupting a substantial part of the maritime traffic for four days. It consequently slowed down the strengthening Allies, whose front lines were now paralysed, and

Hitler had planned a counter-attack to push the Allies back to the sea and on 17 June, 12. SS-Panzer-Division dispatched its hundred or so panzers on a wide front between Fontenay-le-Pesnel and Caen. Here we see a Panzer IV travelling in this area. Its flag at the front of the vehicle allowed it to be recognized by the (rare) friendly aircraft, which was there to support the companies of grenadiers. (SS-KB Woscidlo / Coll. G.B.)

The emblem of 12. SS-Panzer-Division *Hitlerjugend*, which was painted on all vehicles in the unit. Its left flank would receive the full blow of Montgomery's offensive. (Heimdal.)

also provided the German front line troops with an unexpected respite. The storm was terrible: the artificial harbour at Omaha Beach was destroyed, while the one at Arromanches was badly damaged. The British attack was delayed but still took place before the German reinforcements arrived. By the time the storm had ended, Marshal von Rundstedt questioned on 24 June if, after the successful attack on Balleroy and the area north-east of the vicinity, was it then possible to continue the attack towards Carentan? He stated that until the beginning of the offensive, the area around and to the east of Caen remained of upmost importance to the German Army Command in the West, and while he still hoped that the counter-attack at Balleroy would take place, he was determined to draw attention to the importance ensuring German strength in the area around Caen.

As they were waiting for the reinforcements to arrive, the panzer units held the vast areas of the Normandy Front. In the sector where the British attack was later launched, from Tilly-sur-Seulles to the west of Carpiquet, the Germans aligned the following units (west to east): two battalions of grenadiers (II./901 and I./901) from the Panzer-Lehr-Division up to Fontenay-le-Pesnel. From there to the railway line south of Rots, the front was held by one of the two grenadier regiments from the 12. SS-Panzer-Division '*Hitlerjugend*', the SS-Panzergrenadier-Regiment 26., commanded by Obersturmbannführer Wilhelm Mohnke, whose CP was located at le Haut du Bosq (south-west of Cheux). The regiment included III./26, led by SS-Sturmbannführer Erich Olboeter (whose CP was south-east of Fontenay-le-Pesnel) and SS-Sturmbannführer Bernhard Siebken's II./26. The division's engineer battalion held the line north of Cheux, under the command of SS-Sturmbannführer Siegfried Müller, followed by SS-Obersturmbannführer Bernhard Krause's I./26.

SS-Obersturmbannführer Wilhelm Mohnke, commander of SS-Panzergrenadier-Regiment 26, whose CP was located at Haut du Bosq (now Le Bosq), south-west of Cheux. Born in Lübeck on 15 March 1911, he was one of the first 144 *Leibstandarte* members in June 1933. Gravely wounded in 1941 during the Balkan campaign, he became a morphine addict. He may have been responsible for the execution of Canadian prisoners at Le Mesnil-Patry. (Munin.)

1. SS-Sturmbannführer Bernhard Krause, born in Weimar on 11 May 1910, commanded the regiment's 1st Battalion (I./26), which was in position on the regiment's right flank, with his CP at Saint-Manvieu. (D.R.)

2. SS-Sturmbannführer Bernhard Siebken, born in Pinneberg in Holstein on 5 April 1910, commanded the II./26. He would be accused of executing the Canadian prisoners at Le Mesnil-Patry, although the person in charge was probably W. Mohnke. He was hanged at Hameln by a Canadian military court on 20 January 1949. While he was likely innocent, he paid with his life for another. (N/A)

3. SS-Sturmbannführer Erich Olboeter, born in Eberswalde on 26 June, 1917, commanded the III./26 whose CP was located at the Saint-Nicolas farm in Fontenay. (Heimdal)

4. SS-Sturmbannführer Siegfried Müller, born in Krefeld on 18 October 1914, commanded the HJ Division's Engineer Battalion.

This formidable Pak 40 75 mm anti-tank gun is camouflaged behind a wall with only its barrel protruding out. Its anti-tank shells could cover 800 meters, and its explosive shells 7,680 meters. Such weapons reinforced Regiment 26's defensive positions. (SS-KB Woschidlo / Coll. G.B.)

II./SS- Pz.- Rgt. 12 in support

1 & 2. I Battalion of the *Hitlerjugend* Division's tank regiment was in position behind Regiment 26 to provide support it in the event of any adverse attacks. It was under the command of SS-Sturmbannführer Karl-Heinz Prinz and was equipped with Panzer IVs, of which a well-camouflaged example can be seen here, with two members of its crew. The tank commander, an SS-Oberscharführer is on the right, and a young tank crew member is on the left. They wear the black cap of the 1940 tank crews and the two-piece protective netting, as seen in Image 2, which was made from camouflaged cloth and adopted in January 1944. (SS-KB Woscidlo, coll GB and Heimdal doc.)

3. SS-Hauptsturmführer Josef Pezdeuscheg (left) was the head of the command company of this battalion. He is seen studying a map with another officer. (Stephan/G.B.)

4. SS-Ostuf. Friedrich Hartmann and his driver, he was the adjutant to SS-Stubaf Prinz. (Stephan/G.B.)

5. Panzer IV '536' from 5th Company in camouflage behind Regiment 26, east of Fontenay-le-Pesnel. (Willy Kretzschmar.)

6. The same '536' being repaired, having been hit by a shell to its undercarriage during the fighting that took place on 7 June, at Buron. It is being repaired here a day and a half later, near the Juvigny crossroads. Note the mixture between leather outfits and camouflaged jackets. SS-Uscha. Willy Kretzschmar, who commanded the tank, is seen here from behind. (Kretzschmar)

7. SDG (medic) Manfred Stephan, on the right, with one of his comrades from the reconnaissance section of the command company (Stabs-Kompanie) of II Battalion. (Stephan/G.B.)

8. Another of the battalion's Panzer IVs, lined up with forty-four combat-ready units dated 24 June 1944. Allied soldiers would often confuse it with the Tiger because of its angular lines. (SS-KB Woscidlo/G.B.)

In fact, only one regiment and one battalion would face the massive offensive. Until 24 June, the losses within the *Hitlerjugend* Division amounted to 2,500 men and as the division's chief of staff, Hubert Meyer noted:

> Considering the theoretical strength of a regiment of panzer grenadiers (86 officers, 605 non-commissioned officers and 2,502 men), it can be concluded that there are two battalions of grenadiers missing. The losses also correspond to the theoretical strength of a reconnaissance group and a battalion of engineers combined. As of 24 June, the number of panzers fit for combat is as follows: 56 Panzer IVs, 44 Panzer Vs (Panther), 233 SPWs, armoured reconnaissance and artillery observation vehicles and 17 heavy anti-tank guns. In comparison with the numbers on 6 June the losses are as follows: 36 Panzer IVs, 19 Panzer Vs, 44 SPWs and others, as well as 11 heavy anti-tank guns. Half of the losses among the panzers is definitive, while the rest can be rebuilt in a relatively short period of time. The engineer battalion has strengthened its position with its particular know-how and despite the limited time, support points for light infantry weapons were established in previously damaged or destroyed houses, mainly south of the river at Fontenay. The Panzer IVs from the regiment's 2nd battalion are well-camouflaged along a broad front in the following order: 9th, 7th, 5th, 6th and 8th Companies. The first and second groups of the artillery are behind Regiment 26. and are also well-camouflaged and ready for combat. Due to the width of the front, the positions of the panzer grenadiers' companies are not organised in depth and so heavy infantry weapons, panzers and artillery are providing support. The reconnaissance group, A.A.12, is the only remaining infantry near Brettevillette and Missy. The regiment's 1st Battalion is in reserve near Noyers-Bocage, and is available for the division's left flank, where the enemy is expected to attack. Behind 12. SS-Panzer-Division and the Panzer-Lehr-Division (between Saint-André-sur-Orne and Aunay-sur-Odon), the III Flack Corps is in position with its 2nd, 4th and 3rd regiments. The Flak-Sturm-Regiment 4 is in an anti-aircraft position with its three groups in the Mouen/Noyers/Evrecy sectors and is available against terrestrial targets if needed. The Werferbrigade 7 is still engaged east of the Orne.[2]

12. SS-Panzer-Division '*Hitlerjugend*" was formed in June 1943 to compensate for the heavy losses suffered on the Eastern Front, particularly around Stalingrad. The officers and non-commissioned officers mainly came from the elite 1. SS-Panzer-Division 'Adolf Hitler'; the Fuhrer's bodyguard regiment. The recruits came from volunteers born in 1926 and were to be the symbol of the German youth's spirit of sacrifice and its will to conquer. 9. SS-Panzer-Division 'Hohenstaufen' and 10. SS-Panzer-Division '*Frundsberg*' who were also found in this sector, were comprised of a similar age group. The *Hitlerjugend* was engaged in fighting to the north and north-east of Caen, at Ardennes Abbey on 7 June and at Bretteville-l'Orgueilleuse and Norrey on 8 and 9 June. Due to the lack of infantry units, the division was to remain in the front line, exhausting itself in the face of various Allied attacks. It was

---

2   H. Meyer, *12. SS-Panzer-Division Hitlerjugend* (Heimdal)

At the Ardenne Abbey, the staff of the *Hitlerjugend* Division visit the headquarters of the I. SS-Panzerkorps artillery group, the SS-Artillery-Abteilung 101 schwere. Third from the left, with his hands in his pockets, is the head of this heavy artillery group, SS-Sturmbannführer Franz Steineck. SS-Sturmbannführer Hubert Meyer, the HJ Division's Chief of Staff, is wearing a leather jacket and carrying binoculars. In camouflage uniform with his hands in his pockets is SS-Standartenführer Kurt Meyer, known as 'Panzermeyer'. Next is the aide-de-camp, SS-Obersturmführer Bernhard Meitzel and on the far-right, SS-Hauptsturmführer Günter Reichenbach, a member of the General Staff. (KB Woscidlo/G.B.)

therefore a diminished regiment that had to face the offensive, but it was also one commanded by exceptional leaders. The young age of the German soldiers surprised their Allied counterparts, who nicknamed it the 'Baby Division'. But their intensive training led by experienced officers, as well as their strong motivation, meant that they were a particularly tenacious and elite unit that would go on to prove its exceptional ability by resisting an enemy that was far superior in numbers and equipment. Regiment 26 and the division's engineer battalion received their orders from the division's CP, which was now under the command of the charismatic leader, SS-Standartenführer Kurt Meyer, who had led the division since the death of SS-Brigadeführer Fritz Witt on 14 June. Meyer was assisted in this difficult task by an excellent chief of staff, SS-Sturmbannführer Hubert Meyer.

The *Hitlerjugend* Division's Command Post

Hubert Meyer has provided an insight into how the division operated:[3]

> The division's commander, SS-Brigadeführer and Generalmajor der Waffen-SS Fitz Witt, was killed on 14 June, along with some of his officers, non-commissioned officers and soldiers at his command post at Venoix, in the western

---

3   As published in '39/45 Magazine', Vol,64.

1. SS-Sturmbannführer Hubert Meyer participated in all of the *Leibstandarte*'s campaigns. After commanding an infantry company, he attended military school and became First Chief of Staff in the *Hitlerjugend* Division. (Heimdal)

2. SS-Ostuf. Bernhard Meitzel, the aide-de-camp, assisted Stubaf. Hubert Meyer at the division's CP. (H. Meyer)

3. SS-Ostuf. Doldi was one of the staff officers working at the division's CP. (H. Meyer)

suburbs of Caen, after it was hit by an Allied artillery barrage. The divisional headquarters, as well as the radio and telephone facilities, were located 100m east of the crossing between the RN175 road and the Caen - Bayeux railway line. We assumed that the enemy had located our position by either an intercepted radio signal or a betrayal by a civilian, and now know that our command post was discovered after an encrypted message was broken by Ultra.

The CP had to be moved as quickly as possible. After 11 June, enemy fire had moved from the right flank towards the centre and left flanks of the division and so we needed to find a location further to the west. Verson seemed to be the ideal place as it was behind the centre of the division's front lines, which at the time were 16km long as the crow flies. The shortest distance to our front lines, north of Marcelet, was only 5km and as we were north of the Odon, we didn't need to use bridges or fords to reach the front. While it was true that a CP at Verson was within range of the field artillery, but you had to take into account that we were in command of the front and so had to be close to the troops.

My 1st officer, SS-Obersturmführer Bernhard Meitzel, had found an ideal building in the west of the town; the manor house of 'Val Fleuri'. It was located on the south-side of the rue de Verson, at the bottom of a slope, while its gardens stretched down as far as the Odon. Tall trees hid part of the building and acted as camouflage from any aerial reconnaissance. We set off in small groups on the night of 14/15 June and parked the vehicles on a farm on the north side of the road, facing 'Val Fleuri'.

The manor house was well-furnished and belonged to the mayor of Caen. We mainly used the two rooms on the ground floor at the back. I occupied the room on the west side with SS-Obersturmführer Meitzel, after the division's commander, SS-Standartenführer Kurt Meyer, had chosen the room on the east side. The walls in his office were oak-panelled and the paintings were decorated with gothic arches, while my office was also decorated with richly-carved oak panels. We sincerely hoped that the house would not be destroyed in the course of the fighting, not just for our own interests, but for the beauty of the setting also. Fortunately this did not happen, as I would have the opportunity to discover after the war. The right rear corner of the building (looking up from the river) was hit by an artillery shell, but was of little consequence.

This beautiful room served as an office, living room and bedroom for myself and Bernhard Meitzel. In the middle was a large table covered with maps, reports and orders, as well as the telephone. During important phases of the battle, one of us would stay awake while the other laid on a mattress and slept, or at least tried to do so. Each morning I reported to the division's commander regarding the enemy's position and any orders that had arrived in the meantime. Sometimes the intelligence officer, SS-Obersturmführer Günther Doldi, provided more detailed information on the enemy. I would provide my own judgement and make some suggestions as to what to do. After exchanging ideas, 'Panzer Meyer' would give his instructions, which I would then transform into orders (with the help of Bernhard Meitzel, and send them out to the troops. Written orders were forwarded to the regiments and battalions through the staff that had been seconded to us, while shorter orders were transmitted by telephone. The radio was used as little as possible, although if the telephone wires were cut for long periods of time (usually during heavy fighting) then we were forced to use the radio instead. The radio orders were executable immediately, as it would have taken the enemy several days to decrypt them and so the risk was almost non-existent. We were not aware of any possibility that our coded messages could be cracked and were only worried about the radio location being discovered. The radio conversations between armoured units in combat can be listened to and the enemy used them in abundance when preparing for an attack - much to our advantage.

After the morning meeting, 'Panzer Meyer' went to see the regiments and battalions on the line to examine the situation for himself and to discuss the execution of his orders. He gave me his report upon his return, although in urgent cases he would take the telephone with him. I would then provide my own report on the situation and we would repeat what had been done in the morning. In the evening, the decisions for the following day would be made and the corresponding orders give. I would then send off my reports to the army command concerning what had happened during the day and subsequent handling of any combat.

During those days when important fighting was taking place, we reported constantly to the Panzer Corps Chief of Staff, SS-Standartenführer Fritz

SS-Sturmbannführer Fritz Buchsein was the division's 2nd Staff Officer, and responsible for the Quartiermeister-Abteilung, particularly supplies. (H. Meyer)

The rear (south-side, towards the Odon) of the 'Val Fleuri' at Verson in 1975. Hubert Meyer is second from the left, with the owners at the time and other veterans. The HJ Division's CP was installed here from 15 to 27 June 1944. The left room on the ground floor was Hubert Meyer's office, and the one on the right was Panzermeyer's. (H. Meyer)

Kraemer, by telephone, teleprinter or radio. He was a very calm, quick-thinking and thoughtful man who could easily sympathise with the men's situation through his own personal experiences. We had total confidence in him: he even sometimes took it upon himself to issue orders and accepted full responsibility following information we'd provided for him on a given situation.

However, as we have seen, behind the front lines there were only around 100 panzers who were expected to provide the main defensive force against hundreds of British armoured vehicles and who were directed from a strategic point of choice: Rauray.

SS-Panzer-Regiment 12's Command Post

In summer 1944, Georg Isecke was a SS-Hauptsturmführer (captain) in SS-Panzer-Regiment 12. and acted as adjutant to its commander, SS-Obersturmbannführer Max Wünsche. He has provided a description of how the regiment's command post operated from its location in Rauray, which was to become the 'keystone' during Operation Epsom.[4]

From 9 June onwards, the Allies were exerting pressure on the division's left flank and so Rauray was an ideal location for SS-Panzer-Regiment 12.'s CP. As well as being close to the front line it also offered other advantages: it was

---

4   Ibid.

1. SS-Panzer-Regiment 12's CP was installed at the Chateau de Rauray from 9 to 27 June. The terrain, especially the open ground, rises up to this high point (Hill 120), and dominates the surrounding area, and more particularly, the Fontenay/Carpiquet road for around 30 meters. It was an important strategic point, and the main objective of the failed British attack on 25 June. The panzer counter-attacks would be directed from here. (Heimdal)

2. SS-Obersturmbannführer Max Wünsche (right) congratulates an SS-Oberscharführer who had shot down five allied aircraft with his light Flak gun. SS-Hauptsturmführer Schlauss, the communications officer (Nachrichten-Offizier) of SS-Pz.-Rgt 12 is towards the back. The photograph was taken by KB Stollberg. (G.B.)

only a small village and there were plenty of tall trees to provide cover from aerial reconnaissance. In order to maintain a large number of operational panzers, Rauray acted as the head of a large supply chain:

The armoured command station was based at Rauray and comprised of its commander, (Obersturmbannführer Max Wünsche), his deputy (SS-Hauptsturmführer Georg Isecke) and the communications officer (SS-Hauptsturmführer Schlauss). There were eight Panther tanks, the communications department, the anti-aircraft section, the motorcycle section and the regiment's medical officer, SS-Hauptsturmführer Stiawa. Meanwhile, the reserve CP was located west of Grainville, around 2km further south.

The regimental hospital was at Evrecy (around 7km from Rauray) and the company's supply corps and workshop were to be found around 14km away in the forest around Grimbosq, although the mechanic's workshop was based at Neubourg. Refuelling and ammunition supplies were carried out by the supply corps located to the west of Paris: 10-15 per cent of losses were caused by *Jabos* (Allied fighter-bombers).

From 7-9 June the regiment's CP had been set up in a suburb south-west of Caen, as 192 panzers arrived from the Seine Valley along four different roads. On 7 June the first fifty Panzer IVs supported the attack by SS-Panzergrenadier-Regiment 25. on Buron, but there had been difficulties in getting the panzers to the front and so the supply corps had decided to settle in the great forest at Grimbosq. Due to the attacks by the *Jabos*, all troop movements had to be carried out at night and an attack on Bretteville-l'Orgueilleuse took place during the night of 8/9 June. Both this attack and the one at Buron failed in the face of strong anti-tank defence and artillery barrages, and although the commander was wounded in the process, he continued to lead his men.

On 9 June the division moved from being on the offensive to the defensive as the regiment found itself on the division's left flank. The 2nd Battalion (Panzer IV) was at the front, with 1st Battalion (Panther) in reserve and so the regimental CP was established at Rauray. There was a farm at the southern entrance to the village and the administrative sections installed themselves in the buildings around the courtyard. On the other side of the road was a large park and a chateau surrounded by tall trees, thus providing excellent camouflage. Communications with the battalions, companies and even with the main division were maintained day and night, assisted by an observation post installed in one of the trees that provided a view of the battlefield. An officer was stationed up there with a map detailing the front lines, and it was possible to observe the entire area between Fontenay and Cheux, as well as the road leading to Caen, and any reports were sent to the regimental CP by telephone. Once the information had been processed, it was then passed on to the divisional CP. For example, on 14 and 15 June the observer noticed more than thirty armoured vehicles in the area around Cristot and so the commander sent out a company of Panthers that

1. SS-Hauptsturmführer Georg Isecke was the adjutant of the HJ Division's Panzer-Regiment. This photograph was taken in November 1942. (G. Isecke)

2. Georg Isecke in 1984. (G. Isecke)

Max Wünsche decorating the tank crew members of his regiment. On the left is his deputy officer, Georg Isecke. (Heimdal.) This scene took place in front of one of the agricultural buildings located just south of the chateau, which formed part of its outbuildings. The windows are still recognizable, even if the roof has been raised during the post-war reconstruction. (E. Groult/Heimdal)

were in reserve lines. When they reached the ridge line, around 1,500m away, the Panthers opened fire and the bulk of the enemy tanks turned back, while those that were hit were left there to burn. The Panthers were then able to return to their original positions before the artillery or *Jabos* could intervene.

At 11.30 am on 11 June Obersturmführer West warned that during an aerial reconnaissance mission, a Fieseler Storch [a small German liaison aircraft] had noticed that the CP at Rauray had been identified and would subsequently be subjected to an artillery barrage around noon. All wheeled vehicles were immediately sent to the reserve CP, at Grainville, while the panzers and other armoured vehicles in the park remained in the protective shelters that had been dug into the ground, with their crewmen sheltering underneath them. Mattresses were placed up against the chateau's windows as occasional artillery fire rained down. The barrage lasted around a quarter of an hour and there were no casualties; most of the shells had exploded in the trees before they even reached the ground. The broken branches that had fallen on the panzers were removed, but everything else was left as it was so that any Allied aerial reconnaissance could see the 'damage'. It was important to avoid any form of movement when the *Jabos* were in the air. The Fieseler Storch had advised us that the enemy's artillery was guided by an Auster IV and so our anti-aircraft section was now put into action. The Flakvierling were mounted on Panzer IV chassis: a device created by our regiment. The crew was protected by a shield 2cm thick and waited for their target as they hid under excellent camouflage. In the early days they shot down two Auster IVs and so they were now afraid to fly over into our sector.

The HJ Division's guns in action

The Hitlerjugend Division had self-propelled and armoured Flak guns that were feared by Allied aircraft.

1 & 2. The fourth battery of the division's Flak group, 4./SS-Flak-Abteilung 12, was equipped with nine 3.7 cm self-propelled guns, mounted on medium-sized 8-ton tractors. At the front, the cab and the radiator were protected by light armour plating. These two photographs show the guns ready for action and the six-man crew. (Paul Baier/H. Meyer)

2

3. One of the guns has been destroyed by a hunter-bomber. The group was also equipped with eight 2 cm guns and twelve formidable 8.8 cm guns - theoretically. (P. Baier)

4. This *Flakvierling*, a quadruple 2 cm gun, is mounted on a semi-tracked tractor with an armoured cabin and was assigned to the division's artillery regiment. (SS-KB Woscidlo/G.B.)

At dawn we had to check whether or not any fuel had arrived during the night, as well as confirm the losses of any men or equipment. The communications officer, Schlauss, was constantly making sure that the telephone and radio links were working properly, while the regiment's doctor, Dr Stiawa. was in charge of transporting and caring for any wounded: there were always attacks on our ambulances. Almost every day the head of the workshop, Hauptsturmführer Samman, would appear and if we saw him chewing on an extinct cigar then we knew he'd had to jump into the ditches more than once on his way in order to escape the *Jabos*. Our first question was always: 'What's broken down? What's been repaired and can be returned to action?'

The same questions were aimed at the supply officer ('IVa'), Obersturmführer Donaubaner: 'What's happened? What have we lost?' and a small fuel and ammunition depot was soon set up on the northern entrance to Rauray. But the main focus of the CP was always the permanent exchange of information between the regiment's commander and the units, and Obersturmbannführer Wünsche was often gone for the whole day, normally with the divisional commander. As CP of SS-Panzergrenadier-Regiment 26 was located nearby, we often saw its commander, Obersturmbannführer Mohnke. Most of the time we would just sit by the side of the road where we could see what was going on and discuss how we could support each other. What's more, we were also sensitive to the plight of the civilian population, the majority of whom were unable to evacuate the areas surrounding the front lines.

On 13 June we were put on the alert as a dangerous situation was developing to our rear. Divisional reports stated that enemy armoured units were on the march from Villers-Bocage towards Caen and so the panzer regiment immediately began to lock down the area. The commander put himself at the front of the column to guide the two companies and help close the breach. Two hours later, twenty-two panzers (Panzer IVs and Panthers) were moving down the RN175 road. Meanwhile, the primary threat was destroyed by our best tank commander, Hauptsturmführer Michael Wittmann. Our panzers

The *Flakpanzer Wirbelwind* was a vehicle made from a Panzer IV chassis with an open turret on top, armed with a 20 mm *Flakvierling* (a 2 cm quadruple gun). Max Wünsche and the HJ Division's Panzer-Regiment helped to create this machine. Here we see a Flakpanzer IV from II./SS-Pz.-Rgt. 12, which does not have an armoured cockpit around the quadruple gun. Such engines were feared by Allied aircraft. Photograph taken in Normandy, extracted from the album of Wilhelm Krause. (Heimdal)

The HJ Division's Panzer-Regiment also had a reconnaissance section mounted on amphibious vehicles; *Schwimmwagen*. This section is positioned at Rauray, near the CP, and was commanded by SS-Uscha. Harry Wontorra. Here, one of the section's *Schwimmwagen* is sheltering under the trees. (H. Wontorra/Heimdal)

Part of the section's encampment, further along the hedge, with a 4-man tent consisting of four camouflaged individual tent cloths. The helmet was probably placed at the top to prevent rain from coming down the pole. Nearby is a *Schwimmwagen*, a small table covered with a camouflaged canvas, three bowls and a flag with the skull of the Panzer-Regiment. (H. Wontorra./Heimdal)

then returned to base and the incident turned into quite a fortuitous event for our workshops, as we managed to recover some undamaged Cromwell tanks from among the wreckages, which we could take back and use to help repair our own broken panzers.

From 14-25 June the enemy's main efforts were directed against the Panzer-Lehr-Division, on the left flank. Our panzers remained close to the infantry to act as 'firemen'. Unfortunately, our group was not yet ready and we were sorely lacking in numbers. Due to the enemy's superior equipment and their strong anti-tank defences, the tactical engagement of our panzers was not really an option and so the companies had to serve as backup to our brave infantrymen instead.

As there was no way of replacing any of the lost tanks, those that had been damaged had to be recovered from the battlefield, provided they were not totally destroyed, and so every night a breakdown team was sent out to recover the wrecks. The majority of them passed through Rauray and crossed through the hamlet under the careful watch of the sentries. Much attention was given to this problem when the division was first formed, and so the only workshop company (Werstatt-Kompanie) had no fewer than 450 men. They were all specialist tank technicians and excellent gunsmiths, capable of carrying out

1. The lookout platform at Rauray, photographed on 29 June by a British war correspondent. (IWM)

2. The same place in 2008, at the turn in front of the chateau. The trees have been cut down and replaced by poles. (G.B.)

3. The location in 1998. (Heimdal)

exceptional work. The team of mechanics were still located in our former sector to the south of the Seine, in Neubourg and since this was where all repairs were undertaken, every night there would be some form of contact with Rauray.

On 22 June the strong push by the British on the division's left flank and on the cross over with the Panzer-Lehr- Division was contained. An offensive was on the horizon, with the objection of reaching the Odon and then the Orne, before encircling Caen from the south. Many prisoners were brought to us and were especially happy to have been escaped from the area where the artillery was active, or from the aerial threat of the *Jabos*. On 24 June an English officer was brought to our CP at Rauray and stayed with us before being transferred to Grainville, but in the meantime joined us in witnessing how the already dangerous situation was evolving further.

SS-Panzer-Artillery-Regiment 12

The front line was held by grenadiers with anti-tank guns, supported by Panzer IVs held in reserve to counter-attack behind the front line companies. The Panther tank battalion (I./SS-Pz- Rgt. 12) was in reserve in the area around Noyers-Bocage/ Brettevillette, near the Fontenay sector, where the first attack on 25 June would take place. Apart from tanks, there was only artillery behind the front line. Its stockpiles of ammunition were limited, but it would provide effective support to the infantry.

The third group was equipped with 15 cm howitzers, whose maximum range was 24,825 metres. This artillery group was commanded by SS-Stubaf. Bartling. (SS-KB Woscidlo/Heimdal)

The regiment's first group, I./SS-Pz.-Art.-Rgt. 12, was commanded by SS-Stubaf. Urbanitz and was equipped with 10.5 cm self-propelled guns, one of which can be seen here opening fire. The second (Tim Merbeil) and third (Heller) batteries were at le Haut du Bosq during the offensive. (Höke/G.B.)

SS-Stubaf. Schöps' second group was in place in the Salbey area, south of Cheux. It was equipped with 10.5 cm (10.5 cm *leichte Feldhaubitze 18*) howitzers, whose maximum range was 12,325 metres. A young artilleryman can be seen aiming one of the guns (image 1), while a gun commander and gunner stand behind one of these lFH 18s, with the division's emblem painted on it (2). (SS-KB Woscidlo /G.B.)

The Front Line

1. The 1st Battalion of SS-Panzer-Regiment 12 was under the command of SS-Sturmbannführer Arnold Jürgensen. Prior to the offensive, this battalion had forty-four Panzer Vs (Panthers) deployed in reserve south of Vendes, therefore close to the area where Operation Martlet would be launched. Here a tank leader is seen emerging from his Panther. (SS-KB Woscidlo/G.B.)

2. Artillerymen from SS-Panzer-Artillery-Regiment 12 make their plans. Their guns would respond to the British offensive, causing losses in the enemy's compact ranks, despite the lack of ammunition. Notice the camouflaged outfits and headgear allowing them to blend into the landscape. (SS-KB Woscidlo/G.B.)

1. A radio crew using a *Tornisterfunkgerät b/f*, with the forward observer sitting on the left. They are in contact with artillery position and radio operator on the right is holding the microphone. Their instructions would lead to the accuracy of the artillery fire. (SS-KB Woscidlo/ G.B.)

2. In the battery, a telephone operator (right) uses a *Fernsprecher 33*, which allowed him to be in contact with two or three other operators at the same time. To the left is the radio operator, who was in contact with the forward observer. (SS-KB Woscidlo/G.B.)

3. In the front line, in front of the artillery, was the grenadier. They were usually very young, hence the nickname 'Baby Division', used by the British to describe this great unit. Here, with his gun slung over his shoulder, a grenadier eats from the lid of his bowl. In the front lines, hot food could only arrive at night. The camouflaged dress seen here was widely used among grenadiers. (SS-KB Woscidlo/G.B.)

The Front Line (2)

1. This photograph was also taken by KB Woscidlo, a war correspondent attached to the *Hitlerjugend* Division. It was published on 11 July 1944, but was taken a few days before Operation Martlet was launched, along the Tilly-Carpiquet road, north of Fontenay-le-Pesnel. We can see the roadside cross (which we will return to later), located at the crossroads leading leftwards (towards the north,) to the chateau at Boislonde, where terrible fighting would take place. These three young grenadiers from the *Hitlerjugend* are watching this strategic crossroads. Opposite, the main road leads to Carpiquet. A description of the fighting at Boislonde recalls, '[It was] A strategic crossroads. At each tentative approach by English, the German machine-guns, which were well-positioned and camouflaged, would sweep the road. Each time, the British attackers drowned in blood along this road.' (S.Cazenave)

2. A scene of the daily life in Rauray. Near the Panzer-Regiment's CP, two members of the *Erkundungszug* are milking a Norman cow. (S.C./H.W.)

3. The same place today, modified by new constructions and fences, but one can still recognise the cross and the main road. (G.B.)

1. This photograph of a burnt-out Kfz 18 light vehicle from SS-Panzer-Regiment 12, whose white-painted emblem can be seen stencilled on the back, was probably hit by allied aircraft while attempting to reach the Fontenay-Carpiquet main road. (S.C.)

2. Grenadiers from Regiment 26 in the front line. They were usually very young, but would fight with a stubbornness that would surprise the British. (Private Collection)

3. The III./26, positioned in the area of Fontenay-le-Pesnel, was equipped with SdKfz 251s, of which an example is shown here. It would come up against the assault by 49th Division on 25 June. (S.C.)

4. Very young soldiers from SS Panzergrenadier-Regiment 26's heavy company, 13./26, (commanded by SS-Ostuf Polanski), operating a 7.5 cm infantry gun which can be seen here. The road lined with tall trees in the background is that leading from Fontenay to Carpiquet. (KB Woscidlo/ Munin)

1. Another photograph showing the 7.5 cm gun in action. It may have been put out of action by the artillery barrage on 26 June. (KB Woscidlo/Munin)

2. A grenadier makes progress through the corn in the same area. The corn had grown high by this time of year, and provided good camouflage which allowed snipers to surprise the attacking British troops on 26 June. (Heimdal)

Monty's New Attack

On 18 June, the day after the conference at Margival, General Montgomery issued a new directive. It first summarised the past twelve days of combat, in which the Allies had obtained a bridgehead and retained the initiative. He pointed out that Rommel's mobile reserves had been exhausted after being forced to fill in the gaps at the front, not to mention the fact that they lacked any good infantry to relieve them and thus allow him to launch a counter-attack. The general remarked that as their plans developed, the next step for the Allies was to take Caen and Cherbourg. The British Second Army were to launch a pincer movement attack on both sides of Caen in order to gain the high ground north-east of Bretteville-sur-Laize and so dominate the southern exits around Caen. At the same time he urged the First US Army to take Cherbourg and then push south.

He had initially planned to launch the main attack east of the Orne, but there was not enough room from which to launch a powerful enough attack and so there would only be a secondary offensive here, while the main one would take place further west. This also meant he could use VIII Corps, who would land on 22 June, and so the attack was planned for the following day, but the bad weather would upset his plans. Fresh to strong winds, along with poor visibility and rough seas, had slowed the pace of the Allied landings and air activity since D-Day. In the early hours of 19 June, just as the construction of the artificial harbours was making good progress, a strong northerly wind rose up unexpectedly, rising to nearly twenty knots by the afternoon. The terrible weather would rage for the next three days and was the worst June storm in over forty years.

On 20 June 20 Montgomery visited Major General D.A.H. Graham (left), commander of 50th Infantry Division, in the Tilly area, on the right flank of the up-coming offensive.

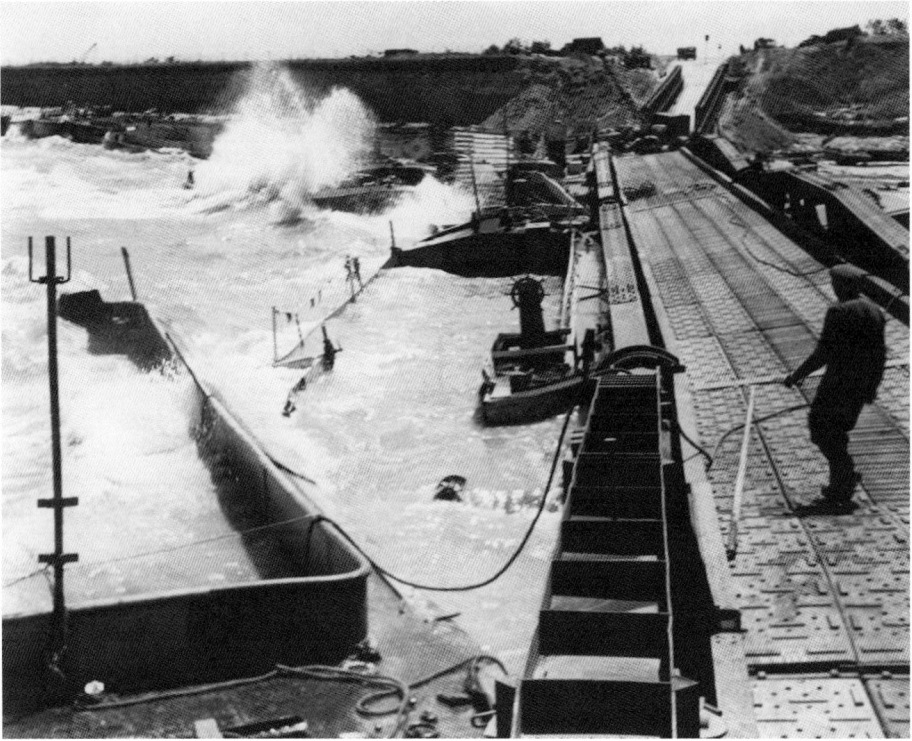

The terrible summer storm disorganised and considerably slowed down the arrival of Allied reinforcements in Normandy, postponing Montgomery's offensive for several days. This photograph was taken on 24 June at Arromanches and shows some of the damage caused. Even though the storm had dissipated, the sea was still strong. (IWM)

The two artificial harbours under construction suffered considerable damage. When the storm struck on 19 June, two and a half miles of Whale roadway were being pulled across the English Channel by tugboats and the majority of it was either lost during the crossing or sunk after it arrived on the Normandy coast in the height of the storm. Rhino ferries, along with numerous other boats and landing craft were torn from their moorings and tossed onto the shore by the enormous waves. By the time the storm finally calmed down on 23 June, the desolation in the areas around the two artificial harbours was complete. The harbour at Omaha Beach (which was less solid that than at Arromanches) was abandoned, and its materials used to help repair damage to its sister port.

Maritime traffic had not been disturbed completely, but it had been considerably reduced. From 15-18 June 15,774 men hand landed in the British sector, and 18,938 in the American. From 19-22 June the numbers fell to 3,982 and 5,865 respectively. Likewise the number of vehicles fell from 2, 965 to 1,375 in the British sector and 2,929 to 1,051 in the American sector. This meant that the volumes of tonnage that landed fell from 10,666 to 4,286 (British) and 14,308 to 3,064 (American.)[5]

---

5   L.F. Ellis, *Victory in the West, vol. 1* (Naval and Military Press, 2009)

For the British Second Army, the losses caused by the four-day storm amounted to the equivalent of three divisions: the great offensive planned for 23 June was consequently postponed by four days. This provided the Germans with extra respite time, and while it may not have allowed them time to launch any counter-attacks, it did mean that reinforcements had time to arrive, as well as the opportunity to strengthen their defensive positions with minefields, barbed wire and small wooden or earthen bunkers.

Montgomery's new offensive was codenamed Operation Epsom and was to be carried out by three divisions from VIII Corps, whose landing had been partly delayed by the bad weather. The operation would be preceded by two attacks, with the first taking place east of the Orne from the bridgehead where the main attack should originally have been launched from. On 23 June 152nd Brigade, 51st (Highland) Infantry Division, surprised elements of the *Gruppe Luck* (21. Panzer-Division), who attempted a counter-attack the following day but without much success. It was more of a large skirmish rather than a real offensive, and the fighting that took place had no impact on the main offensive, which had now turned from a 'pincer movement' into a real 'hammer-blow'.

West of Caen, the Second Army held the front with I Corps by aligning the 3rd British Infantry Division to the north and the 3rd Canadian Infantry

1. North of Caen, I Corps, whose cloth emblem is seen here, aligned the 3rd British Infantry Division and, to the west of that city, the 3rd Canadian Infantry Division, which would provide the basis for the VIII Corps' offensive.

2. Fabric badge from XXX Corps, whose 50th Infantry Division fought in the Tilly-sur-Seulles area against the Panzer-Lehr-Division, on the right flank of the offensive, and had just been reinforced by the 49th Infantry Division.

3. Cloth badge of VIII Corps, who would be engaged in this new offensive. Its first elements arrived on 13 June, with the last arriving on the night before the offensive.

4. Lieutenant General Sir Richard O'Connor would lead VIII Corps' offensive. (DR)

Division to the west of the town. The line was then taken over by XXX Corps, with 49th Infantry Division north of Fontenay-le-Pesnel, 50th Infantry Division in the area around Tilly-sur-Seulles, opposite the Panzer-Lehr-Division, and 7th Armoured Division west of Villers-Bocage, who then linked with the American First Army in the salient at Caumont-L'Eventé. Following the delays caused by the weather, the preliminary attacks of the main offensive would be conducted on the right flank (west) by 49th Infantry Division on 25 June. The main attack would be led by VIII Corps, who would advance from the sector held by the 3rd Canadian Infantry Division. The aim of the preliminary attack was to clear the area around Fontenay-le-Pesnel (which included Rauray and Noyers-Bocage) in order to protect the right flank from the main attack. The latter would have to get beyond the Odon Valley on the first day before crossing the Orne. A new force was needed in order to achieve this ambitious project: VIII Corps.

VIII Corps Reinforcements

In order to carry out Montgomery's decisive offensive, a new army corps had to be engaged: VIII Corps. Its staff had been formed at Aldershot in 1940 by Lieutenant General Sir Harold Franklyn, who was charged with protecting the south-west of England from a possible German invasion. Franklyn retuned to the Yorkshire Regiment in June 1943 to prepare for the upcoming invasion, with three divisions attached to him: the Guards Armoured Division, the 11th Armoured Division and the 15th Infantry Division, as well as the 6th Tank Brigade. At this time, VIII Corps passed under the command of Lieutenant General Sir Richard O'Connor. Born on 21 August 1889 (he was fifty-four in June 1944), O'Connor distinguished himself in the First World War and was promoted to Major General in 1939. From June 1940 he fought in Egypt as commander of the Western Desert Force, which would later become XIII Corps. His success with Operation Compass from 9 December 1940 to 10 February 1941 propelled him to new heights and he was made a Knight Commander of the Order of the Bath, before being captured in April 1941 after leading British troops in Egypt. However, this was far from the end of his military career and after being transferred to Italy and spending two years in captivity, he managed to escape and was back in London by December 1943. His reputation was still very much intact and he was consequently the command of VIII Corps was entrusted to him on 21 January 1944.

The first of the three divisions under his command was the 15th (Scottish) Infantry Division, which had been commanded by Major General H. A. MacMillan since 23 August 1943. The unit had been formed shortly before the First World War, with its emblem representing an 'O': the fifteenth letter of the alphabet, although King George VI suggested the inclusion of the Scottish arms in order to remind people of its origin. On 2 September 1939 is was reconstituted with elements from the 52 Lowland Division and became the First Line Territorial Army when the Secretary of State for War, Leslie Hore-Belisha, doubled the strength of the territorial army without doubling its armament. However, the Territorial Battalions successfully provided the framework, while the volunteers showed a spirit that was reminiscent of those in 1914 and indeed, many of the volunteers were experienced veterans. In September 1939 the unit, whose headquarters were set up in Glasgow, first took its volunteers from the towns of southern Scotland, particularly the Borders. By October 1939 many

15th (Scottish) Infantry Division
(Major General G. H. Mac Millan)

44th Infantry (Lowland) Brigade (Brigadier H. D. K. Money)	46th Infantry (Highland) Brigade (Brigadier C. M. Barber)	227th Infantry (highland) Brigade (Brigadier J. R. Mackintosh-Walker)
8th Battalion Royal Scots	9th Battalion Cameronians	10th Battalion Highland Light Infantry
6th Battalion Royal Scots Fusiliers	2nd Battalion Glasgow Highlanders	2nd Battalion Gordon Highlanders
6th Battalion King's Own Scottish Borderers	7th Battalion Seaforth Highlanders	2nd Battalion Argyll and Sutherland Highlanders

volunteers were taken from the factories by the Ministry of Labour, and the ranks were further replenished by recruits from the Midlands, who soon become 'true Scotsmen'. During the campaign in France it would regroup in the south of England to help face the possible German invasion on the Essex coast. The operations in the Middle East meant that this territorial division was reduced to a Lower Establishment, and it lost its 45 Brigade in the process. But in December 1942 it was reclassified once again as a Higher Establishment and began to receive conscripts once more. On 20 June 1943 it joined VIII Corps and began training in Yorkshire for the planned invasion, before being stationed on the south coast from April 1944 with 790 officers and 15,000 men.

Montgomery announced that it would be participating in the invasion and there were subsequent visits by both the king and Winston Churchill.

The first elements from the division arrived in Normandy on 13 June 1944, but the bad weather from 19-22 June delayed the rest of the invasion. Finally, three infantry brigades were lined up in Normandy:

The 44th (Lowland) Brigade:

- 8th Battalion The Royal Scots (8 R Scots)
- 6th Battalion The Royal Scots Fusiliers (6 RSF)
- 6th Battalion The King's Own Scottish Borderers (6 KOSB)

The 46th (Highland) Brigade:

- 9th Battalion The Cameronians (9 Cameronian)
- 2nd Battalion The Glasgow Highlanders (2 Glas H)
- 7th Battalion The Seaforth Highlanders (7 Sea-forth)

The 227th (Highland) Brigade:

- 10th Battalion The Highland Light Infantry (10 HLI)
- 2nd Battalion The Gordon Highlanders (2 Gordon)
- 2nd Battalion The Argyll and Sutherland Highlanders (2 Argyll)

Among the divisions troops were also a reconnaissance group (15th Reconnaissance Regiment RAC), artillery (131st Field Regiment R.A. and 181st Regiment R.A.), an anti-tank group (97th Anti-tank Regiment R.A.), the 119th Light Anti-Aircraft Regiment R.A., machine gun corps (1st Battalion (MG) The Middlesex Regiment), engineers (15th Divisional Engineers) and signal corps (15th Divisional Signals).

The spearhead of VIII Corps was its armoured division (11th Armoured Division), commanded by Major General 'Pip' Roberts, who at 37-years-old, was one of the youngest generals in the British Army. In June 1940 he was on the staff of 7th Armoured Division, before heading to North Africa and joining the 4th Armoured Brigade as a staff officer, and fighting with them in the Battle of Beda Fomm in February 1941. In 1942 he took command of the 3rd Royal Tank Regiment, followed by the 22nd Armoured Brigade on 29 July and fought with them at the Battles of Alam el Halfa and el Alamein. He led the 4th Armoured Brigade in Tunisia before returning to Britain in November 1943, where he was informed of his appointment as head of the new 11th Armoured Division, with the provisional rank of major general, effective from December.

The 11th Armoured Division was established in Britain on 19 March 1941 and was made up of two armoured brigades, the 29th and 13th, under the experienced command of Major General Hobart, with its headquarters in Yorkshire. The 13th Armoured Brigade was taken away in 1942 and replaced by a motorised infantry brigade (159th Infantry Brigade) from the 53rd Infantry Division. It underwent intensive training from May to July 1942, as well as replacing its Valentine with Crusaders, only for these to be replaced again by Sherman tanks.

11th Armoured Division
(Major General G. P. B. Roberts)

29ᵗʰ Armoured Brigade (Brigadier C. B. C. Harvey)

23ʳᵈ Hussars Regiment

3ʳᵈ Royal Tank Regiment

2ⁿᵈ Fife and Forfar Regiment

8ᵗʰ Rifle Brigade

159ᵗʰ Infantry Brigade (Brigadier J. G. Sandle)

4ᵗʰ Battalion The King's Shropshire Light Infantry

3ʳᵈ Battalion Monmouthshire Regiment

1ˢᵗ Battalion The Herefordshire Regiment

1. Major General 'Pip' Roberts, commander of 11 Armloured Division. (D. Stileman/Heimdal)

2. Brigadier Roscoe Harvey, commander of 29th Armoured Brigade. (D. Stileman/Heimdal)

The division had been based primarily on territorial units, such as the 2nd Battalion Fife and Forfar Yeomanry (F&FY), and newly formed units such as the 23rd Hussars (23H). Its training continued as it carried out manoeuvres in Stanford, Norfolk, and on the bleak Yorkshire Moors. A veteran unit, the 3rd Royal Tank Regiment (RTR) arrived, which was incorporated into the 29th Armoured Brigade. In preparation for any invasion, the division took part in various combined exercises from November 1943 to May 1944 and its vehicles were waterproofed at the base in Aldershot. A reduced staff left Portsmouth in the afternoon of 10 June on an LST and arrived in Normandy the following morning to set up base in Creully. The bulk of the division landed on 13 and 14 June, although it would take ten days for its tanks to arrive in the combat zones and in the mean time, the division was stationed in the Cully-Lantheuil sector while it awaited its orders. The main headquarters was responsible for operations and intelligence, while the 'Rear HQ' took care of refuelling and personnel management. The young General Roberts set up two communication networks; the first allowed him to stay in contact with his artillery commander, while the other meant he had access to his brigades and VIII Corps' headquarters.

The division's infantry brigade, the 159th Infantry Brigade had three motorised battalions:

- 3rd Battalion The Monmouthshire Regiment (3 Mons)
- 1st Battalion The Herefordshire Regiment (1 Hereford)
- 4th Battalion The King's Shropshire Light Infantry (4 KSLI)

The brigade's recruitment had been largely carried out in the Welsh Marches. From south to north; Monmouthshire (now the Welsh county of Gwent), Herefordshire and Shropshire, meaning that the men were either Welsh or English.

However, the most important part of the division was its armoured brigade (29th Armoured), commanded by the calm and collected Brigadier Roscoe Harvey, and made up of three tank battalions:

- 3rd Battalion Royal Tank Regiment (3 RTR)
- 23rd Hussars (23 H)
- 2nd Fife and Forfar Yeomanry (2 F&F), a Scottish regiment recruited from the Dundee area and commanded by Colonel Alec Scott.

The armoured brigade was also supported by a motorised infantry battalion, the 8th Rifle Brigade (8 RB), which used American-made M3 half-tracks. Its men were nicknamed the Green jackets, in honour of the brigade's actions during the Napoleonic Wars. At that time, the British soldiers all wore bright red jackets, but as the Rifles were used as snipers, they were allowed to wear a more discreet, green jacket instead.

The artillery comprised of two regiments; the 151st (Ayrshire Yeomanry) Field Regiment R.A (motorised artillery, 159th Brigade) and the 13th (HAC) Regiment Royal Horse Artillery (horse-drawn artillery, 29th Armoured Brigade). It also included an anti-tank regiment (75th Norfolk Yeomanry A.T.R.), 117th battery for the 159th Brigade and 199th battery for the 29th Brigade, and an anti-aircraft regiment equipped with Bofor guns, the 58th LAA Regiment. Reconnaissance was provided by the 2nd Northants Yeomanry.

For Operation Epsom, the 11 Armoured Division was to be supported by an independent armoured brigade (4th Armoured). This was an experienced unit that had fought in North Africa and carried the emblem of a black jerboa in a white circle on its engines, in recognition of its actions in the deserts. The 4th Armoured Brigade was originally incorporated into the Heavy Armoured Group of the Mobile Division, which later became the 7th Armoured Division, but had been independent since 1943 and had since fought in Sicily and in mainland Italy. Montgomery had chosen it to be the spearhead of the invasion due to its strong regular army units, such as the Scots Greys and the 2nd King's Royal Rifle Corps (2 KRRC), as well as its motorised infantry, a territorial unit, the 3rd County of London Yeomanry (3 CLY) and its tank battalion, the 44th RTR, which had been constituted during the war. At the time when Operation Epsom was due to be launched, the brigade had been fighting in Normandy for two weeks.

Insignia of the 4th Armoured Brigade.

Insignia of the 31st Army Tank Brigade.

Another armoured brigade would also take part in the operation, reinforcing the 15th Scottish Division. The 31st Tank Brigade comprised of an armoured communications company (31st Tank Brigade Squadron), two tank battalions (7th Battalion The Royal Tank Regiment (7 RTR) and the 9th Battalion The Royal Tank Regiment (9 RTR)), B Squadron 22nd Dragoons (Flails) and C Squadron The Westminster Dragoons (Flails), as well as the 31st Tank Brigade Workshop REME.

The 43rd Wessex Division, whose emblem was a Wyvern (a dragoon-like creature that appeared on the arms of the three kings of Wessex), was a classic infantry division and had been commanded by Major General G. Thomas since 2 March 1942. In September 1939 it had been established as a First Line territorial Army Infantry Division and had remained in England, training in Kent from 1940 onwards, before being attached to VIII Corps. It comprised of three infantry brigades:

The 29th Infantry Brigade:

- 4th Battalion The Somerset Light Infantry (4 Som LI)
- 4th Battalion The Wiltshire Regiment (4 Wilt)
- 5th Battalion the Wiltshire Regiment (5 Wilt).

The 130th Infantry Brigade:

- 7th Battalion The Hampshire Regiment
- 4th Battalion The Dorsetshire Regiment (4 Dorset)
- 5th Battalion The Dorsetshire Regiment (5 Dorset)

43rd (Wessex) Infantry Division
(Major General G. I. Thomas)

129th Brigade (Brigadier G. H. L. Luce)	130th Brigade (Brigadier N. D. Leslie)	214th Brigade (Brigadier H. Essame)
4th Battalion Somerset Light Infantry	7th Battalion Hampshire Regiment	7th Battalion Somerset Light Infantry
4th Battalion Wiltshire Regiment	4th Battalion Dorsetshire Regiment	1st Battalion Worcestershire Regiment
5th Battalion Wiltshire Regiment	5th Battalion Dorsetshire Regiment	5th Battalion Duke of Cornwall's Regiment

The 124th Infantry Brigade:

- 7th Battalion The Somerset Light Infantry (7 Som LI)
- 1st Battalion The Worcestershire Regiment
- 5th Battalion The Duke of Cornwall's Light Infantry (5 DCLI)

The artillery included the 94th Regiment R.A. and the 179th Field Regiment, as well as the 59th Antitank Regiment R.A and the 110th Light Anti-Aircraft Regiment R.A. Reconnaissance was provided by the 43rd Reconnaissance Regiment R.A. and the machine guns by the 8th Battalion (M.G.) The Middlesex Regiment.

However, this third division only landed on 24 June. After re-grouping the following day it was sent to relieve the 15th Scottish Division. In spite of this, VIII Corps numbered 60,000 men and was supported by 736 guns, which could provide concentrated artillery every 150 metres. The powerful artillery was supported by another powerful strike force, that of the naval artillery, which was to pin down any German counter-attack in the days to come. This support was provided by HMS *Roberts* and three other cruisers, not to mention further support provided by 250 heavy bombers of the Royal Air Force and the dangerous fighter-bombers that would crush enemy positions and attack any vehicle movements.

As Hubert Meyer, the former Chief of Staff of the *Hitlerjugend* Division, noted: 'The balance of power was in favour of the British. It was 6:1 for the infantry, 7.5:1 for the tanks and 21:1 for the artillery. There was nothing else to say regarding the enemy's superiority in the air (although this did depend on weather conditions). In summary, the numerical superiority of the attacker was such that the success of the offensive had to be considered certain.'(1)

VIII Corps would receive further support on its flanks: to the west was the 49th Infantry Division (XXX Corps), which would launch the preliminary attack (Operation Martlet) with the aim of breaking the German front lines before the full-on attack of Operation Epsom (see following chapter).

In this first sector (around Fontenay-le-Pesnel and Rauray) the 49th Division would line up nine infantry battalions and four tank battalions (from 8 Armoured

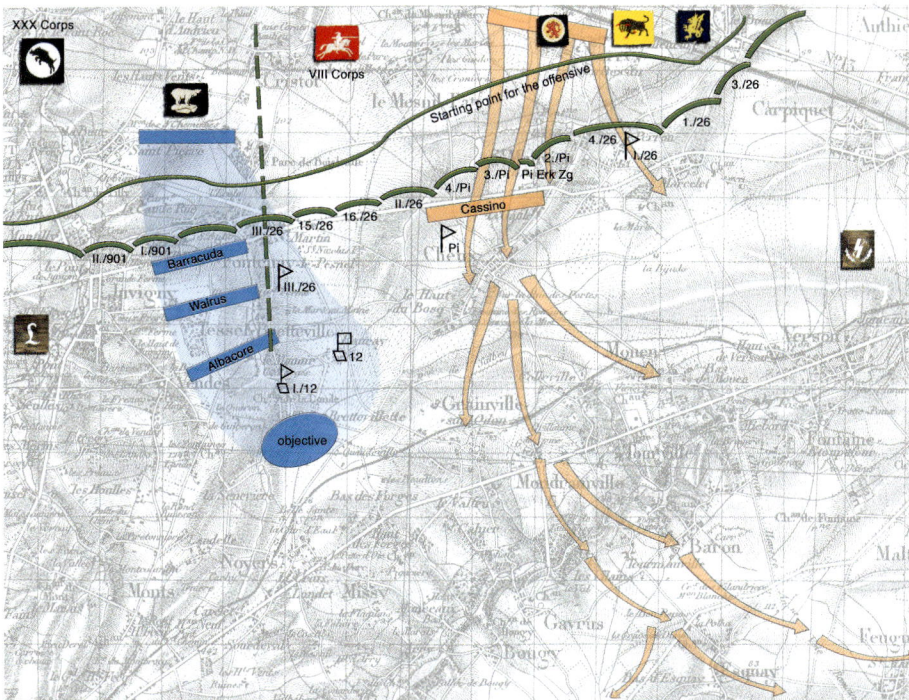

The plan as conceived by Montgomery: the 49th Division would first clear the right flank, particularly the high ground at Rauray, then VIII Corps would push through beyond the Odon and Orne to bypass Caen by the south. (Map L.K./Heimdal)

Brigade). Opposite them were two German infantry battalions (I Battalion Panzer-Lehr-Regiment 130 and III./26), elements from 15./26 and 16./26, and a single tank company (8./12). In the centre (the sector around Saint-Manvieu and Cheux), the British had twenty-two infantry battalions and eleven tank battalions facing three German infantry battalions (I./26, the *Hitlerjugend*'s engineer battalion and II./26) and only four tank companies (5th, 6th, 7th and 9th from II./12).

Faced with what the British called a 'lightly held crust', success seemed assured, and only the terrain presented any obstacles that might hinder their progress. To begin with there was an area of open fields between two railway lines, where compact villages surrounded by high walls provided anchor points along the German front line for the grenadiers to resist any attacks with their defensive 'hedgehog' formations. After this, shortly before the second railway line, came the *bocage*, which was less favourable for the advancing tanks. The *bocage* and villages between this second railway line and the Caen/Villers-Bocage road provided further defensive anchor points for the Germans.

The next obstacle was the Odon Valley. Its sides were steep and wooded, and there were only three narrow bridges crossing the river. It was a considerable obstacle for any tanks and the issue was somewhat underestimated by the masterminds behind the operation. In fact, it became such a problem that in many peoples' minds, Operation Epsom was instead referred to as the Battle of the Odon.

It was clear that a quick crossing of the three bridges over the Odon could be achieved if the weak front lines of the *Hitlerjugend* Division could be broken in the early hours of the attack. If this was the case, and even if the 'hedgehogs' remained on the flanks, because the Germans did not have any reserves in the area at the time, then a rapid British advance by the infantry and armoured forces would be able to cross the Odon immediately.

After the confines of the Odon, the terrain was once more made up of open fields on a large hilltop that dominated the area and included the soon-to-be-infamous Hills 113 and 112. This was ideal ground for a rapid tank advance, provided that the German defences could be overwhelmed in a few hours. From there, the terrain quickly descended to another, even greater, obstacle: the Orne Valley, which like the Odon, was also steep and wooded, but this time was much wider. It had to be crossed in order to bypass Caen from the south via Bretteville-sur-Laize and the Caen/Falaise road. In all, there were a great number of obstacles, perhaps too many, but the overwhelming British superiority over an adversary whose front lines were extremely stretched, allowed for hope.

The official British report described the future battleground as follows:

>…an area of wide, hedge-less fields planted with wheat, descending gently to the Mue; an insignificant stream. From there, towards the south, the landscape once more becomes bocage; its large farms and orchards surrounded by thick hedges, the villages half-hidden among the hills and the landscape interrupted by small woods. From the south-west, a ridge runs north towards Fontenay-le-Pesnel and Rauray in front of XXX Corps' line and that of VIII Corps towards Haut du Bosq, with a prominence south-east of Cheux.(2)

25 June – Operation Martlet

49th (West Riding) Infantry Division
(Major General E. H. Barker)

146th Infantry Brigade (Brigadier J. F. Walker)	**147th Infantry Brigade** (Brigadier E. R. Mahony)	**70th Infantry Brigade** (Brigadier E. C Cooke-Colls)
1/4 King's Own Yorkshire Light Infantry	6th Battalion Duke of Wellington's Regiment	10th Battalion Durham Light Infantry
Hallamshire Battalion	7th Battalion Duke of Wellington's Regiment	11th Battalion Durham Light Infantry
4th Battalion Lincolnshire Regiment	11th Battalion Royal Scots Fusiliers	1st Battalion Tyneside Scottish

The 49th (West Riding) Infantry Division would be responsible for clearing the right wing of the great offensive. Under the command of Major General E. H. Barker since March 1944, it had been formed at the beginning of the war and its elements gradually sent to Norway. It then took up position in Iceland, as the Allies feared that this strategic island in the middle of the Atlantic would be a Nazi objective. As a consequence, the division's emblem was a polar bear and it was nicknamed the Polar Bear Division, even though there are no polar bears in Iceland! It returned to England in 1942 and trained in Scotland in preparation for the invasion, before landing in Normandy on 12 June and being attached to XXX Corps, whose left flank it was to protect.

The division comprised of three infantry brigades:

The 146th Brigade:

- 4th Battalion The Lincolnshire Regiment (2 Lincoln)
- 1/4th Battalion The King's Own Yorkshire Light Infantry (1/4 KOYLI)
- Hallamshire Battalion The York and Lancaster Regiment (Hallamshires)

The 147th Brigade:

- 11th Battalion The Royal Scots Fusiliers (11 RSF)
- 6th Battalion The Duke of Wellington's Regiment (6 DWR)
- 7th Battalion The Duke of Wellington's Regiment (7 DWR)

The 70th Brigade

- 1st Battalion The Tyneside Scottish Regiment (1 TSR)
- 10th Battalion The Durham Light Infantry (10 DLI)
- 11th Battalion The Durham Light Infantry (11DLI)

Divisional troops included the 49th Reconnaissance Regiment RAC, the artillery of the 69th Regiment R.A. (with 147th Brigade) and the 185th Field Regiment R.A. (with 70th Brigade), the 55th Antitank Regiment (218th Battery with 146th Brigade, 219th Battery with 147th Brigade and 217th Battery with 70th Brigade). Anti-aircraft came from the 89th LAA, the machine guns from the 2nd Princess Louise's Kensington Regiment, the engineers from the 49th Divisional Engineers and signals from the 49th Divisional Signals Engineers and 49th Divisional Signals.

Cloth badge of the
8th Armoured Brigade

For this particular operation, the division was reinforced by an armoured brigade (8th Armoured), with three tank battalions (24th Lancers, 4/7th Dragoon Guards and 1st Notts Yeomanry or Sherwood Rangers), an infantry battalion (12th Battalion King's Royal Rifle Corps), an artillery regiment (147th Essex

Yeomanry Field Regiment), an anti-tank battery and a communications unit (8th Armoured Brigade Signal Squadron). Reinforced by an armoured brigade and three infantry brigades (the equivalent of three regiments), the division was now more powerful than the entire *Hitlerjugend* Division. But size and equipment are not the only things that matter; it is the quality of the solider that makes the difference, and as we shall see, there was some concern regarding the 'Polar Bears'.

Montgomery had planned for the division to lead the attack and take the high ground around Rauray, which acted as an obstacle along the valley between Bordel and Fontenay-le-Pesnel. The high ground dominated the area, rising to around 100m, and once taken, the men could push through up to Noyers-Bocage and Aunay-sur-Odon. The attack would be launched first from the western edge of the Bas de Fontenay up to the group of houses that made up the Saint-Nicolas farm (600m south of the crossroads at the eastern exit of Fontenay). Two infantry brigades (the 146th to the west and 147th to the east) would attack, supported by the 24th Lancers and the Sherwood Rangers.

The attack would unfold in four phases:

1) In phase A, 146th Brigade (to the west) would take the Caude Road and the Bas de Fontenay, while 147th Brigade (to the east) would take the hill at Fontenay-le-Pesnel. The objective was codenamed 'Barracuda' and the attack would begin at 4.15 am if the weather was clear, or 4.30 am if it was overcast.
2) In phase B, 146th Brigade were to take the northern part of the wood, west of Tessel and the attack would end after Fontenay had been taken. This part of the attack was codenamed 'Walrus'.
3) In phase C, 147th Brigade would take the crossroads north-west of Rauray and then move forward to reconnoitre the hamlet. 146th Brigade would then advance to the west of 147th towards its objective of the southern edge of the Bois de Tessel. This objective was codenamed 'Albacore',and included the Vendes/Cheux road, with Tessel at the centre.
4) Finally, phase D involved 147th Brigade taking Rauray. The last objective was actually to the south of Rauray, in the east, and the hamlet of Brettevillette, in the west. The 70th Infantry Brigade was to be held in reserve, along with a tank battalion (4/7 Dragoon Guards), in the area west of Audrieu, in case of any German counter-attack along the eastern flank of the offensive.

Thus, in this narrow sector alone, which contained only a handful of German companies, the balance of power was overwhelming. However, the 49th Infantry Division had been on the front lines for a dozen days and had already suffered a crisis within its ranks. After leaving Audrieu on 16 June, which had just been abandoned by the *Hitlerjugend* Division following orders to retreat in order to shorten the front lines, it took part in an attack on the chateau de Boislonde. Situated in the middle of a park, the chateau had been used as a base for the grenadiers of III./26.

Boislonde Chateau

1. The author, Georges Bernage (left) with Len Downs in 1996. Downs is wearing the cap badge of the Duke of Wellington's Regiment and on his sleeve (from top to bottom), the Regimental Flash for The Duke of Wellington's, the Formation Badge with the Polar Bear of the 49th Division, and the two strips for the 147th Infantry Brigade. (G.B.)

2. Helmet and cloth badge of the 49th (West Riding) Infantry Division. (Heimdal)

3. Metal cap badge of the Duke of Wellington's Regiment.

4. A mortar group from 15./26. This picture was taken during training at Beverloo, in Belgium, during the winter of 1943-1944. These men would later take part in the fighting at Boislonde chateau, and their shells would cause heavy losses among the Dukes' ranks. (H. Meyer)

5. Pre-war map showing the Parc de Boislonde, north of Fontenay-le-Pesnel. (Paich)

6. SS-Unterscharführer (but still SS-Sturmmann in this picture) Alfred Steinhausen, who was killed on 17 June 1944 in the Parc de Boislonde. (H. Meyer)

7. Looking south, in the direction of the British attack, is the south-east part of the park where the former chateau stood. (G.B.)

8. Taken from the same place, this photograph shows the right-hand side (south-west) of the park, where the chateau's farm buildings still stand. (G.B.)

9. The remains of the Boislonde chateau after the fighting had stopped. End of June, 1944. (A. Pipet/Heimdal)

10. The chateau's farm toady. (G.B.)

The Dirty Dukes of Boislonde

At 2 pm on 17 June, the 6th Duke of Wellington's Regiment (6 DWR) attacked the park of the chateau de Boislonde, supported by a squadron of tanks and self-propelled artillery. The 'Dukes' were met by a German counter-attack and soon found themselves in Hell. One of the men, Len Downs, was from Newcastle, and had previously worked on the shipyards. He knew straight away that they were entering into a baptism of fire when his sergeant, who was advancing ahead of him, suddenly had his head blown off by a mortar shell. From that moment on, Len Downs would always have tears in his eyes whenever he remembered the horrific struggle at Boislonde. In *la Bataille du Calvados*[1], Albert Grandais states: 'From the outset, the Germans counter-attacked with mortars, which surprised the Dukes. One ran towards the trench, his face slashed by shrapnel, while another collapsed after seeing his arm blown off. Lieutenant David Wood remembers that it was not the sort of battle they were expecting and the sinister shells that came from no one knows where terrified them.'

By 5 pm, the objective had been achieved, but Lieutenant Gledhill's platoon on the left flank had suffered twenty-four casualties, while Lieutenant Hershall's on the right had suffered seven. What's more, two Sherman tanks had been blown up on the chateau's lawn. As the men entered the ruined chateau, Len Downs and his comrades discovered civilians, including the owners, Monsieur Lemaigre-Demesnil and his family, hiding in the cellars and in the kitchen. There were also captured German soldiers, as well as the bodies of those who had been killed, lying in the park.

The next day, 18 June, the Germans counter-attacked at 9 am. The attack was preceded by an artillery barrage that terrified the Dukes, who were still traumatised by the mortar fire they had sustained the day before. The men buried themselves in their foxholes, terrified. As the tumult grew, fear became terror. So intense was the rain of shrapnel that no one dared raise their head out of their foxhole. As the barrage got nearer, 'several of the frightened Dukes rose from their trenches and, abandoning everything, fled towards the trees where they were caught up in a fire storm and died from the shell clusters. The German infantry then looked for other targets on the ground and fired a volley of bullets at close range. At the edge of the wood, A Company was surrounded. Its commander, Helme, was killed and all the other officers eliminated as well.'[2]

The head of 6 DWR's anti-tank company, Lieutenant John Haldane, was at the battalion's CP when he saw the remains of the unit pass by in their desperate attempts to escape. There was nothing he could do to stop them. However, around noon, the 7th Duke of Wellington's Regiment avenged their brothers-in-arms and launched a counter-attack, finally taking back the wood from the Germans after five hours of intensive combat.

In his history of the *Hitlerjugend* Division[3], Hubert Meyer notes that after a brief round of artillery and mortar fire (at around 2.15 pm), the counter-attack

---

1   A. Grandais, *La Bataille du Calvados* (Presses de la Cité, 1973)

2   Ibid.

3   Hubert Meyer, *12. SS Panzer Division Hitlerjugend* (Heimdal, 1991)

of 18 June was led by two companies from III./26: the 9./26 and the 10./26, which would suffer heavy losses and retreat to the northern edge of Fontenay. As for hand-to-hand combat, SS-Oberscharführer Hans-Georg Kesslau recalls that it was a matter of trench shovels against machetes: 'The head of 9th Company, SS-Obersturmführer Zantop, was killed in the middle of the carnage. A comrade from 9th or 10th Company would later tell me that he saw Zantop being attacked by an Englishman, who cut his throat with a machete.' The total number of German casualties for this counter-attack amounted to 151 men, including 40 killed, 93 wounded and 18 missing. Only 7 prisoners were registered by the British, meaning that the remaining 11 of the 'missing' must have been killed.

The park would remain almost a 'No Man's Land' until the chateau was bombed on 19 June, after which the civilians evacuated and headed northwards for the British lines. During the evacuation, Monsiuer Lemaigre-Demesnil noted that there was debris everywhere from tanks and cars, not to mention the bodies of English soldiers. One of the men was still hunched over his gun; his fingers still on the trigger. Following its losses, the 6 DWR was sent to recuperate at Brouay. Here it received reinforcements, with the platoons being reconstituted on a ratio of one third old and two thirds new recruits. But the trauma was particularly bad and on 20 June, when the reinforcements arrived at Brouay, German artillery fire hit the surrounding farm buildings. For those who had experienced Boislonde, the terror from the artillery fire was so strong that the men abandoned their positions, which caused the newcomers to panic. It was at this point that the men were told their former battalion commander had been relieved and that Brigadier Mahony wished to speak with them. He asked the men if they had forgotten their long months of training, as they appeared to have flouted every tactical law during their withdrawal. He told them that their attitude had tainted the image of the whole division and what was worse, a few hundred metres east of Boislonde (south of Mesnil-Patry), members of the *Hitlerjugend* Division had previously executed thirty-five Canadian prisoners on June 8. As a result of their actions at Boislonde, the 'Polar Bears' would acquire a terrible reputation and their use of machetes meant they would be henceforth known at the 'Murderous Bears'. Len Downs points out that they were called the 'Dirty' Dukes, with a drawing even showing their emblem of a polar bear with blood dripping from its claws. On 24 June, the eve of Operation Martlet, the 6 DWR would remain in reserve, while the 7 DWR would stay on the front line.

Two Strategic Routes

As we have seen, the first objective of the attack was the road leading from Tilly to the Caen road. The second was the road from Caumont, which then joined the first to the east of the vicinity. Between the two was a lush valley with a small stream that would constitute a reasonable obstacle. There were houses along the two roads, as well as in the valley, called the Bas de Fontenay, where there were further stone houses dispersed throughout this rural setting. Two churches lay along the southern road: to the west was the parish church of Saint-Aubin, whose choir dated back to the thirteenth century. The Romanesque nave had been redesigned in the Gothic style during the nineteenth century, at the same time when the bell tower was built. The church of Saint-Martin, to the east, stood in the commercial

Saint-Aubin church stands to the west, near the south road. (G.B.)

The bell tower is all that remains of Saint-Martin church. (G.B.)

quarter of the small town, but all that remained was its partially destroyed classical bell tower. According to Arcisse de Caumont,[4] before the revolution each church had its own parishioners, until the latter church was suppressed. Already in ruins before 1944, only its bell tower now remained, although the tomb of the poet Segrais, who died in 1701, remained under its choir.

The road south descends to the level of the stream, which then moves south towards Tessel and Bretteville. There were fields on both side of the valley, which were cut up by thin hedges. Rauray lay to the east and the Bois de Tessel to the west: both were the objectives of the British attack. The commander of III./26, SS-Sturmbannführer Erich Olboeter, had set up his CP at the Saint-Nicolas farm, on the eastern exit of Fontenay, near the Rauray road. His companies were positioned on the north side of the southern road, which ran along the edge of the plateau overlooking the valley, making use of the solid stone houses to be found there.

Fire Storm at Fontenay

At 4.15 am on 25 June (5.15 am German time), nine artillery regiments opened fire on Fontenay. It was hell. Kurt Meyer had spent the night in position with 15./26 along the main road, east of Fontenay-le-Pesnel: 'Grenadiers with haggard faces were crouched in individual foxholes and shell craters. All the officers had either been killed or wounded.' He left his position before dawn, shortly before the artillery barrage:

> In the centre of the village [Fontenay] we were all taken by surprise. I leapt behind a flight of stone steps and waited for this unpleasant morning greeting to end. One of the men who had been with me was now lying in the road with his limbs shattered: a shell had hit him dead-on. Hunted like rabbits, we ran across the village. The violent artillery barrage rained down on Fontenay and we were glad to have escaped the ruins. A bombardment was also unleashed on III./26: could this be the prelude to the large-scale

4   A. de Caumont, *Statistique monumentale du Calvados*, Vol. 1

attack we had been expecting? The battalion CP was only a few hundred metres away, but the journey to it seemed endless, as we ran from one shelter to another before we finally reached it. It was now broad daylight and the first reports were already starting to come in. Fontenay was under attack from elements over in Saint-Pierre and Cristot. Enemy tanks at that moment were clearing a path on a small ridge of land and were preparing to advance on Fontenay. The tank fight began. Our camouflaged Panthers had the advantage with their better guns and the enemy tanks were stopped in their tracks as they caught fire. If only we had had more ammunition! Our artillery had to shoot sparingly and refuelling was almost impossible. Thankfully, the telephone line with the division's CP remained intact and the 1st Staff Officer [SS-Sturmbannführer Hubert Meyer] informed me that it was pretty quiet on the division's right flank.[5]

The British artillery destroyed the houses along the two roads, but spared some of those in the valley. Further south, III./26's positions, which dominated the valley, received direct hits. The fog gathered in clouds on the battlefield, mixing with the smoke from the explosions, which was then made even thicker by the bombs from the German counter-attack. The commander of the Hallamshires, Lieutenant Colonel T. Hart Dyke, noted that, 'It was an audacious plan for a one-day operation.' The fog certainly didn't make it any easier. 'Visibility was limited to about five metres. It was a problem we hadn't anticipated and could do nothing about. I couldn't get any information from either of my advance companies until they finally reported to me that they were both lost in the fog and had lost contact with all their platoons.'[6]

The attack began on the line between Saint-Pierre and Hill 102 (south of Cristot). On the right flank (west) the 146th Infantry Brigade (Brigadier J.F. Walker) attacked using the Lincolns on the right and the Hallamshires, under Lieutenant Colonel Dyke, on their left, followed by 1/4 KOYLI and supported by Sherman tanks from the 24th Lancers. On the left flank (east), the attack was carried out by 147th Infantry Brigade (Brigadier E.R. Mahony), using the Royal Scots Fusiliers on the right and the 7 DWR on the left, supported by the tanks of the Sherwood Rangers (SRY).

Due to the fog, the infantry companies were unable to follow the artillery barrage's advance and so were left to their own devices, completely disorientated. They crossed the northern road and descended into the valley along the labyrinth of small roads before reaching the Bordel stream. Lieutenant Colonel Dyke noted:

The Hallamshires' cap badge.

After understanding that these companies were unable to cross the creek, which was their objective, I sent A and D companies to take it … Five minutes later, seeing

---

5   K. Meyer, *Soldats du Reich*

6   Cited in Grandais, *La Bataille du Calvados*, p.98

that I no longer had any reserves, I went down the slope with the sappers and engineers towards the place I had chosen for the command post for our secondary objective … We couldn't see much … I went to see Sergeant Bennett, the intelligence sergeant, to act as his compass. We had to stop and get our bearings every five metres and it was a slow and worrying business.[7]

As they moved forward, Dyke came across two platoons from the Royal Scots Fusiliers who had got lost and so he put them in the right direction. Shortly after the road, he found the location he'd chosen for his CP, but immediately came under the crossfire from the machine guns and panzer shells fired from III./26's dominant position. However, it didn't prevent him from thinking about the unenviable fate of the German grenadiers, as the houses collapsed all around them and the enemy advanced through the mist and fog. He gave the order to attach bayonets and clear the houses to the west of the crossroads, near the church of Saint-Aubin.

The Juvigny road (from Caumont) at the crossroads at Fontenay was reached around 9.30 am. The Hallamshires, in the centre, reached their objective with the Lincolns on the right, towards Juvigny. On the left, the Royal Scots Fusiliers had come across houses which had now been transformed into mini forts towards the centre of the village. Violent, close-knit hand-to-hand combat followed and the men had to dig-in around the roadside cross, to the north of Fontenay. After reaching the southern road, the Hallamshires no longer had any contact with 147th Brigade's RSF and the left flank was now exposed. They were under fire from the panzers of SS-Obersturmführer Hans Siegel's 8th Company, which wounded many of their men. Lieutenant Colonel Dyke set up his CP at a farm near Saint-Aubin church. His command vehicle had arrived in the meantime and so he was now able to establish contact with the Lincolns, before coming under fire from the German counter-attack launched from the east of the village. However, the positions reached by 146th Brigade (Barracuda) were backed up by the six-pound anti-tank trucks of the 55th Anti-Tank-Regiment (Suffolk Yeomanry). One anti-tank gun, which had been placed to cover the road to the east, succeeded in destroying a Panzer IV using new Sabot ammunition. Sergeant William was in charge and although the next panzer destroyed the gun, William, though wounded, had another gun mounted and attacked the second Panzer IV. Lieutenant Colonel Dyke recalls: 'He was later rewarded with the Military Medal for his courageous action. They were the first enemy Panthers we had met and destroyed in the campaign, which earned us the £5 bonus offered by the division commander.'[8] However, Hubert Meyer's account differs slightly, remarking that it was a Panzer IV. Nevertheless, there are photographs showing a destroyed Panther on the road north of Fontenay.

By 10 am, the fog had lifted. The Lincolns of 146th Brigade had managed to break through in the west, pushing back elements of Major Uthe's I./901, who was killed in the action. This meant that contact with the grenadiers of the Panzer-Lehr-Division was lost, creating a rupture in the German front line at Juvigny. In the centre, the Hallamshires held the area around Saint-Aubin church, allowing Lieutenant Colonel Dyke to call the brigadier to engage the third battalion, the 1/4 KOYLI, who would

7   Ibid. p.98

8   H. Meyer, *12. SS Panzer Division*

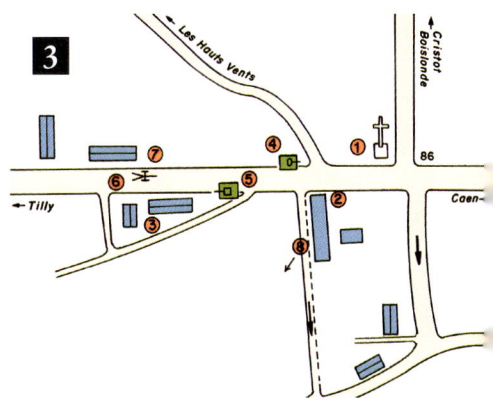

Fontenay-le-Pesnel, 25 June

1 & 2. This dramatic photograph was taken at Fontenay-le-Pesnel on 25 June by Lieutenant Handford. The road is the one leading from Tilly-sur-Seulles (behind) to Caen (ahead), although it was not easy to determine the location as the damaged houses on the right had been razed after the war and rebuilt away from the road. The large agricultural building, which can be seen more clearly in the current photograph, served as a guide. Eye-witnesses also remember the destroyed German tank. The German Pak 40 gun in the foreground was directed towards the junction of the road from les Hauts Vents and the road from Cristot, which is where the British attacked from. This anti-tank gun was therefore very well placed. The wreck of a Sherman tank on the left and a Panther tank on the right are seen further ahead and in the other images. The body of a Waffen-SS soldier lies near the gun and was perhaps a member of its crew. (IWM B 5939/G. Bernage)

3. Plan of the area in 1944: 1. Roadside cross, between the highways coming from les Hauts Vents and Cristot. 2. Agricultural building (see images 1 and 2). 3. Les Ecoles, houses since destroyed. 4. Destroyed Sherman tank heading east, probably having emerged from les Hauts Vents road. 5. Destroyed Panther tank, heading west. 6. German anti-tank gun. 7. House located north of the road. 8. Road leading down to Fontenay and from where you could see the church of Saint Aubin. (Heimdal)

1. Panoramic view showing the north side of the Tilly-Caen road, with the junction of the Cristot road (right), and the great cross dominating the crossroads. This is where the Hallamshires arrived, supported by the tanks of the 24th Lancers. Montgomery-Cuningham, the commander of the 11th Royal Scots Fusiliers, was killed on at the foot of the cross on 27 June 1944. A little further down the road is the location of the two destroyed tanks. (G. B.)

2. This other photograph by Lieutenant Handford was taken in the same direction as the previous picture, and in the opposite direction of the first one. We are now looking west, towards Tilly-sur-Seulles. In the foreground, we can see the back of the 24th Lancers' destroyed Sherman tank. In front of the school buildings, a Panther tank still burns. It belonged to the I./12. (IWM B 59/40)

Fontenay-le-Pesnel

1. This photograph was taken two days later, on 27 June, by Sergeant Christie. We can see the front of the 24th Lancers' Sherman tank that was hit below the turret and caught fire. The school buildings and the Panther tank from I./SS- Pz.- Rgt.12 can also be seen. This tank battalion in the HJ Division was held in reserve. According to Albert Grandais, two Panther tanks were destroyed in Fontenay-le-Pesnel on 25 June and this would be one of them. The SS-Pz.-Rgt. 12 suffered seven killed, fourteen wounded and two missing. Kurt Meyer wrote of the tank battle that took place in this area on 25 June: 'Fontenay was attacked by elements coming from the direction of Saint-Pierre and Cristot. Enemy tanks were just clearing a path on a small ripple of land and were preparing to push on towards Fontenay. The tank battle began. Our camouflaged Panthers had the advantage with their better guns.' (IWM B 6043)

2. Photograph taken at the same place. In the foreground, to the right, can be seen the little road coming from les Hauts Vents, where part of the attack came from. On the left, the razed school buildings were rebuilt away from the road. On the right, behind the trees, stands a large house. (G.B.)

1. This other photograph by Sergeant Christie was taken on 27 June and shows the men of the Durham Light Infantry marching westward. The rain and the intense traffic had turned this axis road to mud; most of the roads were paved and not tarmacked. The two destroyed tanks can still be seen, along with the gables of the houses on either side of the road. The one to the north (right) still stands. (IWM B 6042)

2. This house, north of the road, had been hit by a bomb, creating a hole in its roof and floor. (G.B.)

3. Looking southwards from the road towards le Bas de Fontenay can be seen one of the two churches, Saint-Aubin, which dominates le Bas de Fontenay, and whose bell-tower was hit by a shell. Soldiers used this ideal path to advance southwards towards le Bas de Fontenay. (IWM B 5941)

4. The same spot today. The road descends down to the valley and the large wall of the farm building is on the left. (G. B.)

5. A few meters further along, the church of Saint-Aubin is seen from the same angle as in the photograph from 1944. (G. B.)

6. The Hallamshires advance through le Bas de Fontenay. On the shoulder of the last soldier can be seen the 49th Division's emblem, the polar bear. Photograph taken on 25 June. (IWM B 5942)

7. Away from the two roads, le Bas de Fontenay suffered less damage and remained almost intact, as seen here, looking towards the south road. (G. B.)

press south and attack the Bois de Tessel. East of Fontenay, in the area around III./26's CP, the German grenadiers held firm, preventing 147th Brigade from advancing any further.

At 12.15 pm (1.15 pm German time), the 1/4 KOYLI engaged the second phase of the offensive to reach their objective (Walrus). This phase was supposed to have started at 6 am, but the fog and the resistance by III./26 delayed the advance considerably. From the Saint-Aubin church, which was held by the Hallamshires, the battalion advanced south, climbing the slope leading to the Bois de Tessel through a relatively open field, divided by a few hedges. The 1/4 KOYLI set out from Hill 88, near the church, aiming to reach Hill 114, at the northeastern edge of the wood. During the advance, the battalion suffered seventy-five casualties and although it reached its objective, the men had to dig-in north of the Bois de Tessel due to German counter-attacks from the east (the Rauray sector).

The emblem of the 55th Antitank Regiment (Suffolk Yeomanry) carved on the monument at Rauray. (G.B.)

In the east, the 11 RSF was still engaged in the hard fighting that prevented it from reaching the first objective. Lieutenant Colonel Dyke went to witness the progress of his neighbour on the left for himself, when a panzer opened fire on the farm where his CP was installed, setting fire to the roof. His new brigadier, Johnie Walker, then called him on the radio announcing that, according to a personal order from Major General Barker (the division commander), he would have to delay his push through 1/4 KOYLI's positions for the next phase, meaning the occupation of the southern part of the Bois de Tessel. However, Dyke must first make contact with the 11 RSF on his left and so with great caution, he joined the northern road after crossing the creek and thn moved east, but saw no trace of the RSF. He came under fire from a German machine gun before seeing Corporal Hart calmly descending the hill. He reported that the RSF were entrenched to the north, a long way away from their objectives! Dyke then went back in the same direction on foot and, by chance, met Lieutenant Colonel Montgomery-Cuningham, commander of the 11th Royal Scots Fusiliers. The latter told him that he had only forty men left and that they had been cut off. Dyke reassured him that he had many men in the area, and even more further west. The fog, which by this time (10 am) had lifted, had been responsible for this breakdown of communications. Lieutenant Colonel Dyke described Montgomery-Cuningham as 'amazing guy', but he was killed two days later and buried there near the roadside cross with some of his men.

For the Royal Scots Fusiliers fighting in Fontenay, the struggle against the grenadiers entrenched in the ruined houses was savage and the 7 DWR was only engaged in the late afternoon to support them. It attacked around 9 pm, when it should already have been south of Fontenay and the attack on the left flank was directed towards the eastern part of the village, in the direction of SS-Sturmbannführer's Olboeter's CP, which was seriously under threat.

In the face of these attacks on both flanks, Olboeter realised he was in a difficult situation, as the companies within his III./26 were at risk of being separated and he had already lost contact with the division's CP, in Verson. SS-Sturmbannführer Hubert Meyer ordered SS-Sturmbannführer Gerd Bremer's reconnaissance group to set up a liaison with the front-line sector. Bremer entrusted the task to SS-Untersturmführer Karl-Heinz Gauch, who was in charge of 1. Panzer-Spähkompanie, and below is his remarkably accurate account of what occurred:

> I presented myself to the commander. 'It's a good job you're here, Gauch' [he said] 'Look!' and he showed me the map. 'The enemy is here. He has broken through with infantry and armoured vehicles on our left. Here, near Fontenay, is Sturmbannführer Olboeter's III./26 and there's a dangerous gap between him and the Panzer-Lehr-Division. We don't know any more and there's no contact with battalion.' My thoughts turned to "Putti", the youngest of our officer graduates. His real name was SS-Untersturmführer Gädertz and he was an aide-de-camp at 3rd battalion. SS-Sturmbannführer Bremer continued, 'One of your platoon leaders must take a motorcycle section and get in contact with Olboeter. Only use force if necessary. Understand? Who's going to do it?'
>
> 'Sturmbannführer,' [I replied] 'with your permission, I'll do it myself. I think it's important!'

'No, you're the company commander.'

'But Bartsch could take over that role. Besides, Sturmbannführer, my friend Gädertz is there. I'm asking you to entrust me with this mission. I can't do anything else, I need to do something.'

'Alright, go ahead, but come back as quickly as possible!'

In one move, I took the map off the table and took my leave. Back at the company, I put on my camouflage outfit; did I need the steel helemt? 'Quenzel! Get in the saddle, let's go!' [I said] and jumped onto the Uscha's motorbike. I quickly explained our mission to Paul Quenzel and gave my orders to Bartsch. Off we went! As we passed through Missy, we crossed over the railway line from Caen. Telephone wires were hanging down everywhere and we had to drive very slowly down a sunken road. There were shell holes in the nearby fields and dead cattle with swollen stomachs. The sun was shining and the smell was horrific. Their feet were stuck up towards the sky in a really surreal way. Everything was calm. Our three motorbikes left behind a long ribbon of dust, which was alright because there were trees around us and it was too early for any Jabos. When we arrived at Tessel-Brettevillette, the village seemed dead. Some of the inhabitants passed by cautiously like ghosts. I stopped for a moment to orientate myself. The place seemed melancholy in its silence.

We were soon back among the meadows and hedges. There was a farm on our left and soldiers suddenly appeared. They pointed me in the direction of 3rd Battalion's CP: Fontenay was directly ahead of us. We had to be careful as we knew the enemy had us in their sights, but we continued on. Suddenly, shells were falling all around me and mud burst out from everywhere. Further and further ahead there was nothing but smoke, shell explosions and then more mud. We had no option but to go through it. There was no need to tell my driver what to do: he knew how to act in these situations. As the motorbike was camouflaged, we got off and he laid it down on the ground. In a couple of leaps I was in the fields, when a shell came screaming towards the ground. A pile of straw was burning next to me and my tongue was sticking to the roof of my mouth as I realised I hadn't actually eaten anything all day. I climbed through a

The narrow 'sunken road' leading from Brettevillette to Tessel, which was used by SSUstuf. Gauch on 25 June. (G.B.)

1. SS-Stubaf. Gerd Bremer commanded the HJ Division's reconnaissance group. He sent K.H. Gauch to the CP of III./26. This picture was taken a few days earlier at his CP in Cristot. (SS-KB Woscidlo)

2. SS-Ustuf. Karl-Heinz Gauch was the reconnaissance group's aide-de-camp. (G.B.)

3. SS-Stubaf. Olboeter commanded III./26. His CP was positioned at the Saint-Nicolas farm, south-east of Fontenay. (Heimdal)

hedge and felt a branch hit me in the face, but I had finally reached Olboeter's CP: a bunker covered with earth and straw to cushion the blows from the shells.

I fell inside and landed at Olboeter's feet. My sudden entrance had blown the candle out, which had barely illuminated the interior to begin with, and now everything was completely black. Swearing, someone began to look for some matches and once the candle had been re-lit, I introduced myself: 'SS-Untersturmführer Gauch, reconnaissance, sent to re-establish contact. What's the current situation? Why are you no longer in contact with the division? Are you in contact with the left flank?' Everything around me was spinning and I could hardly breathe. It was as if all the cigarette smoke from the last eight days wanted to come out of my lungs at once. Some of the officers were sat in front of me; muddy, unshaven, their eyes sunken in their sockets, their skin browned by the sun. The one with black hair and a graceful silhouette was Olboeter, nicknamed "Püttmann". I only recognised Lehmann among the others. The commander took both of my hands and said, 'Tell Gerd he has to help us, help us at all costs. Tell him that we're in real shit! I can hardly cope. I'm going to have to pull back my left flank before one o'clock.' He showed me the map and I took notes. 'Here's the breach, up to the small wood of chestnut trees. I can't do any more, our losses are too heavy. Gerd must help us! Now, do you still have any cigarettes?'

SS-Sturmbannführer Olboeter spoke without taking a breath. His eyes moved about nervously. I didn't need to ask what had happened in the last few hours. He loved each of his men as a father and now had to put them in an uncompromising situation. "Pütti" (SS-Untersturmführer Gädertz) was at the front with 10th Company and I couldn't speak to him. He was still alive an hour ago, but now? An hour is sixty long minutes and in a battle, every minute represents a thousand dangers!

We hastily smoked our cigarettes as the enemy artillery rumbled overhead. At each stroke the candle threatened to go out, and the liaison officers came in and out non-stop. Whenever one went out of the narrow entrance it became even darker [in the bunker]. News continued to come in from the front line:

'There's artillery fire on the whole battalion's position!'

'11th Company: the commander was wounded, but continued to take charge. There were four enemy tanks in front of their position.'

'12th Company: short of ammunition.'

'10th Company: a tank had been destroyed.'

'9th Company: the infantry had been pushed back and had suffered losses.'

'12th Company: under this kind of attack, they only had enough ammunition for a few hours.'

'10th Company: the commander had been killed and SS-Untersturmführer Gädertz was now in charge.'

So, "Pütti" was now in command of a company. SS-Obersturmführer Hopf had recently joined 3rd Battalion: he was a good guy. Meanwhile, 12th Company was asking the same as all the other commanders at the time: what was going on? What were their orders? Surely it can't just be "Hold, hold, hold, hold at all costs!" SS-Sturmbannführer Olboeter was shouting down the handset, his voice becoming more and more broken; he was beyond angry. Now that I knew what was happening here, I took my leave and left my last cigarettes to the men and officers in the bunker. Only one metre underground with two metres of straw on top, it was laughable when you considered the power of the British heavy artillery.

'Don't forget, Gauch. Don't forget to pass this on to Gerd, my friend!' [said Olboeter]

I got back on the bike again. A piece of shrapnel hit the sidecar and we were soon back at full speed. We passed by the shell holes and piles of burning straw. On the way we picked up a wounded man who was retreating. Everything I had seen, heard and experienced in those last few minutes was still with me and I knew that those who were still out there needed help as quickly as possible. An anti-tank gun or a tank fired a shell that landed behind us. The wounded man, made even more nervous by his injuries, huddled up at every impact.

I found the commander at Panzer Regiment Wünsche's CP (at Rauray). I made my report quickly, but explicitly. I hadn't forgotten what Olboeter had told me. Near Gerd Bremer was SS-Obersturmbannführer Wünsche, who also listened and appeared relatively calm. 'Tonight Gerd,' he said 'we will have the situation under control. Give me an infantry company to protect my panzers and I'll attack left of Tessel-Brettevillette and push the enemy back to the road!'

My commander quickly turned to a liaison officer: 'Tell Obersturmführer Beiersdorf to join me and let 4th Company get ready.' Then he turned to me and said, 'Well Gauch, it's time to head back!' He was also very calm and so we returned to our own CP and the orders began to flow out.

The situation for III./26 was perilous: its left flank had completely collapsed and there was a gaping breach in the line between the Panzer-Lehr-Division, near

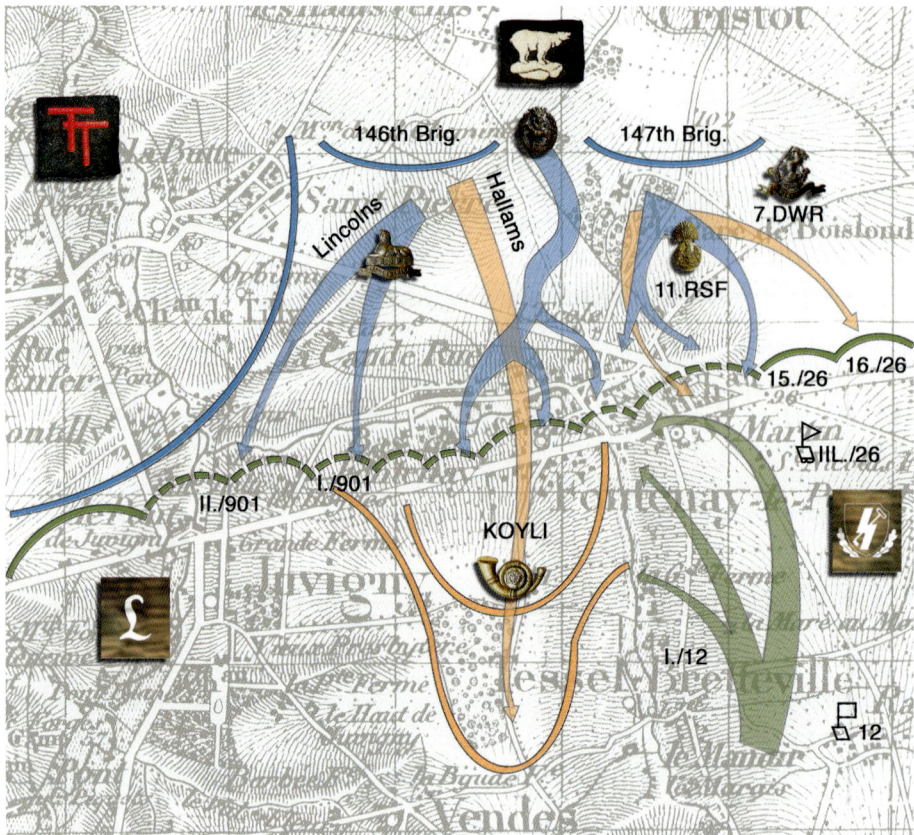

The breakthrough reached as far as the Bois de Tessel. Elsewhere, progress was slow, particularly east of Fontenay. Rauray, Operation Martlet's main objective, was out of reach. (L.K./Heimdal)

The 1/4 KOYLI advanced in the afternoon up to the Bois de Tessel, breaking through the German line.

Juvigny, and the Saint-Aubin church at Fontenay where the 1/4 KOYLI was positioned, north of the Bois de Tessel. The front line was creaking.

To close the gap, I. SS-Panzerkorps ordered the *Hitlerjugend* Division to counter-attack using its 1st Panzer Battalion (Panther) and its only infantry reserves (the 12th reconnaissance group). The Panzer-Lehr-Division would also launch a counter-attack and the two would meet in the Juvigny sector. Help from other elements was also needed, but none were available. The *Hitlerjugend* Division's counter-attack was carried out at the end of the afternoon by three panzer companies, 3rd and 4th companies from the 12 reconnaissance group, 5th (heavy) Company, and elements of III./26 from the Tessel sector, all under the command of SS-Obersturmbannführer Wünsche. SS-Obersturmführer Helmut Gaede's 12th Panzer Regiment would be at the head of the attack and under his orders, SS-Untersturmführer Schröder would take command of the lead platoon.

SS-Ostubaf. Max Wünsche engaged his 1st battalion of PanthER tanks in the area around Fontenay. He would launch a counter-attack at the Bois de Tessel. (Heimdal)

As they came within sight of the Bois de Tessel, the resistance mounted by the 1/4 KOYLI, supported by the tanks from 24th Lancers, increased. Meyer described how the lead panzer was destroyed at point-blank range and SS-Untersturmführer Schröder was killed as he tried to escape.[9] However, by 10.30 pm the counter-attack had brought them to within 500 m of the Juvigny/Fontenay road and allowed them to make contact with III./26's left flank, although they were still unable to establish contact with the Panzer-Lehr-Division's right flank in the area around Juvigny.

To the east, 147th Brigade was still marking time, while the 11th RSF had broken up and the 7th DWR had set off far too late. As for the 6th DWR, its advance was even slower, as most of the men were still in shock following the incident at Boislonde. Albert Grandais quotes the testimony of Luke Wood, who had arrived with

SSOstuf. Helmut Gaede's 2nd Company would be at the forefront of the attack. (Heimdal)

9   H. Meyer, *12. SS Panzer Division Hitlerjugend*, p.268.

the reinforcements, and who was trying to bring his platoon towards the front. The unit was sat in reserve in the Boislonde woods during the afternoon, causing great anguish among those who had experienced the hell there a few days before.

> We were trapped in our own inadequate trenches for most of that stifling afternoon, and a number of the men were shell-shocked. One of them even shot himself in the foot with his rifle, while another was brought to me by his corporal a few minutes later in a state bordering on hysteria. The man had been there during the first battle at Boislonde and didn't think he had the strength to dig up the ground in this mass grave. I spoke to him calmly and tried to bring him back to reason, but my words fell on deaf ears.[10]

As they moved through the park they found the bodies of the 'York men' from 6 DWR. The corpses were rotting quickly and the inescapable stench was everywhere. Soon there were only three soldiers behind Lieutenant Wood and he had to make his way back to find the others who were either smoking or sleeping…

However, at the front, around 9 pm, 7 DWR were fighting in Fontenay, assisted by a tank squadron from the Sherwood Rangers. The fierce combat would last until 11 pm in the eastern part of Fontenay and certain elements of the Dukes finally reached the southern road between the bridge (the Hallamshire's sector) and the crossroads on the eastern edge of the village. In this part of Fontenay, III./26 still held certain key positions, not to mention its CP, which was installed in the Saint-Nicolas farm, 300 m south east of the crossroads. As the tanks withdrew for the night, the Dukes were under orders to capture the CP the following morning.

The losses for 49th Division had been heavy. The 11th RSF alone lost 7 officers and 194 non-commissioned officers and soldiers,[11] and was removed from the front line before being sent back again on 28 June. The *Hitlerjugend* Division had 188 casualties in total, including 45 killed, 120 wounded and 23 missing. The breakdown was as follows:

- 10 killed, 20 wounded and 1 missing from II./26
- 10 killed, 35 wounded and 3 missing from III./26
- 14 killed, 31 wounded and 7 missing from 15./26 and 16./26
- 4 killed, 20 wounded and 10 missing from SS-AA 12
- 7 killed, 4 wounded and 2 missing from SS-Panzer-Regiment 12[12]

In *La Bataille du Calvados*, Albert Grandais notes that, 'according to an Allied report, the 1/4 KOYLI buried seventy-eight Germans in its sector alone and eleven panzers, including six Tigers and two Panthers were destroyed.'[13] The report is somewhat fanciful, as the one given by Hubert Meyer, which is more precise and

---

10   Grandais, *Bataille du Calvados* p.104

11   *War Diary, 147th Infantry Brigade*

12   Meyer, *12. SS Panzer Division Hitlerjugend*

13   Grandais, *Bataille du Calvados* p.104

covers the area as far as east Fontenay, only mentioned fort-five men killed (even if we add those from the Panzer-Lehr-Division, to the west of Fontenay). What's more, there weren't even any Tigers in this particular area at that time and the Allies often used to confuse them with the Panzer IV due to their similar silhouettes.

The end result was not a good one for 49th Division. With the exception of the greater part of Fontenay-le-Pesnel and the breakthrough at Bois de Tessel, most of its objectives had not been met. One of the most important was Rauray, which was supposed to cover VIII Corp's flank for its offensive the following day. This would prove to be a big problem in this sector, as its high ground would become the focus for the panzer's counter-attacks.

Having taken a beating, the *Hitlerjugend* Division began to reorganise. Its front line was extended 1.5km westwards to a bridge over the Bordel river, east of Montilly. In addition, orders were received to establish the main front line south of the Fontenay/Juvigny road.

> Since it was no longer possible to hold our position in Fontenay with sufficient force, overnight the division constructed positions on a line passing south of Saint-Martin, east of the Bordel river, where cover would be provided by elements of the 1st Panzer Battalion and the reconnaissance group, from the Big Farm to the Manor ('Le Montoir', 1.5km west of Rauray). From there we had to find and maintain contact with the Panzer-Lehr-Division in Vendes. The reconnaissance group's 2nd Company provided elements of cover in the area north east of Juvigny.[14]

To counter this threat, I. SS-Panzerkorps ordered a joint counter-attack by the Panzer-Lehr and *Hitlerjugend* divisions for the following day, although the latter replied that its numbers were insufficient for the task. The Panzerkorps planned to send reinforcements of Tigers from Schwere SS-Panzer-Abteilung 101, but they would not arrive on the front lines in time for the dawn attack. To compensate for this, the *Hitlerjugend* Division, in addition to its 1st Battalion Panthers, had to launch its Panzer IVs from 2nd Battalion (5th, 6th, 7th and 9th companies), while they built up reserves from the front between Fontenay and Carpiquet. This meant that the grenadiers from this sector would not have the support they needed to face the upcoming offensive (Operation Epsom), which was due to be launched the next day. The head of the *Hitlerjugend* Division, ignoring the planned offensive, demanded the recall of the transfer of companies from 2nd Battalion, but the Panzerkorps would not be moved: they must first put an end to this initial breakthrough that threatened the remainder of the front line. In addition, III./26 was to be reinforced by 1st Section, 1st Company, Engineer Battalion, which was set up to defend the CP at Saint-Nicolas farm. And so the guns would still thunder in the area around Fontenay and Tessel before the great offensive began.

---

14   Meyer, *12. SS Panzer Division Hitlerjugend*

Fontenay-le-Pesnel, south-east crossroads, 25 June, around 6 pm (1)

1, 2 & 3. Panther tank '219' was involved in the counter-attack on the afternoon of 25 June in the Tessel sector, where the British had just broken through. These three pictures from SS-KB Pachnicke show it breaking through a hedge. (Photos SS-KB Pachnicke/S. Cazenave)

4. This famous photograph shows a grenadier from III./26 at the north-east crossroads, where the attack by the Royal Scots Fusiliers was progressing with difficulty. Behind him, a Panther type G provides protection. In the background can be seen the partially-ruined church of Saint-Martin. (SS-KB Pachnicke/G.B.)

5. The current photograph shows the changes that have taken place: a small garden has been laid by the road in front of the preserved gable. In the background, trees now hide the bell tower of Saint-Martin church. (G.B.)

6. This other photograph from SS-KB Pachnicke shows a group of grenadiers from III./26 advancing towards the crossroads at the eastern exit of Fontenay. It was takendown the road from image 4, as the building can be seen behind the first Panther tank. This is the strategic crossroads of *Départementale 9* (with Caumont, in the west, ahead, and Caen behind), with the D 139 road leading left towards Rauray, 2 km to the south. (SS-KB Pachnicke/G.B.)

7. The same location toady, which looks relatively the same, despite the destruction. The gateway now has a small roof and the rails have been replaced by a cement fence. (E. Groult/Heimdal)

1. Detail of the vintage map showing the crossroads. (BP/Heimdal)

2. Uscha. Mahlke commanded Panther tank '438' and was killed on 25 June. (S. Cazenave/ E. Wenzl)

3. Panther '438' was destroyed on 25 June at Fontenay-le-Pesnel, one of the two declared destroyed. One was destroyed on the road, as seen in the photographs, and the other on the south road by the 55th Anti-tank Regiment, probably the '438' seen here. (S. Cazenave/E. Wenzl)

4. This spectacular picture from *SS-Kriegsberichter* (SS war correspondent) Pachnicke shows three Panther tanks slightly to the west of the crossroads. One of them opens fire in the middle of the ruined buildings towards the Royal Scots Fusiliers, as a soldier, probably a tank crew member, stands indifferently amidst the fire. The sunlight from the west extends the shadows, as seen in images 4 and 6, which gives us a time of around 6 pm, which corresponds well to the counter-attack by the Panthers following the breakthrough by the 49th Division. This photograph was published on 4 July, nine days after the fight. (SS-KB Pachnicke/S. Cazenave)

5. The same location today The agricultural buildings, which were damaged by the morning artillery barrage, are no longer there. The gable on the right and (partially)on the left are our landmarks. (G.B.)

6. Panther '219' (from SS-Ostuf Helmut Gaede's 2nd Company), a model D and recognisable by its turret, enters the crossroads from north of the D139 road, where it had faced The Royal Scots Fusiliers. Two more Panther tanks are behind. (Heimdal)

1. This photograph is taken in the opposite direction image 6. The photographer is now looking east towards the road to Caen, whose rows of trees are visible in the background. Here we can see Panther '219', which has changed position. (Heimdal)

2. The same location now. The two roofs are our landmarks. (G.B.)

Among the anti-tank elements north of Fontenay, a Pak gun, commanded by Otto Berke, a 22-year-old lieutenant and head of section in 8./26, attempted to stop the Polar Bear Division's advance. This is his testimony.

In a large farm with several stables and barns, surrounded by hedges on the northern edge of Fontenay, we wanted to repel the planned attack. A Pak 7.5 cm gun from the regiment's Pakzug *(anti-tank section)* was also assigned to me. The gun commander was SS-Unterscharführer Knaust. The powerful artillery fire, which had lasted all day, indicated an attack, and in the early hours of Sunday morning, a rolling barrage that lasted several hours prevented us from leaving our Bereitschaftsraum *(operations room)* at the farm. Almost all of the houses in the village were in ruins. A few days before, when the presbytery was still undamaged, we picked strawberries in the garden and ate them for our 'farewell dinner'.

Our divisional commander, Panzermeyer, also made an appearance at our outposts to give us courage, knowing full-well what would befall us. When then the rolling barrage stopped, we quickly occupied our positions in the farm hedges. The Pak was ready for combat, with explosive shells to keep the attacking English away from us. In the end, it was practically a melee. When all of the Pak's ammunition had been fired, the soldiers defended themselves with their pistols and rifles. Beside the Pak's protection shield, SS-Uscha. Knaust, the gun commander, knelt down with his submachine gun. 'Untersturmführer, das fetzt!' *('Untersturmführer, that's it!')* He was hit and collapsed on the right-hand side of the gun-carriage.

The 'Sani' *(medic)* had to take care of more than ten injured men in the meantime, so I ordered him to hand them over to the English. I asked the VB *(vorgeschobener Beobachter, the forward observer)* to direct the artillery fire according to his own judgement, so that the British were forced to take cover while we retrieved our survivors.

Sturmmann Weißenborn, who had been wounded by a bullet in the thigh, refused to be taken prisoner and so by dragging him, we both managed to escape being surrounded by the British. As we retreated towards Rauray, I recognised a young fellow who lived near me, who had been mortally wounded. Unfortunately, I cannot remember his name, although he was in the 8.8 cm mortar group.

A Pak 40 gun, probably from SS-Pz. Gren.Rgt.26, in action at the end of June 1944. The 7.5 cm Pak 40 L/46 was one of the best anti-tank weapons of the Second World War and fired a wide variety of ammunition. *Panzergranate 39* (perforating shells), weighing 6.8 kg, could pierce 89 mm of armour (at 30°), at 1 km, with an initial speed of 792 m/sec. (SS-KB Woscidlo/S. Cazenave)

The First Day – Monday 26 June

Prelude at Tessel

During the night of 25-26 June, SS-Obersturmbannführer Wünsche prepared his men for the upcoming dawn attack. Meanwhile, the commander of the *Hitlerjugend*, Kurt Meyer, received the latest reports from SS-Sturmbannführer Hubert Meyer: the front was calm. The radio operators reported no British radio activity that would suggest a movement of armoured troops west of Caen. On the other hand, the British knew everything about the movement of German troops, thanks to the cryptographic intelligence known as 'ULTRA'. However, Kurt Meyer was convinced that something was about to happen, and that the attack at Fontenay-le-Pesnel the day before was just a preliminary.[1] The rolling artillery barrage that had preceded the attack by 49th Division had lasted for three hours; longer than any that had come before it. Kurt Meyer asked his Chief of Staff to keep in contact with the Panzer-Lehr-Division in order that the two attacks could be co-ordinated, before leaving his CP at Verson in the middle of the night and heading to the Panzer Regiment's CP at Rauray. He wanted to make sure that any counter-attack was conducted swiftly so that the panzers of 2nd Battalion could provide cover for Regiment 26.

The British were also planning a dawn attack, which would be launched two hours before the start of Operation Epsom, due to begin at 7.30 am. The attack was to be carried out by 8th Armoured Brigade, reinforced by an infantry brigade from 70th Brigade (49th Division), 1st Battalion the Tyneside Scottish, against III./26's left flank at the Bois de Tessel. Joining them would be two tank battalions: 4/7 Dragoon Guards (minus a company) and the 24th Lancers. The attack would cross the Bordel Valley, north of Tessel, and the objective was Rauray. The right flank (towards Tessel) would be protected by 12th Battalion Kings Royal Rifle Corps (12 KRRC), while 7 DWR would advance south, towards Rauray, in order to take the Saint-Nicolas farm. Their numbers were superior to those of Wünsche's *Kampfgruppe*, and the two attacks would cause some confusion.

The panzers counter-attack at Bois de Tessel

At dawn, the panzers of *Kampfgruppe Wünsche* headed south-east of the Bois de Tessel to launch their counter-attack. The commander of 6th Company, SS-Obersturmführer Ruckdeschel, took part in the attack and gave his account to Hubert Meyer:[2] 'We had been withdrawn from our favourable positions where we had been expecting the enemy to attack between our division and the Panzer-Lehr-Division: more than 100 enemy tanks had tried to break through. We arrived at dawn without any losses and knew that the enemy tanks must be hidden in the

---

1   Or at least this is what he states in his book, *12. SS-Panzer-Division-Hitlerjugend*, p.270.

2   Testimony provided on 15 November 1973 and published in *12. SS-Panzer-Division-Hitlerjugend*.

wood.' Ruckdeschel then goes on to describe the terrain in the area around Tessel, known as 'Le Montoir' (not 'Le Manoir' as is sometimes written in German texts and on maps of the period). He headed to the north-east of the small village, and to the north-west corner of the cemetery, where the church overlooked the Bois de Tessel.

> I observed the wood through my binoculars and could see armoured vehicle tracks in front of it, heading to a large orchard on the right. Fortunately, I was near the cemetery wall and was able to hide my panzers. I got out of my tank and went from one tree to the next, alone, following the tracks with

1. Ludwig Ruckdeschel in the uniform of a Gauleiter. (S.C./via H.M.)

2. Ruckdeschel is seen here in the turret of his Panzer IV during manoeuvres in Belgium. (BA)

3. Tessel church and its cemetery, dominated on the left by the open fields and the Bois de Tessel, and overlooking the Bordel Valley. Behind the church can be seen the trees near to which SS-Ostuf. Ruckdeschel was wounded. (G.B.)

Kurt Meyer, commander of the HJ Division, was in Rauray with Max Wünsche when the attack was launched. (Heimdal)

SS-Stubaf. Arnold Jürgensen commanded the Panther battalion (I./12) which took part in the fighting at the Bois de Tessel. (S.C.)

my binoculars. Suddenly, automatic rifle fire crackled through the air and I instinctively dropped to the ground and headed back on all fours. Enemy shells were now raining down hard and thanks to the start-up flames, we were now able to see where the enemy tanks were positioned: my panzers were still well-camouflaged in comparison to theirs. I was about 50 or 60 metres away from my company when a shell hit the tree I was sheltering under. My right arm was reduced to mincemeat and when I arrived at the division's primary aid station, Doctor Rolf Schulz said, 'The fact that you're still here goes beyond the laws of medicine. You've lost more than half of your blood and there is no way you should have survived.'

Kurt Meyer described the launch of the attack:[3]

In the night, the grenadiers of Regiment 26, exhausted by the hard fighting of the previous day, were huddled in their foxholes awaiting the next attack. A thick, damp mist extended over the fields and hedgerows: the day was beginning to dawn and everything was still quiet. I was near Rauray with Max Wünsche as we rolled the last panzers into position. It was becoming clearer all the time. The first Auster[4] was already circling the sky and the macabre dance would soon begin. We could hear the rumble of the German batteries as the English planes flew over us, firing their rockets towards Rauray. In a loud noise of caterpillars, the first panzers rolled forwards. At first the attack progressed smoothly, but was soon stopped by an English counter-attack and it became a furious tank-against-tank battle. The landscape was covered in hedges, making it difficult to see what was going on and preventing our panzers from taking advantage of their greater firing range.

---

3   K. Meyer, *Soldats du Reich*, p.312.

4   British military liaison and observation aircraft.

It was the lack of infantry that was particularly harmful. The heavy artillery fire seriously hampered cooperation between the units and made any real command almost impossible. We heard nothing from east of Rauray and the whole battle moved westward. The tanks crashed into each other and as the columns of burning fuel rose towards the sky, each one marked the death of another tank.

The attack by 1st Battalion (Panther) and elements of 2nd Battalion (Panzer IV), carried out with 3rd and 4th Companies from the reconnaissance group (SS-Pz.-Aufkl.-Abt. 2), started well, but was then blocked by a counter-attack by the British tanks. The signal officer from 1st Battalion, Untersturmführer Rolf Jauch, was wounded in the battle:

Our attack was bogged down and we were sitting ducks on three sides at once. There was a problem with the gun on my Panther and I had to get down and go get a piece from one of the destroyed panzers on the eastern side of the small valley. Shots were fired at us from the right and my comrade, Gumpert, was killed instantly. I was hit on my right elbow and slightly on my chest, but I managed to bring the piece back to the Panther. Jürgensen, the battalion commander, told me to go east and then south because it was impossible to transport me in a Sanka (ambulance). Through the hedges, I managed to rejoin the road that we had used the day before as we headed for Tessel and Brettevillette. That afternoon, I was taken in an ambulance to the aid station.[5]

Before it had even really started, the German attack was blocked by the British and was soon suspended. The Germans had suffered losses without gaining any real advantage. Operation Epsom had now begun and Kurt Meyer was still concerned about the situation surrounding Regiment 26.

There had been hardly any shelling to the right of Rauray. It began to rain and we thanked God that we would be spared the *Jabos*. But then the earth seemed to open up and swallow us all, and in the space of a few seconds, all hell broke loose. Rauray was now nothing more than a pile of trees and ruined buildings. I lay in a ditch and listened to the sound of the fighting as it drummed and drummed on without any respite. The fog mixed with the gases from the exploding shells and I couldn't see anything. All communications had been cut off. A liaison officer from 2nd Battalion threw himself at me and cried, 'Armoured vehicles! Caterpillar

The battalion's communications officer, SS-Ustuf. Rolf Jauch, was injured. (Heimdal)

---

5   Testimony provided on 6 June 1974 to H. Meyer.

against caterpillar! Battalion right wing!' His message was engulfed by the shell explosions and my ears tried to analyse the noise of the fighting but could not. A rumbling, howling and continual gasping of the shells mingled with the rattle of the tanks' caterpillars was all I could hear. This was the great attack we had been expecting. Now the keystone of the German front line in Normandy was at stake!

Attention now turned away from the area around Tessel. Operation Epsom, which would overwhelm Regiment 26, had now begun, but Kurt Meyer understood the situation and gave his orders:

> All around me were instruments of death. Burning steel whistled over our heads and landed in the damp earth. I cried out towards Wünsche, as liaison officers ran down the road and disappeared into the thick, green hedges. He soon arrived at my side and I knew I didn't have to give any grand explanations to this veteran front line soldier: we had fought next to each other many times. He knew me and knew what I wanted, so I told him, in as few words as possible, what I thought of the situation. I believed the enemy was trying to break through Regiment 26's position with heavy armoured forces and then take Caen. First, I ordered that the attack on Juvigny was to be suspended immediately. I then ordered that as Rauray was the keystone of the division, it was to be held at all costs, and third, that he was to be responsible for holding it.

At Tessel, the British hadn't really benefited from the generous artillery support of the previous day, which had been kept in reserve for the imminent attack. However, the tanks of the 24th Lancers and the infantry from 12 KRRC had managed to reach the edge of Tessel and Brettevillette, and advance even deeper into German territory. Unfortunately, the tanks from 4th/7th Dragoon Guards and infantry from 1st Tyneside Scottish Regiment had failed in their eastward attack to capture the bridge leading to the big farm along the eastern bank of the Bordel, which was one of the main routes into Rauray. The failure seriously threatened the right flank of the 24th Lancers and 12 KRRC, who were now dangerously exposed to the Panthers from I./12. Major Stirling, commander of 4th/7th Dragoon Guards writes:

> This was a wretched day. The scene at the start-line was described as a 'badly organised partridge shoot' because the infantry and tanks did not get lined up properly and our tanks were fired at by the infantry. C squadron was overlooked from two sides. Two to six Tigers and Panthers were operating on the dominant high ground. On the left flank was a small wood in which four Tigers were sitting – cleverly placed so that it was impossible to get at them.[6]

In addition, the Dukes of 7 DWR had also failed in their attack on the Saint-Nicolas farm. After the start of the general offensive, the assessment of 49th Division's

---

6   Tim Saunders, *Operation Epsom* (Pen & Sword Books, 2003), p. 36

attack was that it failed because the strategic town of Rauray remained firmly in the hands of SS-Panzer-Regiment 12, which would thus threaten the offensive in progress.

The start of Operation Epsom

While fighting was taking place around Fontenay and Tessel, 60,000 men were getting ready for the big offensive. The conditions were not ideal: rain had begun to fall on 25 June and the bad weather did not favour aerial support. In addition, the men had had little sleep. Tim Saunders cites the testimony of Lieutenant Robert Woolcombe of the 6th (Border) Battalion the King's Own Scottish Borderers Regiment (KOSB), who had arrived from Secqueville-en-Bessin at the assembly area at around 3 am, in the rain. It was still dark and dawn would not break for a few more hours. They were woken up at 5.30 am by the sentry, having had only two and a half hours of sleep before the attack. They had a morning wash and meal, with two hours before the artillery barrage would start. The rain would finally stop with the break of day. Another testimony from an officer of the KOSB[7] recalls how the men were sheltering under the hedges from the rain and trying to sleep a little. After being woken up at 5.30, they ate and talked to each other, exchanging trivialities without speaking about the upcoming battle. With their weapons carefully cleaned and oiled, the men then applied a green camouflage cream to their faces. At 6.45 am the commanders were told that they would receive less aerial support as a result of the bad weather. There would be practically no aircraft leaving English soil, with only those already stationed in Normandy available to provide limited support. Bayonets were fixed on to rifles and rations, made up of beef pieces, cheese, and biscuits, were stored away. Sweets and chocolate were slipped into pockets and a final cigarette was smoked before the attack.

The guns were already thundering in the west and the commanders knew that the high ground at Rauray had not been taken. At 7.29 am, back in the rear, the artillery batteries began to warm up as they counted down; starting at thirty seconds … and finally, three, two, one, Fire! In total, 630 pieces of artillery opened fire, not to mention those belonging to the Navy. Sergeant Jimmy Blair of the 2nd Glasgow Highlanders (46th Brigade) remembers that, 'It was terrifying to hear our own shells flying over our heads, but it also raised our morale when we thought about the ordeal the Germans must be going through.'[8] Major John How, 3rd Battalion The Monmouthshire (11th Armoured Division) also remembers that:

> Since dawn, the artillery fire had continuously thundered in the direction of the front line. We were caught up in a mixture of excitement and anxiety… Between two bursts, we could see the lights from the batteries through the low clouds: the horizon trembled and thousands of lightning bolts streaked across the night sky. We observed it all for a long time in silence, then someone said what we were all thinking, 'That's where we've got to go!' Our breathing

---

7   I. Daglish, *Over the Battlefield: Operation Epsom* (Pen & Sword Books, 2007), p.41

8   A. Grandais, *La Bataille du Calvados*, p. 110.

1. Major John How, 3rd Battalion Monmouthshire, 11th Armoured Division. (Heimdal)

2. Gunners from E Troop, 521 Battery, 15th Scottish Division, open fire with their 25-pound gun positioned near le Mesnil-Patry. The gun had a maximum range of 12 kilometres, with an average rate of five shots per minute. This photograph was taken on 28 June by Major Stewart. (IWM B6129)

got heavier and our hearts beat a little louder. The 18-year-old boys in the *Hitlerjugend* Division, strong in their beliefs with the folly of youth, would sell their lives dearly.[9]

For ten minutes, the artillery barrage was directed on the lines of the *Hitlerjugend* Division, before advancing 90 metres (100 yards) every three minutes. The British artillerymen were well-trained, but in order for it to be effective, the infantry had to follow behind as closely as possible. It had been five years since the 15th Scottish Division had trained for such an offensive, and they had taken part in an exercise in England, back in April, to try and stick to the barrage. There were always the risks of being hit by shrapnel, but it was decided that it was a risk worth taking. Experience gained since the

---

9   J. How, 'Baptism of Fire', *Western Mail*, 27 June 1981.

Battle of the Somme in 1916 had shown that by arriving in a position which had just been shelled, the enemy was still recovering from the shock and was therefore easier to capture. On the other hand, an enemy who had had time to recover was much more dangerous than the collateral risks of the barrage.

Of the 60,000 men who were to take part in the operation, only a few hundred would follow the artillery barrage. The resources and the artillery would naturally stay behind, but the system of keeping troops in reserve would have infinite repercussions as it meant that front line troops were always thin on the ground: an astonishing feature of British tactics. First, an infantry division

VIII Corps General Staff badge. (Private Collection)

had three infantry brigades. As we have already seen with Operation Martlet, two were engaged while one was kept back in reserve. Within each brigade, two battalions were engaged while again, one was kept in reserve. Then within each battalion, two companies were engaged and two held in reserve, effectively 50 per cent of the workforce, and only sixteen companies out of a possible seventy-two! Within each company, two platoons were engaged, while a third platoon and the command platoon remained behind – still only 50 per cent of the workforce. Furthermore, only two teams from one platoon were on the front line. Thus, as Ian Daglish notes, 'On the morning of 26 June, the leading elements of VIII Corps amounted to only thirty groups of nine or ten men separated by 100 yards or more.'[10]

While the Germans were moving forward in leaps and bounds, adapting to the terrain, the British infantrymen advanced in an old-fashioned line with bayonets fixed. What's more, there were only a little over 300 of them who were to follow the hurricane of fire over the open ground, which itself was drowned in fog. This meant that just over 300 men were to be offered up to the bullets of the surviving machine guns, while 60,000 men followed behind. Thus a privileged few had the unenviable honour of offering themselves before a whole army corps. However, this system also had an advantage: turnover. At each phase of the battle, a front line unit was relieved by a reserve unit, which took over its role, and so on and so on, meaning there were always fresh troops on the front line.

And so to the west (right), the 46th Brigade would advance with the 9th Cameronians and the 2nd Glasgow Highlanders, with the 7th Seaforth remaining in reserve. Tanks from 7th RTR provided support, with their objective being Cheux. To the east (left), 44th Brigade would advance with the 8th Royal Scots and 6th Royal Scots Fusiliers, while the 6th KOSB was kept in reserve. They would be supported by the tanks from 9th RTR and their objective was Saint-Manvieu. Meanwhile, 227th Brigade would remain in reserve.

---

10   Daglish, *Over the Battlefield*, p.42

46th Brigade: Objective Cheux

On the right wing, 46th Highland Brigade, commanded by Brigadier C. M. Barber, advanced from its starting point at Le Mesnil-Patry towards its first objective; the Fontenay/Carpiquet road (codenamed Cassino). Its secondary objectives were the village of Cheux and then the hamlet of le Haut du Bosq. At the front were two battalions: the 2nd Glasgow Highlanders (2 Glas H) on the left (east), supported by the Churchill tanks from B Squadron, 7th Royal Tank Regiment and the 9th Cameronians on the right (west), supported by tanks from C Squadron, 7th RTR. The front of the attack was narrow (about 1000 yards) and the two companies in each battalion were supported by around fifteen tanks each. The front line companies included two platoons, with each platoon assigned two Churchill tank troops, of which there were three tanks per troop. The support elements were to follow behind, including Chenillettes, mortars, anti-tank weapons etc. The flanks of each battalion were to be protected by seven Bren gun carriers, two 3-inch mortars and six Stuart tanks from 7th RTR.

Shoulder badge of the 9 Cameronians, with the Douglas tartan and two stripes for 2nd Brigade (the 46th). (Private Collection)

The battle had been planned meticulously, but the Canadian soldiers of 3rd Canadian Division were already exhausted from fighting, and only had a vague knowledge of the vast German minefield through which they were supposed to lead the Scottish infantrymen. The rest of the units involved were also too 'green'. Thanks to the decryption work of ULTRA, Montgomery was aware that important German reinforcements were joining the Normandy Front to launch a counter-attack. He knew that II. SS-Panzerkorps had arrived in France on 24 June and was currently en route to Normandy, as well as 1. and 2. SS-Panzer-Divisions. The offensive could not be delayed and the Allies had to strike hard and fast, in spite of the bad weather, before it was too late. The Glasgow Highlanders had only landed on Friday, 23 June and not reached their assembly zone until 10 pm the following day. The tanks from 7th RTR had landed in France on 22 June; six were lost in the process after the LCT carrying them struck a mine.

Shoulder badge of the 2 Glasgow Highlanders. The tartan is that of the 42nd Goverment. (Private Collection)

Hundreds of vehicles were piled up in the departure zone behind the front lines. Sergeant Jimmy Blair from 2 Glas H recalls that, 'We had moved through the night and arrived at Mesnil-Patry. The whole countryside was swarming with tanks, trucks and all kinds of transportation. It was already dangerous to try and drive in the muddy ruts with tanks and trucks brushing past you by just a few centimetres.'[11] Following the artillery barrage, at 7.30 am the following companies (from west to east) set off in the attack; A and B (C and D in reserve) from the 9th Cameronians and C and D (A and B in reserve) from 2nd Glasgow Highlanders. The infantrymen would have to travel around 4,000 yards (3,600 metres) to reach Cheux, but the hedgerows that divided up the terrain proved too much of an obstacle for the tanks, and the men soon distanced themselves from their armoured support. The road leading from Mesnil-Patry to Cheux formed the boundary between the two battalions, roughly meaning the line consisted of A and B Companies (9th Cameronians), the road, then C and D Companies (2nd Glasgow Highlanders). Suddenly, C Company was forced to stop in front of a hedge due to machine gun fire. To the right, on the other side of the road, the Carriers and Churchill tanks with B Company hit a minefield and lost nine engines, further disrupting the attack's formation.

Fog further hampered any advance and according to Private McDougal, 7th Seaforth Battalion (who were in reserve behind the front line), the visibility was very poor and the men had to guide themselves using the rattle of the Churchills as they moved through the wheat fields. No one knew where the shots were coming from and only the whistle from their lieutenant allowed them to have any idea of their bearings. In the mean time, they could hear the explosions as the tanks hit the mines.

Their first objective, the Fontenay/Carpiquet road, was still 1,000 yards away as they found themselves confronted by elements of 4th Company from Major Siegfried Müller's Engineer Battalion, who had survived the heavy artillery barrage. Unfortunately, C Company, Glasgow Highlanders, were unable to clear them out and the battalion commander had to ask for one of the two reserve companies (in this case B) to try and get around the Germans on the right and fire on their positions. On the left, D Company (Glasgow Highlanders) arrived at an orchard and came under mortar fire as it tried to cross a small bridge; the Germans having previously noted the coordinates of this important objective. After suffering casualties, the company had to reorganise itself. It had lost its officers and was down to two platoons with no NCOs. By the time it finally reached the main road ('Cassino'), the delays incurred meant that the artillery barrage was now too far ahead.

Sergeant Jimmy Blair describes how:

> Ten minutes after the barrage started we advanced through the corn and soon fell into the firing line of one of the cleverly concealed machine guns. That's where my friend Walker was killed, although I wouldn't know that until a few days later. Many boys were killed by snipers because they didn't take enough precautions, such as not exposing yourself and crawling instead of walking… We reached a hedge at the foot of which lay our company commander and my platoon leader, both wounded. Another officer was killed a short distance away. As I advanced I heard a lot of cries: 'Get down! Get down!' and I knew that the tracers from the snipers were leaving a small mark on each of our chests for a few seconds… Shortly afterwards, two of them emerged with their hands up in the air. A cold rage filled me and I almost finished them

---

11   Grandais, *La Bataille du Calvados*, p. 110.

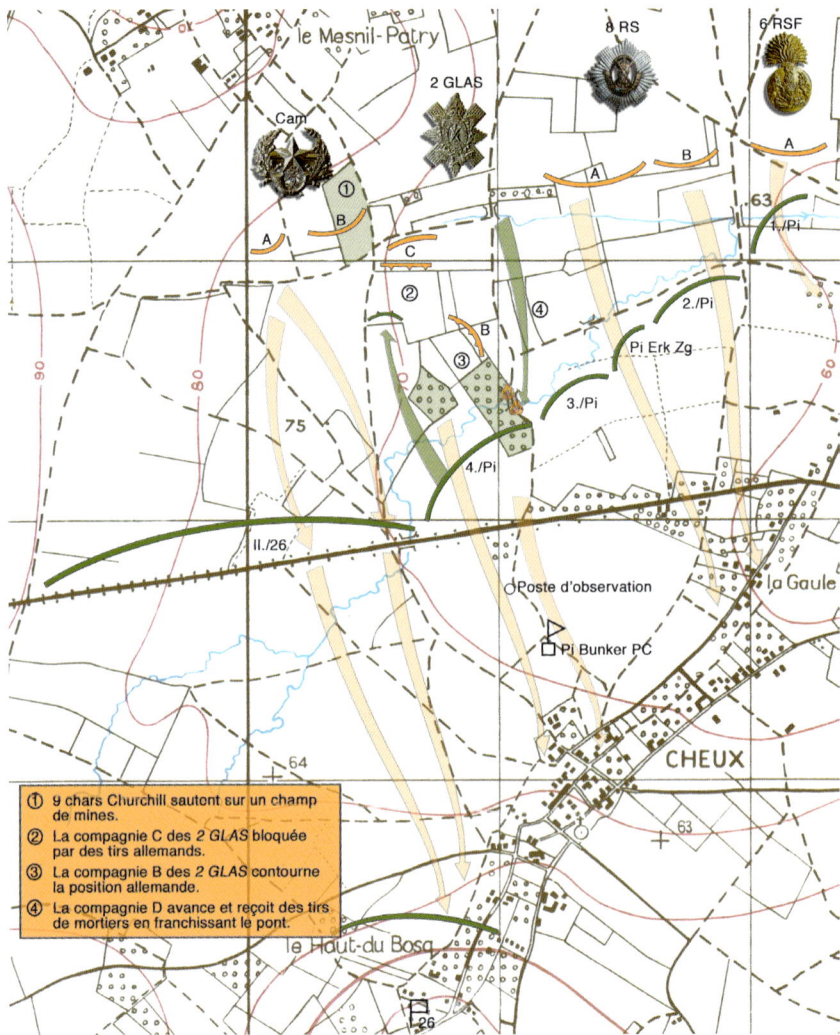

① 9 chars Churchill sautent sur un champ de mines.
② La compagnie C des 2 GLAS bloquée par des tirs allemands.
③ La compagnie B des 2 GLAS contourne la position allemande.
④ La compagnie D avance et reçoit des tirs de mortiers en franchissant le pont.

off as I thought of all of our comrades who had been killed or wounded. However, we shipped them to the rear. At the time, I lost nearly half of my men and there were dead and wounded everywhere from the companies who had advanced ahead. When we reached the main road I had sixteen men left out of thirty, but they were all fit and I decided to press on towards Cheux.

In SS-Sturmbannführer Müller's bunker

The unpleasant surprises seemed to accumulate in the face of an offensive that appeared as unstoppable as a steam roller. Hedges slowed down the tanks, while deadly mortar fire and minefields destroyed them. In the mean time, the artillery barrage had shown that not everything works in practice as it does in theory. The 9th Cameronians found themselves advancing against the positions of SS-Sturmbannführer Berhnard Siebken's II./26, who despite coming under heavy fire, still managed to maintain pockets of resistance. As for the 2nd Glasgow

The bunker belonging to the HJ Division's Pionier-Bataillon still stands in the corn fields near Cheux. (EG/Heimdal)

Highlanders, they found themselves face to face with the *Hitlerjugend* Division and SS-Sturmbannführer Siegfried Müller's SS-Panzer-Pionier-Bataillon 12. Lack of manpower on the front lines had meant that the HJ Division's commanders had been forced to send the engineer battalion to the front, although their specialist skills had enabled them to strengthen their positions (and those of their comrades) with networks of barbed-wire and minefields. Moreover, two bunkers had been built to the north-west of Cheux well before the invasion, and were to serve as SS-Sturmbannführer Müller's CP and the main hub of the German resistance in the area. The position itself was made up of two elements: a well-camouflaged, earth-covered bunker had been dug into the slope overlooking the terrain to the north and the main road. From the bunker, a covered trench linked it to an observation post equipped with a binocular telescope, while a further trench headed southwards into a fallow wheat field covered with weeds and bushes. From the observation post, the Germans were able to monitor the landscape to the north, towards the Fontenay/Carpiquet road, and the hedges where the 46 Brigade had advanced to. The southern edge of the parkland at Boislonde was also visible, as well as the villages of Le Mesnil-Patry and Norrey-en-Bessin, from where the offensive had been launched. Consequently, the two artillery battalion commanders, SS-Obersturmführer Timmerbeil (2./SS-Pz.-Art. Rgt. 12) and Oberleutnant Haller (4th battery), were able to successfully fire their six 105mm Howitzers from the 2nd battery (at Haut du Bosq) and the 4th battery.

A few days later, SS-Untersturmführer Hans Richter, from the battalion's staff, provided an account of the day's fighting to a war correspondent:[12]

Enemy harassing fire was concentrated on the positions of SS-Panzer-Pionier-Bataillon 12 and its CP from 2.45am. The commander, SS-Sturmbannführer Siegfried Müller, immediately requested a report from the companies on what

---

12   H. Meyer, *12. SS-Panzer-Division-Hitlerjugend*, pp.273-4.

they observed. The companies reported no observations or actions. The wires to the units were broken by the harassing fire and contact was maintained by field radios. Telephone connection to the units was re-established at 4.30 am. At 6 am [*sic – it was actually 8.30 am, German time*] the enemy's rolling barrage began. Impact explosions were close together. Slowly, the fire came closer and closer. The wires to the unit were not yet cut. At 6.15 am the commander spotted an assembly of enemy tanks at the southern edge of Le Mesnil-Patry *(46th Brigade)*, and the southern edge of the Parc de Boislonde *(reinforcements for 49th Division)*, through his binoculars. He reported this to SS-Sturmbannführer Hubert Meyer and requested release of the artillery. At the same time, the commander requested panzers or armour-piercing weapons. The artillery was put into action and fired a few well-aimed salvos. Once more the companies were asked for observations or if enemy attacks could be spotted. The companies reported: 'Negative!'

Around 7 am (8 am German time), SS-Obersturmführer Bischof (commander 4. (heavy) SS-Pz.-Pioner-Battalion 12), announced that his neighbour, SS-Sturmbannführer Bernhard Siebken (II Battalion), had retreated following the advance of the 9th Cameronians and that his left flank was now exposed.

The commander reported this immediately and contact with 2./SS-Pi.-Btl. 12 *(on the right flank of 2 Battalion, facing 46th Brigade)* was lost at the same time. Enemy tanks were advancing slowly on the battalion's position and the commander requested panzers, but was referred instead to the commander of Regiment 26 *(Mohnke)*. Communications to the regiment had been cut and radio was no longer available. At 7.35 am the commander ordered the adjutant to bring up the panzers assembled behind our sector for a counter-attack. Radio contact with 3./SS-Pi.-Btl. 12 was good. The squad leader, SS-sturmmann Pötsch, did a particularly good job, although the company signalled that it had still seen no sign of an enemy attack.

Motorcycle liaison officers from 46th Brigade stop in the middle of the wheat fields. Photograph by Sergeant Laing. (IWM)

Caterpillars follow the infantry of the 9th Cameronians. This image was taken by Sergeant Laing, who stayed with the unit until Cheux. (IWM)

Thus, II./26 was struggling and the engineers were under threat from Allied armoured vehicles. On the left, the flanks of 4th Company (engineers) were no longer protected as they faced the advancing 46 Brigade. The head of the company's mortar section, SS-Oberscharführer Ernst Behrens, was set up in an observation post and was able to witness the morning's fighting from there, including the heavy losses caused by the artillery barrage and the destroyed Pak guns. The men huddled in their foxholes during the barrage, but were ready to come out and fight the British after it had passed over. Behrens describes the scene:

> That day SS-Pioner Pelzmann was in the advanced observation post, underneath a tree on a small hill. The shelter was covered by a piece of metal plate from a Panzer IV and then camouflaged using clods of grass. Only a small lookout slit, around the same size as the driver of a panzer would have, allowed him to observe the enemy.

Behrens was captured by the British after they overwhelmed his position. Some of the men were captured before they even had the chance to grab their weapons, while others engaged in close-combat. He continues:

> Although my platoon's CP was 40 or 50 metres behind Pelzmann's position and I had already been captured, I could see Pelzmann was still fighting. There was a semi-circle of British corpses in front of him. Suddenly, the camouflaged cover moved and Pelzmann came out of his shelter, grabbed his gun by the barrel and with all his might, hit the gun against the tree to break the butt. Then I heard him shout loudly 'Well, I'm out of ammunition and I've had enough of you, so now you can shoot me!' I was convinced that Pelzmann would join our group as a prisoner. That didn't happen and what followed was horrible. A tall, red-haired Englishman walked towards Pelzmann, grabbed

him by the jacket collar with his left hand and shot him in the temple with his pistol. As he let go, the body dropped backward to the ground, his right arm in the air. A British officer ordered myself and several men in my platoon to place our killed comrades, and other dead, friend or foe, in sacks and to carry them to a spot he indicated. When we came to the spot where Pelzmann lay, I saw almost thirty dead English soldiers in front of his observation post.[13]

In the front lines, the companies of SS-Panzer-Pionier-Bataillon 12 were gradually being submerged under the rolling artillery barrage and the advancing 46th Brigade, but in the meantime, its CP was also coming under threat. Let us return to the report by SS-Untersturmführer Hans Richter:

At 8.15 am the tanks had still not arrived. The commander sent two liaison offers, one after another, to try and get some panzers. A violent rolling artillery barrage was now falling on the CP. Enemy machine guns were firing nearby and thick clouds of dust and fog surrounded the CP. The lookout could no longer see anything. Around 8.30 am, the head of Pi. Erk. Zug (reconnaissance section), SS-Oberscharführer Vogel, presented himself to the commander, along with some of his men. He had been wounded and reported some enemy tanks along the Fontenay-le-Pesnel/Carpiquet road. He was told to take up positions, with his men, on top of the CP.

As this section had been in front of the CP, north of the road, it must have been hit by the rolling barrage followed by the attack of the Royal Scots (probably A Company). This meant that there was no longer any front line before the CP: the CP now formed the front line itself!

At 9 am SS-Unterscharführer Hemken reported 'Enemy tanks!' The commander leapt out of the bunker and saw tanks and armoured cars, with infantry clinging onto the engines to the left and right as they headed for Cheux. The commander immediately occupied the trench and observation post and ordered the men to open fire on the enemy infantry. The enemy attacked the bunker and the trenches with tanks and on-board machine guns. The men pulled back whilst still fighting on top of the bunker. Scarcely had the last man entered the bunker when the enemy tanks fired upon it three times. Oberleutnant Haller and another soldier were killed, while a large number of the occupants were injured. Then a grenade flew into the bunker. When the smoke cleared a few of the men had only been slightly wounded due to a wool blanket being placed in front of the door, which had deflected some of the blast. It was almost a miracle. The occupants were tense and resolute as they waited for another attack. Nothing happened. The tension grew as the wounded men moaned. The enemy infantry moved to the left and right of the bunker as the self-propelled artillery opened fire

13   Testimony provided by Ernst Behrens on 6 Jnauray 1972 and published in *12. SS-Panzer-Division-Hitlerjugend*, pp.272-3.

1. A group of houses in the centre of the market town of Cheux after the fighting. (Cheux Town Hall)

2. Façade of the church after the fighting. (Cheux Town Hall)

3. The restored church. (EG/Heimdal)

4. Remains of railings marked by the fighting next to the church. (EG/Heimdal)

nearby. We could distinctly hear the enemy's orders and sometimes a man's laugh. Tommy felt completely safe and the tanks rolled on continuously towards Cheux. Suddenly, there was a noise from the bunker's rear entrance. Everyone's senses were on high alert as they pointed their guns towards the door. A man slipped through the entrance with some difficulty: it was a comrade *[according to Meyer, it was Sturmmann Eberle]*. He announced that two enemy armoured cars were on fire outside after being hit by grenades. He disappeared again as he wanted to see what the enemy was doing. The commander placed two uninjured men by the doorway, armed with daggers: any enemy soldiers who ventured into the bunker must be killed quietly. The men became calmer and avoided making any noise. Some of the wounded were exhausted and slept, while others smoked. After an hour, our man returned. He reported that the hill was covered with enemy tanks, armoured cars and infantry.[14]

---

14   Testimony recorded by H. Meyer and published in *12. SS-Panzer-Division-Hitlerjugend*, pp.273-4. Hans Richter's account in preserved in the National Archives in Washington, No.T-534-R154.

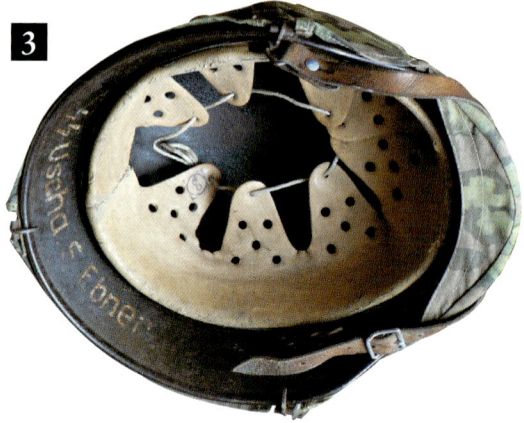

1 & 2. The nave of the church was ravaged in June 1944 (5) and restored (6). (Cheux Town Hall and EG/Heimdal)

3 & 4. Helmet belonging to SS-Uscha. Ebner, who was killed at Cheux. (Private Collection)

As Ian Daglish maintains, the engineers of the *Hitlerjugend* Division first had to recover from the shock of experiencing what was 'unimaginable for anyone who has not lived through such a barrage'.[15] The survivors defended themselves well behind their cleverly-arranged minefields, which caused significant casualties among the enemy tanks. However, their front line was thin and they did not have the panzer support which was in action at the Bois de Tessel. Having reached Cassino (the Fontenay/Carpiquet road), the Glasgow Highlanders, who had been fighting to the north of the road, arrived at the Engineer Battalion's bunker. As has already been noted, the bunker was primarily an observation post and was not necessarily set up as a defensive position. It was taken without much opposition,

---

15   I. Daglish, *Over the Battlefield: Operation Epsom*, p.61

the Germans having found themselves surrounded by the assault wave of the Glasgow Highlanders, who were then able to reach the road leading to Cheux without any further opposition. After passing through the thin defensive line, there was hardly any resistance left. The road ahead was clear and they were even able to set up their regimental aid station in a barn, relatively close to the bunker.

Towards le Haut du Bosq

On their right, the 9th Cameronians advanced across the open ground, observed by the Germans in their positions north of Rauray (15./26 and 16./26 and the rest of II./26), who fired at their flanks of the western-most company (A), which suffered heavy losses as it approached the road. As a result, C Company had to be sent in to reinforce the sector. In order to escape from the gunfire, the Cameronians descended south-east to Cheux and towards the Glasgow Highlanders. The failure of 49th Division's attack on Rauray had seriously exposed the Cameronians.

The Glasgow Highlanders entered Cheux at 9.30 am, but came under fire as they broke through the German front line. Elements of two platoons from 1. Pionier-Kompanie, commanded by SS-Untersturmführer Asmus, had retreated to Cheux following the recent fighting and taken refuge in the houses destroyed by the British artillery fire with the aim of establishing a pocket of resistance there. In addition, SS-Untersturmführer Loren, a technician with the Engineers, formed another *Kampfgruppe* (battle group) to try and help the battalion's staff, who were still trapped in the bunker. The rest of the men who had been cut off by the offensive were in Mouen, where they formed their own *Kampfgruppe*. The fighting that took place in Cheux was fierce, with losses on both sides, but by 10 am the town had been taken. Lieutenant Colonel Campbell's 2nd Glasgow Highlanders suffered heavy casualties on their first day: 12 officers and nearly 200 men.

On the right flank, Lieutenant Colonel Richard Villiers and the 9th Cameronians came under fire as they approached the hamlet of le Haut du Bosq around 11 am, from the four 10.5cm guns of 5. SS-Panzer-Artillerie-Regiment 12, which were positioned between le Haut du Bosq and Cheux. The *Hitlerjugend*'s artillery was particularly strong in this area, with two batteries from 1st group (2nd and 3rd) equipped with 10.5cm Wespen self-propelled guns positioned around 500 metres south-west of Cheux. The group retreated during the day, heading to the north-west and west of Grainville. The three batteries belonging to 2nd group (SS-Sturmbannführer Schöps) were positioned south-west of le Haut du Bosq, in the Salbey sector, surrounded by barbed-wire and ready for close-combat. SS-Obersturmführer Kurzbein's 5th battery was on the right-hand side of the road leading from Cheux to Brettevillette, and positioned behind a hedge (to the west) and a row of trees (to the east). The battery CP was set up behind the trees in an earth-covered bunker, with a further two Flak batteries set up a few hundred metres behind. SS-Oberscharführer Hartmann had to go into the nearby football field and climb onto one of the goalposts in order to see what the British were doing; the advance observation post having been evacuated during the morning. The battery's four guns then sent concentrated fire right into the middle of the Cameronians and their accompanying Churchill tanks from 7th RTR.

The small hamlet of le Haut du Bosq was also defended by SS Panzergrenadier-Regiment 26, commanded by SS-Obersturmbannführer Mohnke, who was determined to resist the Allied advance and was supported by two artillery batteries. At first, the Cameronians came under machine gun fire along the open slope towards the north of the hamlet. Crocodile tanks with flame throwers from 141st Regiment RAC were put into action, but were unable to hit their targets. The hamlet was finally gained at 11.30 am at the loss of 6 officers and 120 men from Lieutenant Colonel Villiers' regiment: the equivalent of an infantry company.

As the two battalions advanced, they were followed by the brigade's reserve battalion, the 7th Seaforth Highlanders, who were tasked with assembling the German prisoners. Losses among the Seaforth Highlanders were small and its B Company arrived on the southern slope at Cheux in the afternoon (accompanied by Churchill tanks), before having to stop due to German fire. But what of SS-Sturmbannführer Müller's men who were still trapped in the bunker?

> Slowly, very slowly, the hours passed. The guards stood quietly at the entrances and watched. Time and again there were voices quite close to the bunker. In between, there were the harsh discharges from guns very close by. Ammunition was exploding in the enemy armoured cars. This was what was holding Tommy off. Sporadic explosions from our own artillery made us heave sighs of relief.[16]

The shots were fired by the batteries belonging to Heller (4th) and Timmerbeil (2nd), who were positioned south-west of Cheux.

The war diary of VIII Corps summarises the conditions under which the offensive took place:

> The enemy was holding his positions and let us pass when he was not directly attacked, overwhelmed or overrun. He only revealed himself when presented with promising targets. There were numerous points of resistance, which had to be cleared long after objectives had been reached, in the forward as well as the rear areas ... It was remarkable that in all cases, the enemy in these positions fought until the defenders had been killed or the positions captured.[17]

The stubbornness of the German defences had surprised the British, but before following 227th Brigade and the advanced elements of the 11th Armoured Division, let us return to the offensive on the left flank.

44th Brigade (1)

The following images are from a remarkable collection by Major Stewart as he advanced across the open ground with 12 Platoon, B Company, Royal Scots Fusiliers (44th Infantry Brigade), towards Saint-Manvieu. Major Stewart was accompanied by a cameraman, Sergeant Connoly. It was 7.30 am on Monday, 26 June. The Royal Scots Fusiliers had awaited the order to attack and then advanced through

---

16   H. Meyer, *12. SS-Panzer-Division-Hitlerjugend*, pp.274

17   Tim Saunders, *Operation Epsom*, p.55

the middle of the wheat fields, after the 700 guns based near Norrey-en-Bessin had opened fire. Major Stewart gave the following comment on these photographs:

12 Platoon advanced immediately, and stuck close behind the artillery barrage. From what I could see among all of noise and the flames, the enemy returned our fire with guns, machine-guns and mortars. Our first objective, an orchard, was successfully achieved, although we suffered some casualties. During this phase, we crossed a wheat field and a barley field. We waited in an orchard for about fifteen minutes and then resumed our attack on Saint-Manvieu, with A Company. *(IWM - B5950/51/52/54)*

44th Brigade (2)

Five more images from Major Stewart showing 12 Platoon (B Company), 6 Royal Scots Fusiliers, progressing across the open ground towards Saint-Manvieu, through the morning fog and a thick smoke curtain laid down by the British to cover their advance. Supporting the Scots Fusiliers are the Churchill tanks from 9th RTR, 31 Brigade, moving through the corn. The infantry then dug themselves in along a sunken road near Saint-Manvieu, before the assault began. (IWM - B5953/55/57/59/60)

44th Brigade: Objective Saint-Manvieu

The 44th (Lowland) Brigade attacked at Saint-Manvieu with two battalions from the 'Royals': the 8th Royal Scots on the right (west) and the 6th Royal Scots Fusiliers on the left (east), commanded by Lieutenant Colonel Buchanan. Both battalions attacked in the same formation, with A Company on the right (west) and B Company on the left, followed by C Company (right) and D Company (left), each accompanied by Churchill tanks from 9th RTR. The 6th KSOB battalion was kept in reserve. The 8th RS advanced on the small hamlet of La Gaule and the 6th RSF on Saint-Manvieu; each company advancing along a front of 250 yards, and thus 500 yards for the whole battalions, just as it had been with the 46th Highland Brigade.

The 44th Brigade, commanded by Brigadier Money, left Norrey-en-Bessin, whose magnificent church had been destroyed by the fighting, along the Paris/Cherbourg railway. However, it was not long before the 6th RSF suffered heavy losses as the sunken road it was travelling along, although lying diagonally to the axis of the attack, was also only around 125 yards (114 metres) away from the artillery barrage, meaning the men were hit by shrapnel. What's more, the morning mist had now been replaced by smoke from the explosions, creating a kind of thick 'fog' in which the men found it difficult to orientate themselves. In addition, the infantrymen of 6th RSF were on the left flank of the offensive, and were thus subjected to German fire coming from the Carpiquet sector, including artillery and mortar fire from the HJ Divison, which continued to rain down on this moving mass that was almost drowning in the 'fog'.

Their first objective, Saint-Manvieu, located north of the Fontenay/Carpiquet road, was very close. In the midst of the random German shelling, the 6th RSF infantry quickly reached the small valley of the Mue river (which was actually just a large stream in the middle of a slight depression). The German front line had been established behind the small stream and was held by the grenadiers of I./26. Once more, B Company, on the very left flank, after already being exposed to the artillery barrage, was now exposed to the German front line as it ran diagonally north-east and came under fire from I./26 or 3./26.

The 6th RSF crossed the remnants of the German line and arrived in Saint-Manvieu at 8.30 am. The large village was made up of two parallel segments, the first of which, in the west, included the church and the large Manoir farm, as well as groups of solid stone houses with orchards. The eastern segment was aligned on both sides of the north/south road with a well-built farm to the north (a real stronghold) and various other houses and properties. On the east of the road, the Perron residence, with its house in the middle of parkland and its farm buildings on the northern side, was the CP for SS-Sturmbannführer Krause's I./26, and became a focal point for the German defenders, as we shall see. With its strong walls forming a complex of smaller defensive strongholds, Saint-Manvieu would prove very hard to capture.

Despite their favourable positions, the Germans suffered under the heavy artillery barrage and their situation was not an easy one, as confirmed by the testimony of SS-Oberscharführer Erich Wohlgemuth, the head of 4./26's anti-tank section:

> We were awoken by violent artillery fire very early. We could tell by the level of artillery fire that an attack was coming. We entered the trench which had

been covered with soil, branches and earth, which was useful because during the attack we were hit by at least four shells. Nothing happened, however, because the shells had been fitted with very sensitive detonators and there was just a lot of dust. The whole area was dotted with shell holes: I'd say around two for every square metre. When the fire moved behind us, we left our shelter and ran to the company CP because we knew that the tanks and infantry would be arriving behind the curtain of fire. The farm, which was next to the school, was already occupied by the British, and they tried to get to the school by climbing over the walls. As we were unable to hold them back using our firearms, we fired a *Panzerfaust* at the wall, but the charge didn't explode. At this point, the attack seemed to slow down, but we suddenly had several enemy tanks on our backs. Following the orders of our company commander, SS-Obersturmführer Alois Hartung, we pulled back to the battalion CP. Hartung remained behind enemy lines and our medic, SS-Unterscharführer Gesswein, remained in the company CP along with two dead and six seriously wounded. No one knew what became of them later.[18]

The men without taking their Pak gun, which was abandoned 30 metres from the battalion CP after being damaged by the artillery. The British artillery also damaged other German guns, as shown by the testimony of Heinrich Bassenauer, who worked in one of 4./26's mortar teams:

Three of our mortars had already been decommissioned by direct hits, and many comrades in our section had been killed or wounded. The enemy had already reached the trees and hedges around our position and we were surrounded by tanks, who directed their guns at us. We retreated to the battalion CP with our two remaining mortars and set them up between the buildings, making sure they were well-camouflaged so the enemy couldn't see them. We returned to our old position several times to fetch mortar shells, but suffered further losses from enemy machine gun fire. It seemed that the whole world was sinking when, suddenly, a British tank with a flam-thrower appeared at the entrance leading to the battalion CP and the horizon turned red and black.[19]

SS-Ostuf. Alois Hartung commanded 4./26.

At around 10.30 am, after six hours of fighting, the 6th RSF were steadily pushing back the small pockets of German resistance from the north of the village towards their battalion CP in the south-east. The British were exhausted by their heavy losses and struggled to progress any further: the infantry had to be helped by the special Churchill tanks

---

18   Testimony recorded by H. Meyer on 23 February 1975 and published in *12. SS-Panzer-Division-Hitlerjugend*, pp.274.

19   Ibid.

from B Squadron, 9 RTR, who could help with the demolition. The difficult and confusing battle would continue all day and last for ten hours.

A liaison officer from I./26, SS-sturmmann Aribert Kalke, was at the Perron residence, the location of the battalion CP:

> The artillery fire got bigger and bigger, and finally fell on the centre of the village. There were impacts on the park side, overlooking the street, in front of the entrance to the CP. The house was hit by shells and between the explosions you could hear the banging of the tanks' guns. The battalion staff were sheltering in the cellar and only a few men remained on the upper floors. Radio links with the companies had been interrupted and the situation was unclear. The battalion commander, SS-Sturmbannführer Krause, was just about to send a liaison officer to 2nd Company, when one appeared through the smoke. The man was wounded and reported that the company commander, SS-Obersturmbannführer Gröschel, and his deputy had been killed. The company had been overwhelmed following hard fighting, and enemy tanks and infantry had broken through the line where 2nd and 1st Company joined. There were now enemy tanks near the CP. The commander (Krause) ordered his officer, SS-Untersturmführer Hölzel, to make contact with a panzer company in the Bijude sector (2 kilometres south-east of Saint-Manvieu) and tell them to counter-attack immediately; a new defensive line had to be formed. Hölzel took me as his liaison officer, along with another untersturmführer who was one of the regiment's liaison officers who had been seconded to the battalion.
>
> When the artillery fire started to diminish, we exited by the rear door, one after the other. There was a small grove opposite the house that provided some protection. After passing a high fence we found ourselves in a cereal field which provided excellent camouflage, but also meant that I lost sight of the two officers. As I crossed the Fontenay/Caen road I came under rifle and machine gun fire from the right. I arrived at the aid station which was in the process of being dismantled due to the proximity of the enemy. Soon after, I met up again with SS-Untersturmführer Hölzel and together we reached the panzer company. The company commander categorically refused to engage in a counter-attack in an area with no infantry support, and so while the untersturmführer tried to set up new areas of support with the other isolated men, I was ordered to contact 1st Company. I came across 1st Platoon, commanded by SS-Untersturmführer Gross, but when I arrived the section was no longer in any contact with either the other platoons on the left flank, or with the CP. Liaison officers were sent out several times, and they finally brought back a seriously-wounded man; SS-sturmmann Hans-Joachim Forth.[20]

Aribert Kalke was the liaison officer for 1./26. (G.B.)

20   Testimony sent by Aribert Kalke to H. Meyer in April 1975 and published in *12. SS-Panzer-Division-Hitlerjugend*, pp.275.

Saint-Manvieu

1. A continuation of Major Stewart's report as he accompanied B Company, 6th Royal Scots Fusiliers. They are now in Saint-Manvieu, in the western part of the town. Some infantrymen are seen examining the ruined church from a breach in the cemetery wall. (IWM B5963)

2. It was futile to look for the church steeple; it had disappeared after being hit by artillery fire. The church no longer exists, all that's left among the tombs is a renaissance chapel and the remains of the flat Gothic chevet. (E.G.)

3 & 4. Walking along the cemetery wall on the south side, the Scottish infantrymen are seen heading for the Manoir Farm. (IWM B5962 and G.B.)

5. The men advance along the village streets. Progress would be particularly difficult in the face of elements from I./26, who clung on to the area and would hold parts of it until nightfall. (IWM B5964)

1. Major Stewart follows their advance along the same street. (IWM B5965)

2. The men's faces are particularly tense and casualties were heavy against a determined opponent. Major Stewart advanced at the forefront of the offensive with 12 Platoon (commanded by Lieutenant Robertson, a Canadian officer), B Company, which would suffer a 50 per cent casualty rate, including its leader, Major Agnew. The first soldier is armed with a Sten gun with a 32-cartridge loader, which was the weapon of a corporal who commanded a group of six riflemen, armed with MKI No. 4 rifles. Some of the men are carrying a pickaxe attached to their bag as an individual tool. (IWM B5964)

3. The farms, behind their large walls, were real fortresses. One of them is inspected here by some particularly nervous Fusiliers. (IWM B5966)

While the two officers and Aribert Kalke went to look, in vain, for support from the panzers – who would have been destroyed in the streets of Saint-Manvieu – and while 1st Company was in disorder, the fighting in Saint-Manvieu itself raged on. Having suffered heavy casualties and blasting the high stone walls that were acting as strongholds, the Scottish soldiers tried to advance. The battle would last all day. Only the special tanks, including the formidable flame-throwing Crocodiles, were able to overcome the last German entrenchments, primarily the battalion's CP.

The fight for I./26's CP

While the Scottish infantry gradually made its way through Saint-Manvieu, the CP of I./26 became the focal point for the German resistance in the middle of this tidal wave of attack from 44th Brigade. As Bernhard Krause sent his two officers and SS-sturmmann Kalke off to seek reinforcements, the CP became a rallying point for all the dislocated sections, as well as the last link in the defensive chain in this area. At the CP was a non-commissioned officer from 4./26's anti-tank section, SS-Unterscharführer Emil Dürr, who would lose his life at the CP after fully-committing himself to fighting the flame-throwing Crocodile tanks. In this desperate situation for the German front line, his sacrifice would become emblematic of the relentless resistance displayed by the *Hitlerjugend* Division, when all hope for Regiment 26 appeared to be lost. An unknown German war correspondent arrived at I./26's CP the moment after Dürr had been mortally wounded and now lay dying. His narrative has, of course, been used in several German texts, as well as English and French, and his 'heroic' style is typical of texts published during wartime, no matter the country:

> In the early morning hours of 26 June 1944, while the sun was still resting behind the Norman hills, the English barrages had set in. When, three hours later, the enemy guns fell quiet and only shrapnels were whirling and howling through the air, enemy tanks advanced through the smoke, stench, and fog. They broke through the positions and overran Saint-Manvieu. Like a pack of hungry wolves they surrounded the park. The handful of men in the battalion CP could count fifteen Shermans with their naked eyes. They were sitting in front of the wall which enclosed one side of the park and the grain field on the other side. Whoever had arms left to fight was sent into action in the park; messengers, clerks, orderlies. If they roll over the bridge, thought the Grenadiers, if they break through the walls, if they push into the park-well, then it will be over. The battered battalion would lose its leadership and the cornerstone of the uneven battle would be overthrown. Then the desired English breakthrough would succeed, because that is what they wanted: to break through here, to the Orne river, to the last undamaged bridge near Saint-Manvieu to reach the Caen/Falaise road and encircle Caen from the south. The battalion CP had suddenly become an important bastion, but it had no heavy weapons. They had sub-machineguns and rifles. They had *Panzerfausts* and magnetic explosives, but only a hand full of men... They also had SS-Unterscharführer Dürr. But no one could foresee the outcome at this critical hour. The young, blond corporal didn't even know it himself yet...
>
> But two mortars were still sitting in the park, massive and mighty. And their crews had twenty-five shells left. These they fired among the tanks, into this corner and that. The shells exploded with bangs and caused confusion. Sharp shooters crept to the hedges and wall ledges, firing at the commanders who came out of their hatches too soon. Some of the tanks turned away. They assumed that the forces in the park were much stronger and did not dare to break through. But the calm did not last long, the tanks returned and fired from all barrels. They picked the house as their target and damaged it so badly that the wounded had to be carried out.
>
> Then, suddenly, there was a shout of alarm: a flame-thrower tank had set up at the entrance to the park, dominating the path to the CP, and able to harass any movement. 'That tank has to go', the commander ordered. He

said it as he was walking by; he had no time to stop. He was needed out there with his men, here and there and everywhere.

SS-Unterscharführer Dürr had heard the order. He did not hesitate. 'I'll go', he said, and was gone. He took a *Panzerfaust* and went to scout the situation. It was difficult to get close to the tank as it was sitting in a position that dominated the terrain on all three sides. Dürr did not hesitate for long. He jumped across the inner wall of the yard and ran straight at the tank. But the *Panzerfaust* did not pierce the tank. Maybe he did not aim accurately in his excitement. Then Dürr felt a blow to the chest, and immediately a warm substance was running down his thighs. Hit! Shot in the chest!

Angry, Dürr pulled himself up and ran back the path he had come down. He picked up another *Panzerfaust* and ran up to the tank a second time. This time, since the distance was more difficult, he aimed at the tracks. The tank rattled, the track ripped. But again, Dürr was covered by violent machine gun fire. Crawling, he worked his way back. With one jump he scaled the wall, out of the range of fire. He spotted a magnetic charge and quickly grabbed it. A comrade wanted to hold him back: 'You're already bleeding…' But Dürr did not let himself be stopped. The tank had to go.

For a third time he set out on his dangerous journey. For the third time, now quite weakened, he jumped across the wall. He ran, stumbling, toward the tank, paying no attention to the bullets. Now he was very close, once more he put the charge into positions and was about to get away when he heard a thud behind him: the charged had dropped to the ground. Not even seconds were left for him to consider, no time to contemplate his duty, desires, wishes: the tank had to go. Once again he was at the flame-thrower tank like a flash. He grabbed the charge with a strong fist, pressed it against the tank, staggered once, pushed, gasping, against the diabolic dynamite. Everything exploded in fire and flames, and night fell before his eyes.

As he hit the ground, he saw that the tank was burning. He wanted to jump up, but he could not, and he lay on the ground as if paralysed. He tried once more and felt a stabbing pain in his thighs … he looked down at his bleeding legs and his heart turned cold with shock.

Was it desperation which gave him superhuman strength now? He crawled back down the path, now cleared, to the CP. His comrades spotted him, pulled him in and took him to the medic. Four hours later his life came to an end. Not a word of complaint had crossed his lips. 'You must not let them into the park', he said.

The above was the story as told by Emil Dürr's comrades to the war correspondent, detailing what had happened before he arrived. What follows is his direct testimony after his appearance at the CP:

They had carried him from the burning house, which the enemy tank guns had picked as their target, to a pond under the old shady trees. There he lay, both thighs wrapped in makeshift dressings, quiet and withdrawn. His blue eyes were clear and calm, his lips pale and pressed together in pain. His comrades stood around him, wishing they could do something to help him through those last moments he had to live. But there was nothing to do or say: he only had moments to live. Sighing, the medic had turned away from him, the dressings dripping with unstoppable blood. Did he know that he was going to die?

The company commander asked him if he had a wish. Yes, please lift his head a little. If only they had a pillow to offer him a soft headrest, but there was only a gas mask which they carefully pushed under his head.

The guns of the enemy tanks surrounding the park sent shell after shell, without pause, into the tree covered terrain. The gable of the house in which the battalion CP was located blew apart with a bang. The beams were smouldering. Here and there the dry ground, set afire by the searing tongues of the flame-thrower tanks, was burning. Smoke and dust were creeping through the trees to the pond. A fine rain drizzled with hopeless monotony on the leaves. The wounded man turned his head a little. He tried to see something. But he only saw the smoke, the fumes, and the clouds of dust. 'You must not let them into the park', he said. He spoke calmly, as if there was nothing to worry about for him. Then he asked for a cigarette. Many hands were extended towards him. He smiled. His comrades knew he was about to begin a long journey, but they did not sense that he knew it too.

He smoked, composed, as was his manner. He held the cigarette in his right hand, black with Normandy soil, a few blood stains on the crust of dirt. His hand, too, was steady, eerily so. His left caressingly stroked the grass on which he was laying. Under this grass, he would soon be sleeping, sleeping forever.

'There is nothing behind us', he said. 'You must hold on until they have a new line behind us...' He seemed to want to say more because his lips continued to move, but no words were formed. His left hand gripped the grass more firmly as if it was looking for a hold. 'Give my love to my wife', he said. 'And the little one ... take care of them ... and do not be sad, there is no need to be sad.'

Then the cigarette dropped from his hand. He closed his eyes. Once more he breathed, deep and heavy. Then the blood stopped, as did his heart. His comrades took off their helmets and instinctively folded their hands. Tears were running down quite a few cheeks. They were not ashamed in front of each other.

Heavier and heavier, the shells from the tanks hammered the park. The beams of the house were splintering, bricks were flying from the park wall. The earth was trembling. He had calmly smoked a cigarette as if he was saying goodbye to his comrades before going on extended leave. Over his grave the commander awarded him the Knights Cross as the first non-commissioned officer of 12. SS-Panzer-Division '*Hitlerjugend*'.[21]

---

21   H. Meyer, *12. SS-Panzer-Division-Hitlerjugend*.

The actions of Emil Dürr were often described as 'fanatical' in post-war literature. It is clear that members of the *Hitlerjugend* Division were particularly motivated and determined, with a certain ideological indoctrination. Emil Dürr knew the importance of the situation and split-second decisions are often made in the heat of the moment. As in any troop of well-trained, elite soldiers, such selfless acts are numerous, especially for those in armies with a solid military tradition. In the British Army, the prestigious Victoria Cross more often than not honours the heroic dead, rather than the glorious living. In Normandy, Corporal Sidney Bates of the Monmouthshire Regiment was killed on 6 August 1944, near Chênedollé, who despite being wounded, continued to fire his weapon until his last breath. In the French Army, one recalls the 'spirit of the Camarón', so often represented in action by the Foreign Legion.

The fight for I./26's CP

The Perron residence. On the left are the farm buildings where the battalion's CP was installed. The house is on the other side of the wall, on the right. (G.B.)

The house is surrounded by a park. The area remained almost intact even though some districts of Saint-Manvieu were completely devastated. (G.B.)

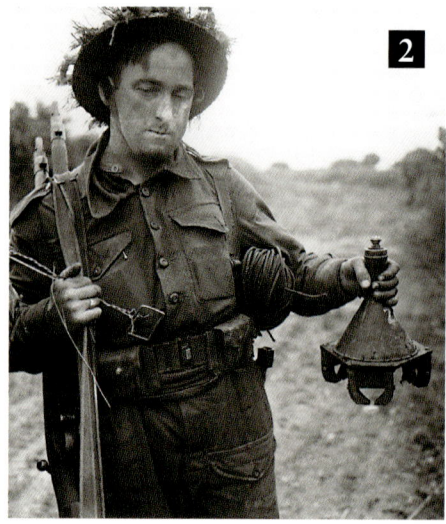

1. Map showing: 1. The church (largely destroyed - the current, modern church was rebuilt in the eastern part of the town). 2. The Perron residence and I./26's CP. 3. The hole in the wall through which the Crocodile Tank entered.

2. In this photograph, taken on 26 June, L/Cpl Lodge of the Royal Engineers' 278 Company is seen holding a German anti-tank magnetic mine, like the one used by Emil Dürr. This image was taken in the 46th Brigade's sector. (IWM B6015)

3. A grenadier from the HJ Division armed with a *Panzerfaust*. As used, in vain, by Emil Dürr. (Heimdal)

4. SS-Unterscharführer Emil Dürr of 4./26. This photograph was retouched after his death and the Iron Cross was added. (Munin)

5. The Churchill Crocodile was a Churchill tank that had been fitted with a flame-thrower in the machine gun's position. A two-wheeled armoured trailer was used to transport the flammable liquid. (IWM)

The Royal Scots at La Gaule

While 26 June had been a black day for the 'Royals', with the infantry of the 6th Royal Scots Fusiliers coming under continuous fire from the beginning of the artillery barrage, followed by similar fire on their left flank and finally their exhausting ten-hour battle in Saint-Manvieu, the advance by 44th Brigade on the right flank was much easier.

The 8th Royal Scots attacked the positions held by 2nd Company, SS-Panzer-Pionier-Bataillon, who quickly lost contact with their battalion CP after being overwhelmed by the Churchill tanks of B Squadron, 9th RTR. It took the Royal Scots and B Squadron just two hours to reach their objective; 'Cassino'. The small hamlet of La Gaule lay just to the south of the main road and had been completely cleared of German soldiers by 11 am (11.30 am according to Meyer). The civilians there who had survived the hell of the artillery barrage were certainly relived. The Rouitour farm, not far from the Bouille crossroads and ran by Gustave Renault, had been hit by a large shell that had exploded in the corner of a stable, mortally wounding a woman who had taken refuge there, as well as most of the cows.[22] Renault asked the Scottish soldiers to evacuate the woman, who was transported to Bayeux hospital and died of gangrene a few days later.

---

22   A. Grandais, *La Bataille du Calvados*, p. 113.

The 11th Armoured Division advances

1. The armoured vehicles of the 11th Armoured Division waited to the north of the Fontenay/Carpiquet road until midday. This photograph by Sergeant Laing shows us the machines that belonged to 29th Armoured Brigade's HQ, identifiable by the number 50. For Operation Epsom, this armoured brigade had 138 Sherman tanks, 35 Sherman Firefly tanks and 30 light Stuart tanks. (IWM B6019)

2. Taken in the same area, this spectacular photograph by Sergeant Laing shows a vehicle loaded with ammunition exploding after being hit by a German mortar shell. (IWM B6017)

3. Sherman tanks from 29th Armoured Brigade advancing along a corridor that has just been cleared and marked with white tape. The tanks would suffer losses in the middle of the German minefields. Photograph taken by Sergeant Leeson in the area around Cheux. (IWM B5976)

4. Sherman tanks from 29th Armoured Brigade, probably the 23rd Hussars, advancing towards the main road which they would cross in order to reach Cheux. Photograph taken by Sergeant Leeson. (IWM B5977)

5. An Achilles; a British variant of the American M10 tank destroyer. This one belongs to the 91st Anti-Tank Regiment, directly attached to VIII Corps. The tank was named Glengarry II. Photograph by Sergeant Laing. (IWM B6006)

6. Cromwell tanks (Taureg II in the foreground) of the 11th Armoured Division. (IWM B6011)

The second phase of the offensive

Although two objectives had been achieved by midday – Cheux and La Gaule – the offensive was slowed down on the flanks. This included the 9th Cameronians, who had been stopped at le Haut du Bosq and the 6 Royal Scots Fusiliers, who did not capture Saint-Manvieu until the end of the afternoon. This meant that around noon, the second wave of the attack was launched, including the infantry that had been held in reserve and the tanks from 11th Armoured Division.

At the *Hitlerjugend* Division's CP, in Verson, the alarm bells that had rung at the beginning of the day began to sound once more. Apart from Regiment 25's sector, where no attack was reported, the rest of the front line held by the HJ Division began to crack under the pressure exerted by VIII Corps. Their positions between east of Fontenay and Saint-Manvieu had already been overwhelmed, with the latter (containing the CP of I./26) being taken from the north and the south-west. To the east, the positions of 1./26 and 3./26, behind the river Mue, were outside the areas where the offensive was taking place and so remained in German hands. The 9th Panzer Company, whose assistance had been demanded by SS-Sturmbannführer Krause, was behind the battalion's main position, to the west of the Carpiquet aerodrome. All of the battalion's right flank was held, but I./26's left flank was breached and contact with the Engineer Battalion, located at the heart of the offensive, was lost. Nor was there any news from II./26, whose right flank had also been overwhelmed during the attack. To the west, Rauray remained the cornerstone of the division's front line, after the Allied attacks at Tessel and Fontenay had been repelled. The risk of a British breakthrough lay mainly in the area south-west of Cheux, and the HJ Division had very few resources to deal with it, mainly just elements of the reconnaissance group, Panzer IV companies that had been re-routed from Tessel and 15th Company (reconnaissance) Regiment 25 (15./25). Finally, a Tiger company from I. SS-Panzerkorps, (3 Company, s.SS-Heavy-Panzer-Abteilung 101, under the command of SS-Untersturmführer Amselgruber), came to provide reinforcements at Grainville-sur-Odon, 2.5 kilometres south of Cheux. In addition, 21. Panzer-Division were ordered to provide a panzer and assault-gun company in the Verson sector, and two battalions from 1. SS-Panzer-Division *Liebstandarte* 'LAH' were also made available, but at present were still too far away.

11th Armoured Division head for the Odon

By noon, the tanks of Major General Roberts' 11th Armoured Division were still waiting at their starting points, even though they were supposed to have crossed the Odon before nightfall. The Cromwell tanks of the 2nd Northamptonshire Yeomanry, the division's reconnaissance group, were to lead the advance. General Richard O'Connor pointed out that, 'If the 2nd Northamptonshire Yeomanry were able to get as far as the Odon and cross it, the 29th Armoured Brigade would follow them as soon as possible.' The reconnaissance group had only two squadrons, A and C, who had only just arrived in Normandy and the commander of the division, Major General Roberts, was sceptical about the

2nd Northamptonshire Yeomanry

possibility of them succeeding: 'I never hoped that they would succeed until the enemy had been completely disrupted and was already taking flight.'[23] This belief was based on erroneous intelligence reports, which believed that the Germans, as was their custom, had formed a single line of advanced positions with their main line of resistance behind, which included armoured reserve. At the time he was unaware that the 'advanced positions' were, in fact, the only German lines of defence and that there was virtually nothing behind them. The inaccurate reports led the British to be over-cautious as they waited for the 'real', hypothetical line of resistance; an excessive prudence that would lead to the failure of the operation. The lessons of 'Blitzkrieg' had not yet been fully understood and the British Army of 1944 was still acting as it had in 1918, while its generals, and Montgomery, were as unable to adapt to the situation as the French generals had been in 1940.

As the historian Alexander McKee has pointed out, the courageous and arrogant 'snipers' of Regiment 26, who would keep fighting until the end even though they were overpowered by the offensive, constituted the main line of defence and gave the ultimate sacrifice. Indeed, as they advanced deeper into the German front lines, the Scottish infantrymen found themselves under fire from all directions. The obsession of the sniper was now born. The insolent courage of the *Hitlerjugend* Division had disrupted all of the intelligence collected by the staff of VIII Corps.

At 12.50 pm, the lead tanks of the 11th Armoured set off. This included nineteen Cromwell tanks from A Squadron, 2nd NH Yeo, accompanied by a single Crusader anti-aircraft tank and a Sherman for the forward observation officer (FOO). The young, British tank crew members, who were used to hunting foxes across the open fields of Northampton, were now confronted with narrow roads encumbered by a chaos of vehicles between their departure point at Norrey and their first objective, Cheux. The village itself had been ravaged by the artillery barrage and its narrow streets were filled with rubble, while the thick stone walls of the houses had collapsed under the shelling. On top of this it began to rain, creating potholes in the roads and making the crossing through Cheux particularly difficult. Under the command of SS-Unterstunführer Asmus, a handful of Pioneers were still fighting, which caused further concern among the assailants. A Squadron's second in command, Captain Raynsford, was killed by a bullet to the head after he stood up in the turret of his Cromwell tank. Corporal 'Reg' Spittles, the leader of 2 Troop, described the prevailing situation in Cheux: 'The village was totally destroyed and the Germans were there, there were as many of them as there were of the 15th Scottish! They just couldn't locate each other.' Spittles even had to throw phosphorous grenades at the German grenadiers as they tried to place magnetic mines on his tank. They reached Creux shortly after 1 pm, following the artillery barrage that was re-launched again at 1.30. Behind this steel curtain, the four troops of Major Peel's A Squadron were deployed: 4 Troop moved up on the left and 3 Troop took up its position on the right. 1 Troop and the command echelon were blocked by a ditch, while 2 Troop (Corporal Spittles) were held in reserve at the back. Corporal Spittles suddenly saw Cromwell tanks on fire as they were deployed up on the hill and Major Peel radioed him to go and see what was happening. He headed for the front of 2 Troop, which had positioned

---

23   G. Roberts, *From the Desert to the Baltic*, (Kimber, 1987), p. 159.

itself in a corner formation, advancing rapidly through the burning Cromwell tanks and hoping that the smoke would hide him from the enemy. From the turret of his Cromwell he observed the terrain and could see the Panzer IVs that had hit the two tanks from 3 Troop. The Cromwell tanks then opened fire and destroyed several Panzer IVs who were attacking from Rauray, on the right (western) flank (possibly Panzers from 7./12). However, all the tanks from 3 Troop had been destroyed and troops 1 and 2 (Spittles) had been halted by the German resistance south of Cheux. Only 4 Troop, under the command of Lieutenant Stock, passed unnoticed by the Panzer IV's counter-attacks (thanks to its more beneficial position on the left flank), and reached the railway line near Grainville around 2.30 pm. After crossing the railway line, the few tanks were able to look out over the Odon valley and sent their observations back by radio. They stayed there for ten minutes, even destroying a 2 cm Flak and its crew in the process. However, despite their success, it would seem that a tank advance towards the Odon was not possible due to the arrival of the Panzer IVs in the area. At 2.50 pm, A Squadron, 2 N Yeo received orders to pull back.

Yet behind this little vanguard, all the tank battalions of the 11th Armoured Division were ready to follow. At 12.30 pm Major General Roberts ordered the 2nd Northants Yeomanry to advance towards to Odon bridges, followed by the 23rd Hussars and 2nd Fife and Forfar Yeomanry, supported by the 3rd RTR. The 2 F&FY would advance west of Cheux and the 23rd Hussars to the east. None of the regiments had any battle experience and the drivers, accustomed to the open spaces of East Anglia, were unpleasantly surprised when they came across the *bocage* and its hidden traps. Progress would not be swift.

The reserve battalions head for the front

Following the losses sustained after four hours of battle, the four infantry battalions were exhausted. Consequently, the 7th Seaforth Highlanders were sent in to reinforce 46th Brigade, and the 6th KOSB to reinforce 44th Brigade. The latter headed to Saint-Manvieu where the exhausted Royal Scots Fusiliers were being held by SS-Sturmbannführer Krause's grenadiers. As previously noted, the flame-thrower Crocodile tanks of the 141st Royal Armoured Corps (the Buffs) had attempted to destroy the CP of I./26 and for Operation Epsom, its A Squadron had been placed under the command of the 31st Tank Brigade and Troops 4 and 5 under that of the 9th RTR. It was the latter who would support the 6th RSF at Saint-Manvieu. Each troop comprised of three tanks, and it was Lieutenant Harvey's Crocodile tank which had driven through a breach in the northern wall of the Perron residence and the one that Emil Dürr had attacked in single combat. While the Germans claimed that Dürr had destroyed it, the Buffs declared that the mine had only immobilized it by destroying one of its caterpillars. The British managed to recover the empty tank the following day; Harvey and his crew having been captured, according to the Buffs' battle log. To the west, three of the four 6th KOSB companies moved forward: A Company taking the Manoir farm and ruined church to the south, with C Company in the middle and B Company to the north. The men from A Company came across twenty-four Scots Fusiliers who had taken refuge in a German bunker. It was all that remained of a company who had left that morning, after their commander, Major Goring, had been killed and a captain had finally accepted the inevitable. Having lost their company commander, these twenty-four Royal Scots Fusiliers were amalgamated into the Borderers, and together they would defend the entire western half of the vicinity against German counter-attacks from the east, including an attack by a weakened company of Panzer IVs from 21. Panzer-Division around 6 pm. All of the German counter-attacks were halted by the 181st Field Regiment, Royal Artillery's 25-pound guns, which were fired from Saint-Manvieu. The Borderers were amazed by the relentless resistance shown by the isolated grenadiers, who they called 'snipers', thanks to the few who stayed behind to fight to the bitter end. Finally, the last pocket of resistance pulled back from Saint-Marvieu during the night and headed east, meaning that the area was under the complete control of the 43rd Division by the following day.

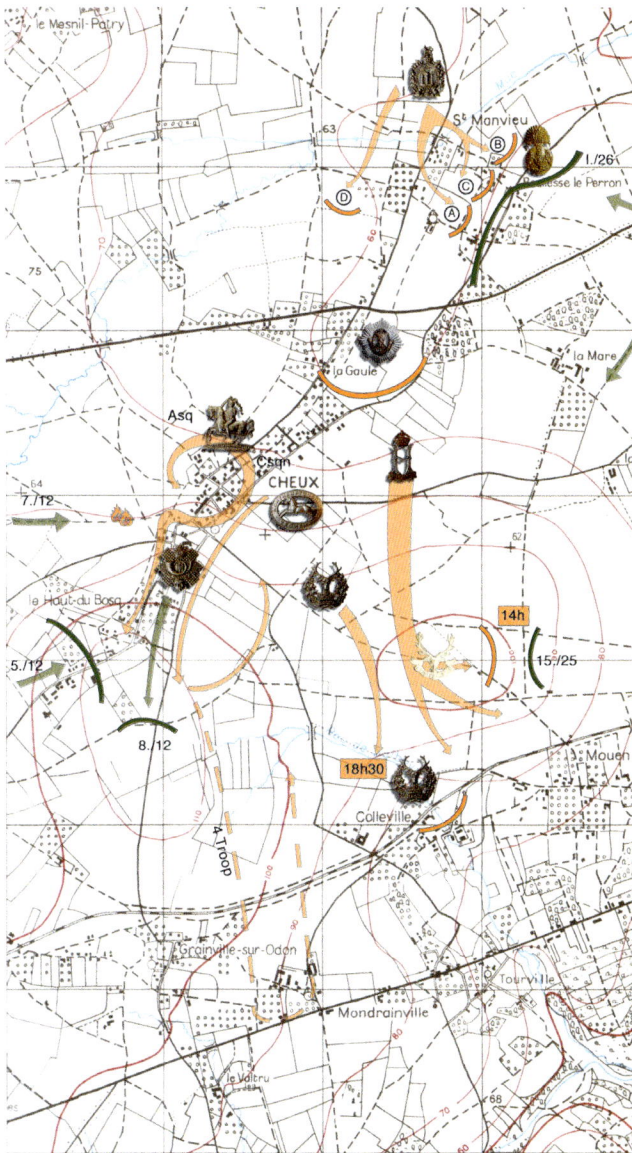

Meanwhile, the 7th Seaforth Highlanders were sent to Cheux, where according to Lieutenant James Hayter, 'there was nothing but mud, water, ruins, smoke and rubbish, and the air was full of projectiles.' He also saw two destroyed German tanks. At 2 pm they were ordered to continue on to occupy an area of high ground called Ring Contour 100, located around 1,500 yards (1,350 meters) from Cheux. According to Lieutenant Hayter:

> I had lost my little compass and my sense of direction. Then a captain arrived in a scout car and showed us the way before he left. But as soon as we set out, the Jerries attacked us with their various rocket launchers and all hell was let loose. We were forced to retreat into the ruined buildings and mark time. Then there was a break in the enemy barrage and we could rush out of Cheux and head in the right direction, along with others from a different unit. The fog had dissipated and we came under fire from all directions, including mortar fire. I was hit on my right leg but kept moving forward.

The battalion was then confronted with a German company whose numbers had been severely diminished following losses it had suffered since 8 June. The company in question was Regiment 25's reconnaissance company (15./25), now under the command of SS-Hauptscharführer Boigk, following an injury to SS-Obersturmführer Reinhold Fuss. The 15./25 had arrived at Hill 100 in the morning in order to contain the British advance around Cheux. The following German testimony provides a detailed description of the agonies experienced by this company as it tried to halt the Allied advance.

Counter-attack by 15./25

The 15./25 was the reconnaissance company of SS-Panzergrenadier-Regiment 25 and had suffered heavy losses during the fighting at Bretteville-l'Orgueilleuse on the night of 8/9 June. It had since remained in the area around Rots and Franqueville, but had been ordered that morning to stop the breach in the front line near Mouen, opposite Saint-Manvieu (south of Cheux). The remnants of the company would be severely tested on this occasion and what follows is the testimony of Otto Funk.

> We were put on alert during the night of 25/26 June. According to my recollection, we were at Franqueville at the time. Our commander, SS-Hauptscharführer Wilhelm Boigk, told us that the English had broken through the area around Cheux and that their forward elements had already reached our artillery positions … 15./25 was the only reserve unit available. We stayed by the road for half of the night and waited for our orders to engage. I was in the middle of my comrades and said, 'Who will be the of us to be hit today?' Boigk replied, 'Funk, stop talking nonsense!' Morning arrived, but it was still dark. The naval artillery suddenly spat out shells and fired them towards Cheux and Mouen. The order to engage arrived and we climbed into our *Schwimmwagens* and headed for a new day of fighting. The road took us via Saint-Germain-la-Blanche-Grass, past the prison at Caen, then via Venoix, Bretteville-sur-Odon and Verson and finally towards Cheux. The firepower of the artillery had been unleashed; there were only

the trunks of the trees left, the branches having been torn off by the shells. After this little wood, we reached an open space and left our *Schwimmwagens*, which continued to follow behind us at a certain distance.

We crossed a cereal field and reached a meadow with a hedge in front of us. We took shelter first and then the *Schwimmwagens* followed us into the cereal field before stopping to camouflage themselves. After a short break we moved on again and walked along the hedge on the right. At the end of the hedge was 10 to 12 metres of open ground, followed by a sunken road that ran perpendicular to the hedge we were hiding behind. When the first man crossed the open ground, a machine gun began to fire and proceeded to sweep the area. We crossed the ground one by one to reach the shelter of the sunken road which, miraculously, we all reached safely! We then advanced along the road and after about 80 metres, came across another sunken road, which crossed the one that we were using. We all gathered there and then Boigk divided the three groups from 3rd Platoon along the path. The third group, which I found myself in, was the last and we advanced along the left-hand side of the road.

After 30 or 40 metres the road rose up to ground level and we had to crouch down as there were only a few bushes between us and the enemy, including a small hedge that had been thinned-out by the shells. SS-Hauptscharführer Boigk said to me, 'Funk, get into this shell hole!' And then about 80 yards in front of me I saw two houses surrounded by many trees. After a while, I saw some "Englishmen" running between the houses and disappearing into their individual foxholes. Boigk crawled back and ordered me to open fire with my machine gun if I saw anyone. Suddenly, a few "Englishmen" appeared again and my MG 42 started to crackle. At the same time I got a shock in my upper left arm, which threw me over to the side. My comrade, Klaus Schuh, immediately took over the machine gun and SS-Hauptscharführer Boigk tried to dress my wound, which was not easy as we had little shelter. The blood continued to flow down my

SS-Hascha. Wilhelm Boigk commanded the third section of 15./25, on the east side of Hill 100. (Heimdal)

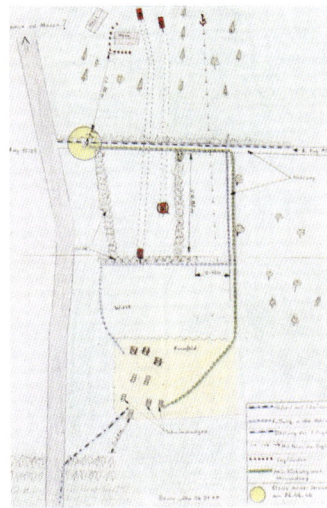

Sketch by Otto Funk showing the fight for Hill 100. (Heimdal)

Klaus Schuh, machine gunner with 15./25 and a crew member of Otto Funk. He was killed on this day after receiving three bullets to the forehead. (Heimdal)

Otto Funk, seen here in 1944 and 1996, was a key eyewitness to the fighting that took place. (G.B.)

left sleeve and Boigk told me that we had to get to the sunken road. He pulled me by the leg using his right hand and when we reached the road, I stood up and took a few steps before, as Wilhelm Boigk informs me, I fainted.

When I came to I was lying in the bushes that lined the sunken road, my comrades having already strapped up my arm in order to stem the bleeding and to dress the wound. To stop the blood, they placed three packs of dressings under my armpit: an artery must have been hit. I then drank two flasks of tea, one of which belonged to SS-Unterscharführer Mohr, whom I had met here, but who actually came from Giessen, the same region as me. Boigk said to me, 'Tonight you'd asked who would be the first and now it's you! I'm going to leave you here. We're going to launch a counter-attack and a *Schwimmwagen* will be able to pick you up.' He turned to Mohr and said that he must make contact with the first group, who were in position to the left of the road leading to Mouen. Mohr said goodbye to me and then left (I visited his parents in Giessen after the war and learned that their son had gone missing on 26 June, 1944 ...). After a while, I heard the rumble of armoured vehicles and saw two English tanks coming from the houses I had seen. They crossed the sunken road and headed for our *Schwimmwagen*. One of them was destroyed with a *Panzerfaust*, while the second one fired towards the *Schwimmwagen*. Then Boigk said to me, 'Go back down the sunken road where we came from and get yourself to the aid station.' I took my leave and headed for the vehicles. I came under fire several times as I worked my way along the road before I finally managed to reach them. When I got there, three of them were on fire after being hit by the tank, including the one which I had previously travelled on and which contain all of my personal belongings. A comrade immediately took me to the Chateau de Louvigny, where one of our field hospitals was located. I received first aid in the afternoon when the doctor realized that the bullet had also crossed over to the left side of

Men from D Company, 7 Seaforth Highlanders waiting for the order to attack. (IWM B6003)

my ribcage. In the evening, a wounded soldier from the third group announced that Klaus Schuh has been killed after receiving three bullets in the forehead, just below his steel helmet. I never found out where he was buried.

In order to take the southern slope held by 15./25, the 7th Seaforth would lose fifty men, including four officers, and several tanks. They then dug in on the north side, leaving a no-man's land between themselves and the Germans.

The 227 Highland Brigade provides reinforcements

Rain had begun to fall by the early afternoon and while the bulk of 11th Armoured Division's tanks were preparing for the offensive, the 15th Division's reserve brigade, the 227th Highland Brigade, was sent to reinforce the other two other brigades, who were exhausted after hours of battle.

The brigade advanced with two battalions as they followed the 11th Armoured's reconnaissance group, the 2nd Northamptonshire Yeomanry (2 N Yeo). With the 10th Highland Light Infantry (HLI) on the right (west) and the 2nd Gordon Highlanders (Gordons) on the left (east), the brigade's objective was to advance on Cheux, then onwards towards the Odon valley, behind the 2 N Yeo. They were then to clear it of any German resistance so that it was ready to be crossed the following day. But the corridor of attack was narrow: everything had to pass through the village of Cheux, which was difficult to cross because of the ruins and resulting rubble caused by the artillery barrage. The rain also slowed any progress on the ground, as well as hindering any covering aerial support. The narrow corridor between Rauray, which could not be taken, and Saint-Manvieu, which had yet to be so, dangerously exposed the flanks of VIII Corps, and Operation Martlet's failure now weighed heavily. During the early hours of the offensive, the threat of the Panzer IV companies who had been sent to support the front line units was negated due to the counter-attack by *Kampfgruppe* Wünsche in the area around Tessel. However, they were now returning to the area, not only on the western flank of the offensive, but also to the south. The companies were arranged as follows: on the west, 6./12 (east of Fontenay-le- Pesnel), 7./12 (Bräcker) east of Rauray and who were to attack Cheux, then 5./12 (Bando) who were positioned at le Haut du Bosq. 8./12 (Siegel's unit) settled in a position south of Cheux, from where they could block any breakthrough towards the south. In the south-east, another redoubtable panzer threat existed in the shape of the Tigers from 3rd Company, s.SS-Panzer-Abteilung 101. As we have seen, this narrow corridor, with country roads and a terrain covered by *bocage*, did not necessarily allow for the easy deployment of tanks, which could only advance slowly amid the many traffic jams.

The 10 HLI, supported by C Squadron, 7th RTR, and commanded by Lieutenant Colonel Young, passed through Cheux then le Haut du Bosq and Grainville-sur-Odon, before finally crossing the valley. The 2nd Gordons, supported by C Squadron, 9th RTR and commanded by Lieutenant Colonel Colville, also passed through Cheux before turning south-east towards Tourville-sur- Odon, where it would cross the river. When the two battalions arrived on the other side of the valley, the 2nd Argyll and Sutherland Highlanders (2nd SH), who were following behind, made sure that the bridges over the Odon were protected. But the objectives that were actually achieved were much more modest.

When the two battalions reached Cheux they passed through using two parallel streets. Navigation was a nightmare due to the narrow streets which were cluttered with debris, water and mud, while several Churchill tanks from 31st Tank Brigade had been immobilized after crossing through minefields. By 6 pm, the two battalions were still in Cheux and were unable to reach their starting line for the attack. Isolated without their accompanying infantry, some of the Churchill tanks fired their BESA machine guns in every direction, which frightened the Scots as much as the Germans. According to Sergeant Green, the HLI was advancing towards its objectives by the late afternoon. After crossing the main road, a young grenadier from the *Hitlerjugend* had leapt up from among the corn wearing a camouflaged uniform, right in the middle of the 10th HLI, and was immediately killed by a Sten Gun. This sudden appearance caused a panic among the Scots, who now imagined snipers were all around them and so began firing at the treetops. The rising panic, rain and smoke did nothing to help with their orientation, and although the battalion was supposed to head south, it

1. MK II artillery helmet of 2 Argyll and Sutherland Highlanders, 227th Infantry Brigade. (Heimdal)

2. Glengarry beret of the Argyll and Sutherland Highlanders. (Heimdal)

instead took the wrong direction and headed west towards Rauray. This direction led them straight towards a German stronghold and meant that they came under machine gun fire. A shell decapitated a tree which fell on one of the carriers, killing Lieutenant Bell in the process. Lieutenant Colonel Young realised they were going the wrong way and had to reorganise his battalion and put it in the right direction. However, because of the rainstorms, the overcast skies meant that the night had already begun to draw in, and so the HLI had to suspend its advance and dig in south of le Haut du Bosq. It remained stuck there, in the pouring rain, for a truly 'miserable night'.

The Gordons, commanded by Lieutenant Colonel Colville and supported by C Squadron, 9th RTR, advanced east of Cheux before reaching Ring Contour 100, which was being held by 7th Seaforths. A Company advanced on the right and B Company on the left, coming under fire from the *Nebewerfer* and the remnants of 15./25, suffering a number of casualties as a result. Around 5 pm, several Churchill tanks from A squadron, 9th RTC, were confronted by panzers, and a battle took place on

Lieutenant Colonel E.C. Colville being decorated on 15 September 1944, when he was promoted to Brigadier. (IWM)

the hill. The Gordons were at the front around 6.15 pm and the battle ended around 7 pm, by which time many of the Churchill tanks were on fire. They were followed by the reinforcements from 11th Armoured Division (C Squadron, 23rd Hussars), who tried to support the Scottish infantrymen but, in turn, also soon found their Sherman tanks on fire, probably after coming under fire from the Tigers of s.SS-Panzer-Abteilung 101. As soon as the first ones appeared on the ridge, they began to fire: 'It was the first of the regiment's tanks to be destroyed in action' notes the regimental diary, adding, 'Those who witnessed it will never forget the shock of seeing a regimental tank becoming a brazier for the first time.' A Squadron, 23rd Hussars, were positioned on the right flank and Lieutenant Robson was killed and three other Shermans from 23rd Hussars were destroyed. The 2 Gordons then crossed the Salbey stream and Lieutenant Colonel Colville reached the high ground that dominated the road leading from Cheux to Colleville. The strange circumstances of war thus leading this battalion commander to a village that bore a similar name to his own.

Five Churchill tanks from C Squadron, 9th RTC, and four Sherman tanks from C Squadron, 23rd Hussars, were destroyed while defending the hill. Trooper Jack Wods, who drove the armoured car for C Squadron, 9th RTR's reconnaissance officer, saw the Churchill tanks on the hill, along with the thick clouds of black smoke emanating from them, as the rounds of their ammunition exploded. Their crews retreated on foot through the wheat fields; their eyes still startled by what they had experienced. Wods also saw the retreating infantrymen who had not been able to reach their objectives. Everyone had believed the Churchill tanks were invincible and the two squadrons were ordered to withdraw before dark, leaving the 2 Gordons infantry on their own. Its B Company crossed the railway track (since replaced by the high-speed rail), and reached the first houses at Colleville. The civilian population had suffered heavy casualties under the artillery fire: Monsieur

1. SS-Ustuf. Dr Wolfgang Rabe.

2. SS-Ustuf. Thomas Amselgruber.

Bellanger, who had suffered terrible injuries in the previous war, was now seriously wounded in the head, while his wife was wounded in the hand. Having been at the forefront of VIII Corps' offensive, the Gordons had lost five officers (four killed and another wounded), before they had to retreat north of the Salbey after dark. The losses sustained by 9th RTR and 23rd Hussars were, in fact, due to the powerful 8.8 cm guns of the Tiger tanks. Patrick Agte notes:

> The 3rd Company of s.SS-Panzer-Abteilung 101 was moved to Grainville-sur-Odon, 2.5 km south of Caen. There the company commander, Unterstürmführer Amselgruber, and another Tiger engaged the onrushing enemy. The two Tigers guarded the break through point with no infantry support. Amselburger knocked out three enemy tanks during an attack and successfully engaged the following infantry. After its heavy losses, the enemy suspended its attack. Tanks from 1st Company also fought there and SS-Unterstürmführer Stamm was injured. Further east, near Mouen, a single Tiger was able to stop an attack by the 227th Infantry Brigade. Several tanks from the 9th RTR and the 23rd Hussars, which were escorted by the 2nd Gordon Highlanders, were destroyed.
>
> The remaining committed elements from the Tiger battalion joined the tanks of the *Hitlerjugend* in the heavy defensive fighting. The British attacked repeatedly with tanks and infantry, supported by artillery, and had to be beaten back. Radio contact with the Tigers was lost. SS Hauptstürmführer Dr Rabe, who was once again close to the fighting, volunteered to convey orders. In a display of skill and bravery, the Viennese doctor slipped past the British forces that had broken through and re-established contact with the Tiger company fighting at the front. During the hours-long battle, the Tigers destroyed a number of enemy tanks. Nevertheless, there was no hope of recapturing the old main line of resistance with the Tigers and II./SS-Panzer-Regiment 12. Also in action at that location was SS-Hauptstürmführer Möbius' 1st Company. The difficult terrain often prevented the Tigers from exploiting their longer-ranging guns and the shortage of infantry made it more difficult for the panzers to carry out their mission.

Armoured vehicles halted at Cheux

The 11th Armoured Division's armoured brigade (29th Armoured Brigade, commanded by Brigadier Harvey) finally arrived at Colleville, with his 23rd Hussars on the left flank of the offensive. The 2nd Fife and Forfar Yeomanry advanced on the right flank, with the third tank battalion, the 3rd Royal Tank Regiment, following behind. The three battalions were accompanied by an infantry battalion, the 8th Motor Battalion The Rifle Brigade. Lieutenant David Stileman was a member of the battalion's G Company (commanded by Major Noel Bell). After graduating from Wellington College, he joined the Rifle Brigade at eighteen and became an officer in 1943. This young, rugby-minded lieutenant stood out for his gentle humour and on that day, he had crossed the battlefield but remained north of Cheux:

> We passed through several villages before crossing the main road that goes from Bayeux to Caen. The state of the ruined houses and shops was a testimony to the heavy toll of the bombardments. A disgusting and repugnant smell of decay prevailed everywhere. On leaving the deserted villages we encountered other signs of destruction: dead animals, shredded, lying in a pestilential odour around the burned-out farms. The column stopped near a crossing [the Paris-Cherbourg railway] as some shells fell close by. The surrounding wheat fields were strewn with corpses of Canadian soldiers. We quickly realized that the ground was filled with mines. Having crossed the railway a kilometre further west, we began descending a grassy slope framed by two small woods. We stopped in a hollow and our 25-pound guns opened fire. Tea break, new orders. The corpse of a dead horse lay near a hedge.[24]

And so in the late afternoon, G Company, 8th RB, was still on the start line of the offensive, which it has only just joined. It would not leave until the following day and was to cross through Cheux just before noon on 27 June.

Once again, the compartmentalised terrain and the narrowness of the offensive sector - the Rauray sector not included - did not allow for the deployment of any resources, and the tanks from 29th Armoured Brigade were still stuck in traffic jams. Two squadrons from the 2nd Fife and Forfar Yeomanry, commanded by Lieutenant Colonel Scott, advanced into Cheux. They

1. Major Noel Bell commanded G Company, 8th Rifle Brigade. (G.B.)

2 & 3. Lieutenant David Stileman commanded the company's 11th Platoon. (G.B.)

had been preceded by B Squadron and the Recce Troop (light Stuart tanks). A Squadron advanced to the right, west of Cheux and C Squadron, commanded by Major Nicholls, who had a long experience of desert warfare, attacked through Cheux, along the main north-south axis, towards Grainville.

---

24   Published in *39/45 Magazine*, Vol. 8, October 1985

SS-Ustuf. Willi Kändler, a section commander in 5./12.

To the west, A Squadron advanced along the western edge of Cheux, heading north-west of le Haut du Bosq. The narrow road was crowded and the squadron lost two tanks to the panzers of 7th Company (Bräcker), and the grenadiers equipped with *Panzerfäusts*. Major Nicholls' C Squadron took the road leading from Cheux towards the north of le Haut du Bosq at around 2 pm, although the squadron had to progress in single file. 3 Troop was in the lead, formed of Corporal Goddard's tank, then Sergeant Stewart's tank and Corporal McCaffern's tank. They approached slowly and then suddenly, as they emerged onto the open ground at the top of the road, the lead tank was hit and Corporal Goddard and his gunner were killed. Sergeant Stewart's tank was destroyed in turn and the rest of the squadron had no choice but to stay stuck where they were. Over the radio, Major Nicholls received the order to advance from his commander, Lieutenant Colonel Young. But the Major, who had no accompanying infantry, replied that he would not move forward unless he judged the amount of ground gained would justify the losses incurred. He remained where he was. With his experience, he was not willing to risk the lives of his men unnecessarily, who loved him for this reason in return. Night fell and the tanks remained where they were, very close to the Germans. The British soldiers stayed in their tanks, hand-grenades at the ready in the case of an attack. Tensions were high. Then the order to withdraw came over the radio and they had to retreat, even though they were unable to turn around. As they reached open ground, they entered an empty field north of Cheux, where they spent the night. Seven tanks had been lost during the day, and of the ninety-one crewmen from C Squadron, at least ten had been killed and five others wounded.[25]

Opposite the Fife and Forfar's C Squadron were the Panzer IVs from 5./12. SS-Untersturmführer Willi Kändler was in command of one of the company's platoons and had noticed British tanks on the slope to the left. Before they were able to re-take their previous position behind a hedge, they found themselves engaged in a violent battle, with losses on both sides. A few yards in front of him, SS-Unterscharführer Buchholz stood at the turret of his Panzer IV and received a direct hit, which decapitated the tank commander. After a squadron of British tanks had broken through, they retreated to a new position on the Cheux/Noyers road. SS-Oberscharführer Junge then saw Sherman tanks advancing in a parallel direction and destroyed five of them. As a result, the panzers had locked up all of the roads by the evening. In the south were four tanks from Hans Siegel's company (8./12) facing the HLI and what follows is his particularly detailed account of the events that took place.

Hans Siegel on the Salbey

In the morning, Hans Siegel was at the head of 8th Company, SS-Panzer-Regiment 12. He was facing north with his Panzer IV, to the right of the road leading from

---

25   According to the report by radio operator Cox, who was in Corporal McCaffern's tank. Grandais, *La Bataille du Calvados*, p. 117.

Rauray to Fontenay-le-Pesnel. In front of him, on his right, were the Panzer IVs from 6th Company, while further ahead, the panzers of 5th Company were ready to go. Thus the Panzer IVs from 2nd Battalion were covering the area north-east of Rauray. To the left of the road, towards Tessel, the Panthers from 1st Battalion were fighting the attacking Englishmen at Fontenay-le-Pesnel, on SS-Panzer-Regiment 12's left wing. In the rear, Max Wünsche directed his regiment of panzers from the chateau at Rauray.

SS-Hauptsturmführer Hans Siegel had already had many victories. Two weeks earlier, on 11 June, he had thrown himself into the Canadian assault on Le Mesnil-Patry, destroying six Sherman tanks from the First Hussars in two minutes, and thus contributing greatly to the failure of the Canadian offensive. The First Hussars left thirty-four tanks behind after the battle.

Hans Siegel commanded the 8./12. This picture was taken after he had received the Iron Cross on 23 August 1944. (Heimdal)

Today, however, the situation was more worrying. The panzers were sent in regular counter-attacks to try and stem the assault, and fuel and shells were quickly spent during the ensuing combat. Within the panzer companies, the platoons took turns in pulling back to gather supplies. Between 4 pm and 5 pm, it was Hans Siegel's turn to leave, accompanied by three other Panzer IVs from his company, and they headed to the north-east of the Rauray chateau to refuel. The crew had barely had time to drink from their flaks, because the fighting had been raging since dawn. He met Max Wünsche, who told him, 'The front is breached on our right flank. We must go immediately to try and stem the enemy assault south of Cheux!' There was no accompanying infantry for the panzers and as Siegel notes, 'The engines howled, the hatches were closed, the guns and turrets were positioned for combat. The commander's final words disappeared in the clank of the caterpillars.' Without waiting a moment longer, Hans Siegel left with his four Panzer IVs. The rest of the company was positioned in front of Rauray, under the command of Herbert Höfler, the head of 1st Platoon. Hans Siegel ran across the fields to the east and reached a hill where there was a large bush. Beneath him was the little road which ran northwards from Grainville-sur-Odon to Cheux. On his left was the small Salbey stream, whose name had Scandinavian origins (probably: the 'brook of the Saules') thanks to the Vikings, who had settled in the area more than a thousand years earlier. It was usually a small brook, but had been swollen by the heavy rains and now the whole surrounding area had become swampy. Hans Siegel saw his target and opened fire. Three British chenillettes were demolished on the road. He rejoined the unpaved road, which was really more of a narrow path (the current road has since been widened), and which was flanked by tall trees. He proceeded north, towards Cheux, with caution.

The four Panzer IVs advanced in a line along the narrow road, which by now was lined with meadows and hedges. At 6 pm Hans Siegel arranged three of the

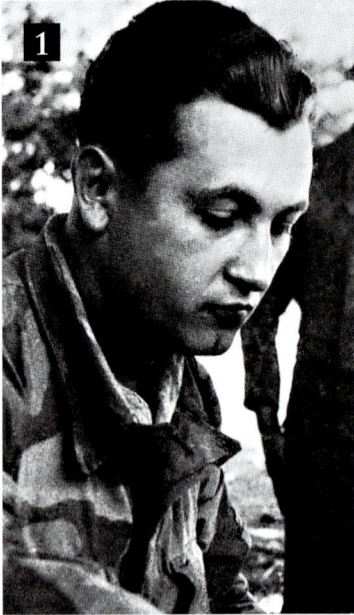

Panzer IVs in a field on the left, 300 metres north of the Salbey, positioning them in a line facing north. They were camouflaged behind the hedge, with only their gun barrels protruding through the foliage. His own Panzer IV remained on the road, facing north. At 6.05 pm he went to reconnoitre the meadow on the right, where he saw four abandoned 10.5 cm howitzers from a battery belonging to the HJ Division's artillery regiment. Further down, he also found a coat in an abandoned vehicle, bearing the insignia of an artillery major. In the north-east corner of the field he could see a bunker covered in earth and wood. He approached, thinking it had already been taken by the British and entered with a pistol in his hand shouting 'Hands up!' What he actually found were around forty artillerymen from the division who had hidden in the bunker and were ready to defend themselves. They had

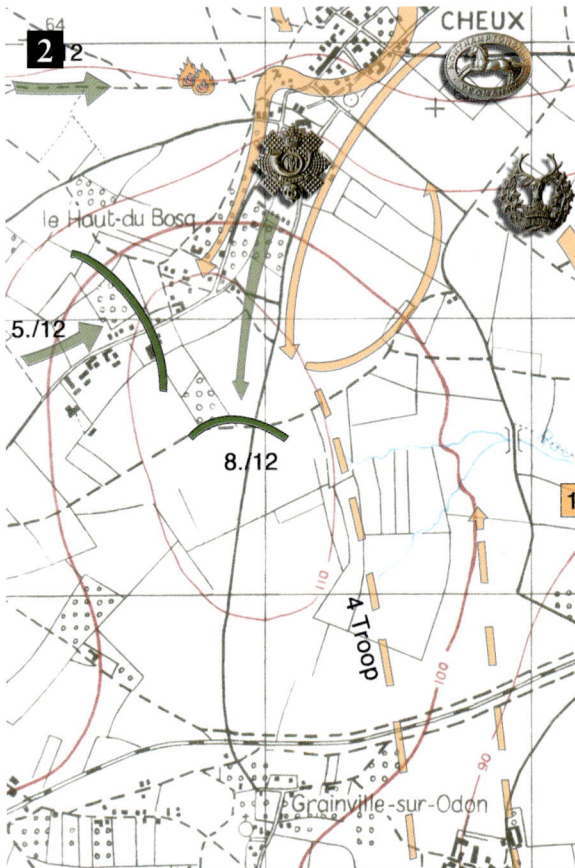

1. SS-Ustuf. Herbert Höfler was the leader of 1st section, 8./12. Hans Siegel entrusted him with command of the action that took place in the Rauray sector. (Heimdal)

2. Positions of the four Panzer IVs from Hans Siegel's 8./12 on the Salbey. (L.K. Heimdal)

3. The field where Hans Siegel positioned his four Panzer IVs, pointing north (towards Cheux), on the right. (Heimdal)

4. One of the Panzer IV's position, hidden in the hedge, looking towards Cheux. (Heimdal)

no shells left after their battery had been overwhelmed by the British, who had since continued on their way after breaking through the front line, not caring for the artillerymen who had taken refuge in the bunker. Hans Siegel decided to have the four howitzers repaired, but the tractors were behind the railway that passed in front of Grainville-sur-Odon, and they would have to wait until nightfall before they were able to evacuate them.

Hans Siegel returned to his own panzer back on the road, and was joined by the reconnaissance patrol he had sent to reconnoitre the left flank. They told him they had come across elements from SS-Panzergrenadier-Regiment 26 on a hill, 500 meters away. It was covering the division's left flank and had been hit by the British offensive, but was unable to link up with the four Panzer IVs because it did not have enough men. Hans Siegel then noted, 'We were thus in the front line, without any contact with the left or right flank. The enemy pulled back, probably to the southern edge of Cheux. The breach was plugged and our mission fulfilled.' It was now 7 pm and Siegel decided that he would make contact himself with the elements from Regiment 26, which were a few hundred meters away on the left. He followed a hedge and arrived at an earth covered-bunker, identical to that where the artillerymen were. It was the battalion CP of Bernhard Siebken's II./26. He then returned to his panzers and night began to fall. The torrential rain penetrated everything and the men were soon soaked through. Siegel had no radio contact with anyone and the night was as black as ink. Suddenly, a *VW-Kübelwagen* stopped near the Salbey and brought a canteen with food for the twenty soldiers. A man from each panzer went to fetch supplies for himself and his four comrades, while Siegel took the opportunity to write a quick message to the regimental CP, pointing out that his mission had been accomplished and that he was holding his position. A quarter of an hour later (about 11 pm), another *Kübelwagen* arrived and came down the road between the trees, towards Siegel's panzer. It brought with it SS-Sturmbannführer Schöps (whose coat Siegel had found in the abandoned vehicle), the artillery commander for the entire area. He spoke with Siegel and they decided to move the howitzers at around 1 am, but with no tractors, and using one of the Panzer IVs instead. The *Kübelwagen* was about 35 metres behind Siegel's panzer and was unable to turn around on the tree-lined road. With a 'Hau Ruck!', in four manoeuvrers the vehicle was carried at arm's length, turned 180°, and put back facing the right direction (facing south, towards Grainville-sur-Odon). Suddenly, someone shouted 'Hands up!' as several silhouettes emerged from the bushes. They moved towards the group, which quickly split up and sought the shelter of Hans Siegel's panzer, and in an instant, Siegel found himself alone in the middle of the road.

Acting on reflex, Siegel lunged towards his assailant's throat as he raised his automatic rifle to his shoulder, preparing to fire. He squeezed his neck with his left hand, swung him to the ground, and grabbed the rifle with his right hand. The triangular bayonet had cut the right leg of Siegel's leather trousers and as the British soldier fired into the material, the bullets brushed Siegel's leg. The gun's magazine was soon empty and the Briton, half choked moaned, 'Help me, help me!' The two men rolled around on the ground, struggling. At this moment, another Briton appeared to try and help his comrade. He fired, but hit the wrong target, as Siegel's opponent cried out, 'Oh, I'm wounded!' and collapsed. Siegel stood up and then, realising that he still had his pistol with him, drew out the weapon. He removed the safety with his right hand, all the while with his left hand still holding the first soldier's neck, and emptied his P08 at the silhouette of the second British soldier, who disappeared through the hedge, as quietly as he had first arrived. Hans Siegel removed the bayonet stuck in his trousers and left the British soldier, who had been killed by his panicking comrade, on the ground. He recalls:

> There was a ghostly silence. Only the rain fell on us from the tops of the trees, as the blood cursed through our veins. I went back to my panzer. Ten metres in front of it, on the left, I saw a man on his knees leaning on one arm: it was Schöps, the artillery group commander. His head was hanging down and he was moaning slowly. I knelt beside him and I tried to raise his head with my right hand. Blood gushed from his neck. I pulled him under my panzer to protect him. Where were the others? There was no sound or movement, only the rain.
>
> The panzer crews had to be on the alert. I sent my gunner over to the right while I headed for the panzer on the left, putting a new round of ammunition in my pistol. Suddenly, I saw two flat helmets above the tank, standing out against the night sky. I was now next to the panzer and saw the two silhouettes jumping up, trying to open the turret's hatch, while at the same time the hatch was being pulled in the other direction, from below. There was a rhythmic clicking: open, closed, open, closed. One of the English soldiers shouted for a grenade and I said to myself, 'Wait for it'. Then quietly, just as if I was at a shooting range, I moved the pistol from bottom to top, firing two shots at close range. That was enough, the turret was free! Suddenly, a burst of bullets gushed from the turret's machine gun just above me. It was our sentry, who was positioned in front of the panzer and had been woken up by the two pistol shots. The crew had been completely surprised by the British patrol. No wonder: the rain, the exhaustion, the night time.

After the tension of the recent fighting, and particularly those of the last moments, Hans Siegel was exhausted. He lay down on the ground with his face in the wet grass and slept for five to ten minutes, as if he were dead. He was woken up by his gunner who said, 'Returning from captivity, chief!' Indeed, after being sent away (by Siegel), the gunner had been captured by some of the men from the British patrol that had attacked them. The patrol had caught him without making any noise, pointed a rifle butt in his back, then arms in the air, off they went. Having made it a third of the way towards Cheux, the patrol sent out a flare and a British machine gun opened fire to provide cover for the men returning with the prisoner. The shots forced the patrol to get down on the ground, the gunner too. He jumped into a ditch full of water that ran along the road, rolled over, and stayed in the water without moving. 'God dammed, where is our prisoner? - Where are you?' said the men in the patrol, as they swept the bushes with their torches before the shots resumed again. As they took shelter and fell back, the gunner took the opportunity to rejoin his lines, with only aches in the arms and back to show for his ordeal. As he stood before his leader, exhausted by what he had just been through, Siegel decided to send him back to the rear to rest. The reserve gunner, a motorcycle liaison officer, would take his place in the panzer. But suddenly, Siegel heard the sound of his panzer's engine. Had the British patrol, who had already failed twice, managed to capture his panzer? He ran towards the tank, which was not heading in the direction of the British. Instead, it turned and entered the meadow, stopping after few moments before the engine was switched off.

Nothing moved; there was only the sound of the rain. It was a black night. I removed the safety on my gun and with a jump up, I leapt towards the back of the panzer, then underneath it. Finally some shelter! I crawled up to the exit hatch, which was at the bottom of the panzer. With my back against the tank and my stomach in the wet grass, there was no going back and no turning around. I hit the door with my pistol, but no one responded at first. 'Password!' 'It's me!' *[I said]* They had witnessed the previous scuffle and as they had not seen me, had left the road.

The British patrol had failed because it had suffered too many casualties and was unable to bring back a single prisoner. They had no information on

1. Hans Siegel showing where he fought with the British soldier. The south and the Salbey river are behind him. The other British soldiers left through the hedge on the left. Hans Siegel is seen here with a former tank commander in his battalion. After the Battle of Normandy, Hans Siegel commanded the Panzer-Regiment's 2nd Battalion and lost his left arm during the fighting in Hungary in 1945.

2. The same place today.

the importance of Hans Siegel's forces, which would be important for the following day's attack. It was now midnight and Siegel gave orders for one of the Panzer IVs to bring the 10.5 cm howitzers back to Grainville. He told them to roll slowly and make no noise, as they didn't want the operation to be noticed by the enemy. However, he would leave beforehand in SS-Sturmbannführer Schöps' *VW-Kübelwagen*, taking him along as well. Siegel knew Schöps was not only wounded, but most likely dying, having suffered a cut to his jugular artery and losing a lot of blood.

Hans Siegel knew the Panzer Regiment's CP had just been transferred from Rauray to Grainville, and so headed south. The new CP was set up in a farm near the medieval church. He parked his car in front of the building, asked the medics to look after SS-Sturmbannführer Schöps, then went in to make his report. Max Wünsche was there in a dark room, examining the maps on the table using only the light of a flickering candle. The windows had been blocked by wardrobes to protect them from the shelling.

1. Hans Siegel mimics the position of the injured SS-Stubaf. Schöps, although this scene took place slightly further north along the road, on the west side. (S. Varin)

2. Hans Siegel describing his action on the Salbey river to the author. This picture was taken in 1991. He has since passed away. (G.B.)

The aides-de-camp and the officers leaned tiredly on the backs of chairs or lay on temporary couches. A cup of coffee was stretched out to me. It felt good. The door creaked and, almost noiselessly in comparison to the crash of the fighting, a sergeant, the head of a Pak section in position along the railway track, stumbled in, saluted and breathlessly announced that he had heard the engine noise of armoured vehicles approaching! Max Wünsche threw me an inquisitive look and said to the non-commissioned officer, 'Calm down, those are our panzers from 8th Company bringing the vehicles back! Siegel, you go back there immediately, give your orders and keep your eyes open. Good luck!' I left, leaving half of my cup of coffee behind.

Night covers the retreat

The dusk did not mean the British could leave their valuable armoured vehicles in the front line, where they could be destroyed by German patrols, and all squadrons were ordered by radio to retreat slightly and fill up with fuel and ammunition, as well as regroup (as we saw with the 2nd Fife and Forfar Yeomanry and 23rd Hussars). The Scottish infantrymen were left alone on the front line: 10 HLI south of Cheux, and the Gordons and Seaforth to the south-east. To the west, in 49th Division's sector, following their morning failure the 7 DWR attacked the Saint Nicolas farm for the second time at 3 pm, backed by Sherman tanks from the Sherwood Rangers Yeomanry (SRY). This time, thanks to the strong support of the artillery and benefiting from the departure of many of the remaining panzers further east, the Dukes finally took the farm. The tanks of the SRY advanced along the road leading from Tessel to Cheux, up to 500 yards (450 metres) from the hamlet of Rauray. But the tanks of the Sherwood Rangers had no infantry and so were unable to exploit the advance. It wasn't until 9 pm when they were joined by infantrymen from 11 DLI that they were able to settle west of Rauray, and be in a favourable position in order to take the hamlet the next morning. This threat then led to the evacuation of the Panzer regiment at Grainville, as we have seen.

Despite being only modest successes, Montgomery felt triumphant, and at the end of the day sent the following communiqué to the Commander-in-Chief, General Eisenhower: 'Very bad weather with heavy rain and low clouds, but very good progress has been made and the leading elements of VIII Corps are now at the railway line in Colleville.' He went on to add that, 'the fight will continue all day and all night.' This was, of course, completely untrue. As we have seen, all tank squadrons had been ordered to retreat and there was no night time combat. Those on the British front line settled down for the night and did not to continue the advance. Moreover, the objectives (the bridges over the Odon and the Orne), were still far away and a few dozen men from a weakened company, north of Colleville, still remained. All brigades from the Scottish 15th Division received the following order: 'Top secret: enemy now reduced to its last reserves on our front. It is essential to guarantee the crossings over the Odon River as soon as possible tomorrow, 27 June.'

The Germans, meanwhile, used the night to fall back and reorganise. The rain and darkness allowed isolated and surrounded groups from the HJ Division to rejoin their own lines. The line itself was reconstituted and covered (from west to east) Vendes, Rauray, the high ground southeast of Cheux (remains of 15./25) and Marcelet. Among the reinforcements who were trying to reconnect to the main line included those retreating from the Engineer Battalion CP's bunker. SS-Untersturmführer Richter recalls:

Only nine men took part in the breakthrough, because we had two seriously wounded men with us. As far as I know, one of them was an artilleryman, but I do not remember his name. The other was SS-sturmmann Thile, from Hamburg. He was courageous and patient, and one of the best men in the *engineers*. In the autumn of 1944, I learned that he had been exchanged as a seriously wounded prisoner, and had had one of his legs amputated. While in hospital he received the wound badge in silver and the Iron Cross, 2nd class.

The HJ Division's situation report, signed by its commander, 'Panzermeyer', shows that by the evening, the General Staff were well aware of the situation, in spite of the relative confusion resulting from the fighting around Cheux:

While in the north-east sector of Rauray, the enemy is massing its armoured forces (fifty-three enemy armoured vehicles have been counted), the remains of SS-Pi.-Btl. 12, SS-Pz.-Gren.-Rgt. 26 and SS-Pz.-Aufkl.-Abt. 12, and above all those of SS-Pz.-Rgt. 12, under the command of SS-Obersturmbannführer

Wünsche, pushed back all enemy attacks. After several crises had been overcome, by the evening of 26 June 1944 we held a new, albeit weak, front line. During the day's fighting, at least fifty enemy tanks were destroyed by Panzers and Pak guns. It is not yet possible to count the tanks that were destroyed in close combat or by mines. Our own panzer losses are high, and those of particular concern are among the grenadiers. SS-Pz.-Pi.-Btl. 12 can be considered to be annihilated. The particularly high number of losses among SS-Pz.-Gren.-Rgt. 26 cannot yet be assessed. II./SS-Pz.-Art.-Rgt. 12, who calmly engaged its artillery and infantry despite being surrounded, was able to pull back in the course of the night and alter its position. The group's commander, SS-Sturmbannführer Schöps, was killed. In the area where the enemy broke through, the grenadiers, sappers and artillerymen fought until their complete destruction. Those who merit particular mention include: SS-Obersturmbannführer Wünsche, SS-Sturmbannführer Olboeter, SS-Sturmbannführer Bremer, SS-Sturmbannführer Krause, SS-Hauptsturmführer Siegel, SS-Unterscharführer Dürr (4./SS-Pz.- Gren.-Rgt. 26). In spite of heavy losses, the division estimates that the enemy will attack again on 27 June 1944 from the sectors of Cheux/Saint-Manvieu/ Norrey in order to seize Caen. The division will defend its positions with all its strength. It still has: 30 Panzer IVs, 17 Panzer Vs, 233 SPWs, armoured reconnaissance, armoured artillery observation and 14 Pak guns.

The total losses for the HJ Division amounted to 730 men, including 88 killed, 230 wounded and 412 missing, and were distributed as follows: I./26, 6 killed, 23 wounded, 40 missing; II./26, 15 killed, 26 wounded, 60 missing; III./26, 8 killed, 23 wounded, no missing persons; Pionier-Battalion, 18 killed,

Grainville. The farm near the church was where SS-Pz.- Rgt. 12's CP was located. (G.B.)

23 wounded, 280 missing; A.A. 12 (reconnaissance), 5 killed, 18 wounded, 6 missing; Panzer Regiment, 4 killed, 37 wounded, none missing; Artillery Regiment, 8 killed, 26 wounded, 2 missing; Regimental companies (including 15./25, 15./26, 16./26), 17 killed, 46 wounded, 23 missing. In two days, the division had lost half of its panzers, going from 100 to just 50. The losses for VIII Corps were also heavy (645 men, 104 of them killed), but they did have considerable reserves and the *Hitlerjugend* command was certainly aware of the gravity of the situation. *SS-Brigadeführer* Kraemer, head of I. SS-Panzerkorps, submitted the following report to the head of the 7th Army at 8.10 pm:

> Enemy breakthrough between Saint-Manvieu, Tessel and Brettevillette to the south, with advanced elements at Grainville two hours ago. Some elements are still on either side of Cheux. If reinforcements are not brought in tonight, the enemy breakthrough cannot be stopped. The first elements of 1. SS-Panzer-Division are in the area around Saint-Germain, without any fuel. Werfer-Brigade 7 may be engaged with a group on 27 June.

Kraemer was informed that new forces were not available and it would be another two nights before any infantry could arrive in the area around Villers-Bocage. I. SS-Panzerkorps would have to try and gain assistance from 2. Panzer-Division. An hour later, a discussion took place between Generaloberst Dollmann (head of 7th Army) and Marshal Rommel. The first proposed that II. SS-Panzerkorps launch a counter-attack, which Rommel agreed to. However, the corps could not be engaged before 29 June and so it was decided that a battalion of panzers from 2. Panzer-Division and a *Kampfgruppe* from 2. SS-Panzer-Division would be immediately engaged instead. Elements from 2. Panzer Division could be deployed the following day near Cheux, from line at Noyers/Rauray. On that day, VIII Corps lost 645 men, of which 104 were killed, including the commander of 4th Armoured Brigade, Brigadier John Cuvrie. The losses suffered were close to those of the HJ, but with a very different balance of forces.

The 15th Scottish Division were in the area around La Gaulle and Saint-Manvieu (44th Brigade), while its 227th Brigade was in the Haut du Bosq sector and also south-east of Cheux. Its 46th Brigade was still fighting pockets of German resistance within Cheux itself, with the 43rd Division arriving to relieve the battalions and allow the offensive to continue. The objectives set down by Montgomery had not been achieved, but the losses suffered by the *Hitlerjugend* Division meant that, theoretically, it would not suffer any secondary setbacks. About fifty panzers and a few hundred scattered grenadiers were facing a 5 kilometre-wide offensive and were unable to stem the attack. Only reinforcements could help prevent the breakthrough and, apart from elements from 2. Panzer Division and a Tiger tank company, they were still too far away. It would appear that even though he had not made a decisive breakthrough, Montgomery (who was informed by ULTRA of the approaching II. SS-Panzerkorps), was winning the race to supply reinforcements. For the moment, it was just VIII Corps against elements of I. SS-Panzerkorps, but they still needed to break through to the Orne before II. SS-Panzerkorps arrived.

To conclude the assessment of this particular day, let us return to the combativeness of the grenadiers from the *Hitlerjugend* Division. It was their extraordinary resistance that slowed down the British offensive and saved the German front that day. The artillery barrage was terrible, and any army subjected to such ravages would generally collapse. The effects of the barrage could clearly be seen on the villages that had come under its fire; they were ruined. Following the artillery fire, the German survivors had immediately resumed the fight, causing losses among the Scottish infantry. Surrounded and overwhelmed, these survivors had continued to open fire in all directions, creating the impression of snipers in the area and thus slowing down the offensive's progress. Artillery and mortars also caused losses among the Scottish infantry. The minefields, Pak guns and, as of mid-afternoon, the Panzer IVs, also resulted in heavy losses among the British

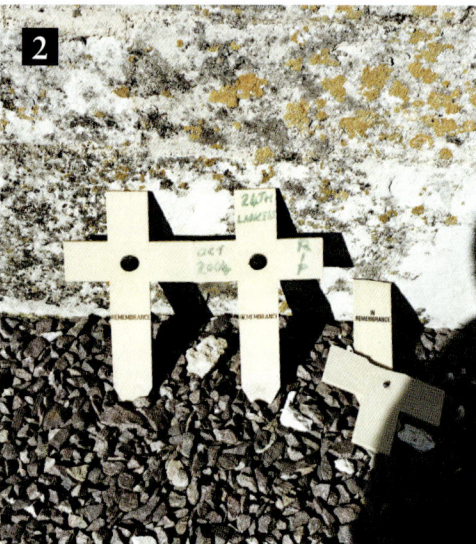

1. The Saint-Nicolas farm was only taken until 3 pm on 26 June. The ruined house was rebuilt after the war. The agricultural buildings, including the one seen here on the left, have survived. (G.B.)

2. At the foot of the commemorative plaque at Tessel church, small crosses have been left in memory of the 24th Lancers and its action in this area on 26 June 1944. (G.B.)

armoured vehicles, not to mention individual weapons such as magnetic mines and *Panzerfausts*. This permanent insecurity had made an already prudent army even more cautious when the offensive was halted south of Cheux. However, experienced men such as Major Nicholls, who refused to advance further unless absolutely necessary, showed that this cautiousness was, at times, justified.

The unexpected defensive success was due to several factors. First of all, the terrain, which had been favourable at the start, one more turned into *bocage*, surrounded by large villages that had become defensive focal points, such as Cheux and especially Saint-Manvieu. The failure of Operation Martlet also had serious consequences; the corridor of attack was narrow and three Panzer IV companies were able to attack the British flanks and front lines, resulting in heavy casualties. But there was also the human factor. The *Hitlerjugend* Division was, clearly, the best German division on the front line. Its leaders mainly came from 1. SS-Panzer-Division *Leibstandarte* Adolf Hitler, an elite unit whose officers had plenty of battle experience, mostly in the Polish campaign. The young soldiers they mentored were particularly motivated fighters and the majority were conscripts, such as those from the *Hohenstaufen* and *Frundsberg* divisions, which were units from II. SS-Panzerkorps that were sent to the front. Despite the obviously strong military qualities of the latter, the *Hitlerjugend* Division still surpassed them in terms of military strength, as the British testimony on this subject has shown. The exceptional strength of the division stems from its origin, its commanders and officers, but also from many of its non-commissioned officers from the SS *Leibstandarte* Adolf Hitler. This was a highly-motivated, elite unit with leaders of exceptional calibre and was to commend itself during the various campaigns in Poland, France, the Balkans and the USSR. Among these, the new divisional commander SS-Standartendführer Kurt Meyer, known as 'Panzermeyer', demonstrated an extraordinary level of initiative. These leaders aided their young soldiers particularly well, giving them extensive experience, and in turn the soldiers adulated their commander, thanks to the newspaper and cinema propaganda reports who detailed their magnificent achievements. Every elite corps can transform a simple conscript into an elite soldier, by the example of its peers and the pride of being one of the best. The young soldiers were certainly proud to wear such a prestigious uniform.

Veterans have said how they would 'show off' in front of girls when on leave. It is important to imagine what wartime Germany was like; shaken by the bombings, which in turn aroused a desire for revenge on the Allied planes that had caused relatives and neighbours to suffer, it was a nation energised and inspired by the propaganda films that showed panzer units on all fronts 'heroically' defending the threatened Reich. These young teenagers arrived on the Normandy Front full of such images. They were physically well-trained, motivated, often volunteers and had a desire to take revenge against the destruction they had suffered. Not to mention the fact that they wanted to wear the prestigious medals on their jackets that would dazzle when they back home.

Ernst Eischen, from Luxembourg, was a member of the division's tank regiment. He describes how the tank officers had a '*halsweh*' ('sore neck') as they called it, which basically meant the ardent desire to hang the Knight's Cross around their neck at all costs. In a totalitarian state where military value is the of the highest

1. This picture by Sergeant Leeson shows soldiers from the Seaforth Highlanders bringing four HJ Division prisoners to the rear. (IWM B5972)

2. This other image, also taken on 26 June by Sergeant Laing, shows other prisoners from the HJ Division (including a non-commissioned officer). (IWM B 6007)

importance, the soldiers of such an elite unit wanted to be exemplary, whatever the price, even if it meant giving the supreme sacrifice. What they wanted was to return home covered with decorations and to have helped change the fate of the army. They admired their leaders and were willing to follow them, without question, into the line of fire. The best elements from the *Leibstandarte* had been drawn on in order to make up this new division, including officers and also non-commissioned officers. Indeed it had been done to such an extent that afterwards, the *Leibstandarte* was a shadow of its former self, as was seen seen during the battle of Normandy, where it did not exactly shine as it would normally have done.

The leaders in the *Hitlerjugend* Division knew each other and the fact that they had fought together was a major advantage when it came to their cooperation. This was not the case for the leaders of the *Hohenstaufen* or *Frundsberg* Divisions, who despite being good soldiers for the most part, came from various backgrounds. A more debatable area concerns the particular fierceness of these young soldiers. What had they been told before going up to the front? Their commanders had fought on the Eastern Front, where it was often better to die than to surrender the Red Army, and where conditions were often abominable. Although they had been affected by their trials on the Eastern Front, they knew that the fighting they would experience with the Western Allies would be more similar to the general rules of war. But did they still tell their young soldiers that they would be executed if they surrendered? In some cases this was probably true. There were several cases of executions of Canadian prisoners by the *Hitlerjugend* Division in the first few days, such as those at the Ardenne Abbey, the Chateau at Audrieu and le Mensil-Patry (near the Fontenay-Carpiquet road). In the latter two cases, it appears that they were motivated by the ill-treatment and subsequent death of Oberst Luxemberger in front of the HJ Division's lines. However, there were no other such occurrences after this. The stress of the first battles often provoked such acts and the Allies committed similar actions in Normandy during the early days, especially in the sectors of the American paratroopers. On 26 June, a Scottish soldier, Trooper Les Arnold, recalled, 'The infantry captured some "Hitler Youth" soldiers who came swaggering into our lines; this attitude annoyed us, particularly because we had heard that some of their units had shot Canadian prisoners.'[26] Another testimony from Lieutenant Woolcombe, 6th KOSB, who were marching on Saint-Manvieu describes how:

> Suddenly, we froze at a burst of fire from Black's Bren gun, firing from his hip, and instantly an apparition rose screaming from the corn and rushed towards us, throwing itself at my feet. It was an SS soldier … But he was in no state for offensive action, by a neat bit of shooting by Black, who had hit him in the shoulder. He knelt at my feet clutching my knees, frantic with pain and terror. 'Don't shoot – don't shoot – have pity'. He knew that much English. We understood. To strengthen their resistance, they had been told the British shoot all prisoners. He now expected death in cold blood … We carried him into the Company position.[27]

---

26   Tim Saunders, *Operation Epsom*, p.49-50.

27   Ibid. p.52.

A captain from VIII Corps interviews a young officer (an SS-Ustuf.) from the HJ Division, who had been captured in the area around Cheux on 26 June. (IWM)

This testimony appears to reinforce what we have already seen. Another testimony, that of Captain Mike Peppiatt (Royal Artillery), who was captured in Colleville on that day but later escaped, throws a slightly more complementary light on the young soldiers he met:

> With one or two exceptions, the soldiers of the *Hitlerjugend* were chatty and friendly. They were amazed at the power of our artillery. I suggested that they surrender themselves, but they refused. In the evening we drove through Tourville and the Odon valley. At night, we were loaded on various vehicles and gun tractors. We tried to escape when we came to a halt, but we were scarcely at the mouth of the gun when hands grasped us, and we were threatened with being shot if we tried again. We spent the night with these same soldiers in a farm and they shared their pitiful rations with us.[28]

These were the elite soldiers who had contained the Scots' offensive. Montgomery's soldiers would still have to face them the following morning if they wanted to cross the Odon and reach Hill 112 and the Orne.

---

28   A. Grandais, *La Bataille du Calvados*, p. 122.

Part Two

The Offensive Stops At Hill 112

On 29 June near Hill 112 (near Eterville), a trio of infantrymen from 8th Rifle Brigade (11th Armoured Division) went on patrol. The men were B. O'Neill, from London, G. Wood, from Uxbidge and Jack Pearson, from Mill Hill near London. This image illustrates the reality of Operation Epsom. It was supposed to involve a blazing tank charge, but the tanks had found it difficult to advance. When they were able to get beyond Odon, by dawn on the third day, the panzers had already reached Hill 112 where they blocked any further progress. Epsom had reached the end of its offensive after two days, trapped in a vice established by the gradual arrival of German reinforcements. The first phase of Operation Epsom had been conducted by the infantry, with bayonets fixed, as seen here. These infantrymen from 8 RB had accompanied the armoured vehicles that had now been halted at Hill 112. In the end, the operation was quite the opposite of the German Blitzkrieg. When the German lines faltered on the first day, the tanks were kept back in reserve and when they were finally engaged, albeit cautiously, it was too late. Operation Epsom would end in a stalemate due to the Allied misuse of its armoured forces.

The Hohenstafen moves towards the Normandy Front

Formally activated on 31 December 1942, 9. SS-Panzer-Division *Hohenstaufen* was set up in 1943, mainly from young conscripts directly from the RAD. Its name was officially registered on 19 March 1943 in honour of the imperial Hohenstaufen dynasty of medieval Germany. The division was sent to counter-attack the new Soviet offensive, which had surrounded German units in a pocket near Tarnopol, in Galicia, along with II. SS-Panzerk orps (made up of this division and 10. SS-Panzer-Division '*Frundsberg*'), from Lemberg. The counter-attack took place in April 1944, breaking through the Soviet lines and clearing a path for the encircled units. However, when the Allies landed in Normandy, this new threat on Western Front demanded the urgent transfer of all II. SS-Panzerkorps. The transfer was decided as early as 12 June 1944, and began the following day. Trains were used initially, crossing the whole of the Reich at the incredible rate of seventy-two trains per day: an average of three trains per hour! When the division landed in France, still far away from the Normandy Front, a long road journey then began.

1. This picture shows a Panzer IV from 5th or 6th Company engaged in Galicia. SS-Panzer-Regiment 9 had four Panther tank companies in its 1st Battalion. On the other hand, 2nd Battalion had Panzer IVs for the 5th and 6th companies and only *Sturmgeschütze* (assault cannons) for 7th and 8th companies. (P. Tiquet)

2. An assault cannon from 7th or 8th Company and its crew in Galicia. (P. Tiquet)

1. Another Panzer IV from 6th Company in Galicia. (P. Tiquet)

2. Transfer by rail to the Normandy Front from Galicia, here showing a Panzer IV from 6th Company. Ready for a long journey, the crew are drying their clothes on the machine. (P. Tiquet)

The (heavy) SS-Panzer-Abteilung 101

This heavy tank battalion originated from a company from 1. SS-Panzer-Division 'Leibstandarte SS Adolf Hitler', which fought on the Eastern Front, mainly in the Charkow sector, in February 1943, and in the Kursk sector from 5 to 17 July. It then moved to Italy before returning to the Eastern Front in November 1943, where it remained until 20 February 1944. It was during this period that Michael Wittmann distinguished himself, receiving the Oak Leaves on 30 January 1944. The (heavy) SS-Panzer-Abteilung 101, was set up on 19 July 1943 and the remains of the heavy tank company were amalgamated together.

The battalion's command was entrusted to SS-Sturmbannführer Heinz von Westernhagen, with SS-Hauptsturmführer Rolf Möbius in command of 1st Company, SS-Obersturmführer Michael Wittmann that of 2nd Company, and SS-Obersturmführer Hanno Raasch of 3rd Company. The battalion was put on alert in the Beauvais sector directly after the invasion, but took six days (from 6 to 12 June) to reach the Normandy Front due to routing difficulties. Arriving in the Villers-Bocage sector on 13 June, it was surprised by the unexpected arrival of the 7th Armoured Division and so immediately responded to SS-Ostuf Wittmann's actions, as he destroyed the head of the armoured column and acquired the reputation as a 'tank ace'. On the night of 14-15 June, a bombardment crushed Evrecy and hit 3rd Company; eighteen of its members were killed and eleven wounded. The battalion was then engaged against the British offensive of Operation Epsom.

The Tiger I Ausf. E was a formidable opponent for the Allied soldiers, with its powerful 88 mm (8.8 cm KwK 36 L / 56) gun and its thick armour providing protection: 100 mm for the frontal turret and 80 mm for the sides, 120 mm for the front bumper, 100 mm for the frontal hull of the vehicle and 80 to 60 mm for the sides. But it was also a monster, weighing in at 57 tons and capable of travelling at 38 km/h on road with an operational range of 195 km on the road and 110 km cross country.

The battalion's insignia is similar to that of the Leibstandarte, but with two passepartout. (Heimdal)

May 1944, Beauvais sector

1. Tiger 232 of 2nd Company (2./SS-Pz.-Abt. 101), which was under the command of SS-Unterscharführer Kleber on 6 June 1944. (BA)

2. Tiger I markings of SS-Panzer-Abteilung 101. Each company had a special way of marking tactical signs on the front and back of its Tiger. 1) 1st Company: on the left is a diamond with an 'S' for schwere (heavy) followed by a '1', and on the right is the armoured unit's emblem. 2) 2nd Company: the company's emblem is on the left, rounded at the bottom. 3) 3rd Company; same emblem, but placed on the right. 4) 1st Company, the emblem on the left and the diamond 'S' on the right. 5) 2nd and 3rd companies: emblems on the left. The numbers are painted in red with a white border. Tiger 131 belonged to SS-Ustuf. Walter Hahn. Tiger 221 belonged to SS-Ostuf. Georg Hantusch, who had provided testimonies concerning Operation Epsom. (Heimdal)

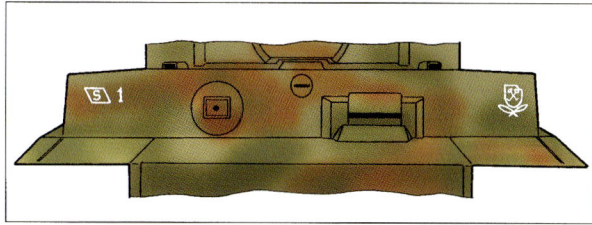

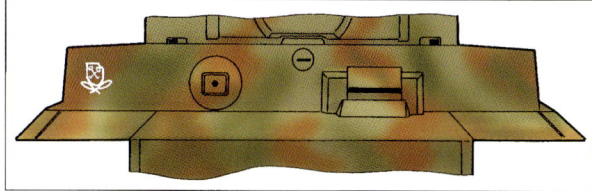

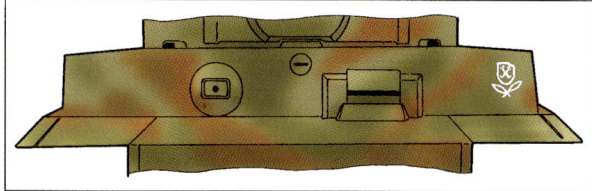

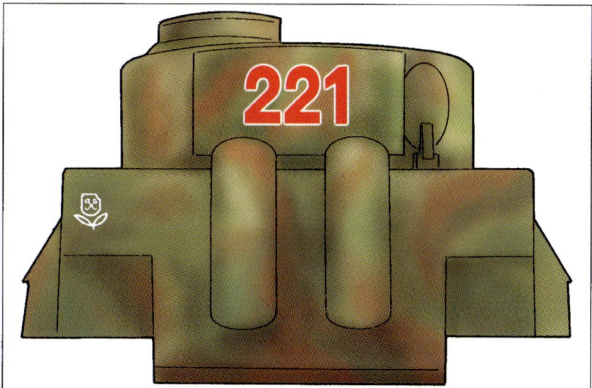

Hans Siegel on the Salbey river

1. SS-Obersturmführer Hans Siegel commanded 8th company, SS-Panzer-Regiment 12. On the previous day he was facing the Salbey and was up against the centre of the British offensive. On 27 June his role would be even more decisive, completely blocking the HLI's attack and the tanks from the 7th RTR who were supporting it. This picture was taken after he had been awarded the Iron Cross on 23 August 1944, in recognition of his victories at le Mesnil-Patry and on the Salbey. (Heimdal)

2. While three of his Panzer IVs remained west of the road leading to Cheux, SS-Ostuf. Siegel moved his tank east of the road to roughly the area in foreground, on the right. Ahead and to the left is the field that the Jocks of the 10 HLI advanced through. Their supporting tanks came up against the three other Panzer IVs camouflaged behind the hedge. In the centre is the road leading to Cheux. (G. B.)

3. The field on the right (east) of the Grainville-Cheux road, where the artillery guns were positioned on the previous day, and where Hans Siegel's Panzer IV was positioned on 27 June. It was from the right, behind the trees, where the Allied tanks that destroyed his panzer appeared. (G. B.)

4. This Panzer IV from 8./12, No. 837, was occasionally used by SS-Untersturmführer Jeran, who commanded the company's 3rd section. The large numbers were roughly painted in black, with a white border. In theory, the head of this section should carry the number 831 on his tank. This Panzer would be lost on 6 July and recovered by the British. (Heimdal/Erik Goult)

5. Here we see SS-Ustuf. Jeran in the turret of his Panzer 837 with his crewduring an inspection by Marshal von Rundstedt, in Beverloo, Belgium, in March 1944. (Heimdal)

6. In this picture, taken by Sergeant Hardy on 6 July, a Cromwell tank crew member from 11th Armoured Division is towing Panzer 837, which had been lost near Cheux. The turret is turned towards the rear and the badge of the *Hitlerjugend* Division can be seen on the rear, to the right. (IWM)

3

Rauray, 27 June

1. The DLI launched an initial attack in the morning, using one company, from the site of the present British military cemetery, before the main attack took place around noon. This photograph was taken at the crossroads of the D139 and D173 roads, located north of Rauray. A Panther A tank has been destroyed near this intersection and partly burned. It bears the number 204, indicating that it was the commander of 2nd Company's (ISSPz.-Rgt. 12)fourth tank, a unit commanded by SS-Ostuf. Helmut Gaede. The tank belonged to SS-Uscha. Süsse, whose Panther was destroyed here on this day, injuring Süsse in the process. Further away, in front of the tall trees, a destroyed Sherman tank still burns. Süsse had destroyed three of them. A 6-pounder anti-tank shotgun (average range: 1,000 metres, calibre: 57 mm) has stopped and its crew are examining the defeated monster. (IMWM-B 6045)

2. The same location today. (EG/Heimdal)

3. Another view of No. 204 showing the hole left by the projectile that pierced the 40 mm-thick armoured plating and blew up the fuel tank, which was placed at the back. The armoured plating that overhung the undercarriage was shredded. (IWM B6046)

1. A Tiger I, from 3rd Company, SS-Pz.-Abt. 101 is driven back towards the rear. It is being examined by Sergeant Dring and his crew members from the Nottingham Sherwood Rangers Yeomanry. He reported having destroyed four Tigers with his Sherman, which was impossible because only two Tiger tanks were put out of service in Rauray, both from 3rd Company. Sergeant Dring, who received the Military Medal, was a well-known farmer in Grimsby. This Tiger tank had taken many hits, one of which had resulted in the death or evacuation of the crew, but it was still operational. (IWM-B 6047)

2. Another image of Panther 204 taken two days later, as Sherman tanks arrived from Fontenay to support the offensive by 49th West Riding Division. In the foreground can be seen the remains of a small building near the crossroads, while in the background are the rows of trees along the Fontenay/Carpiquet road. (IWM – B6226)

3. The same location today. The trees on the main road have been cut and then replanted. The two groups of trees to the right mark the present British military cemetery, where the 11th DLI attacked from on the morning of 27 June. (EG/Heimdal)

4. Detail of the crossroads with vestiges of the small buildings that were destroyed. (G.B.)

5. This other photograph was taken west of the crossroads, near the Panther tank. It was taken on the following day, 28 June, when the offensive was conducted towards the south of Rauray, as infantry and tanks moved towards the front. (IWM B6132)

1. The same crossroads today looking towards Cheux: the trees and hedges have disappeared. (G.B.)

2. The wounded are evacuated to Rauray by British medics. This scene may correspond to the testimony of SS-Oberscharführer Hans-Georg Kesslau, who reported that a truce took place that day from noon to 2 pm, in order to evacuate the numerous wounded on both sides. (IWM)

3. A Bren Carrier passes near Panther 204, heading up towards Fontenay to evacuate the wounded. (IWM)

Le Haut du Bosq, 27 June

A report made by Sergeant Leeson on 27 June 1944, showing destroyed German tanks. On this day he went to Bretteville-l'Orgueilleuse/Norrey, to Rauray and finally to le Haut du Bosq, where the two photohraphs shown here were taken.

1. Two of the six Panther tanks destroyed on 27 June. One of them is still burning, while the other has fallen into a ditch in its haste to get away. These two panzers were probably destroyed near DCLI's CP, whose roof can be seen on the right. (IWM B 6055)

2. A photograph by Sergeant Leeson of a 17-pound anti-tank gun, with its crew standing proudly in front of the gun that destroyed the Panther tank from I./3, which is seen burning. (IWM B 6056)

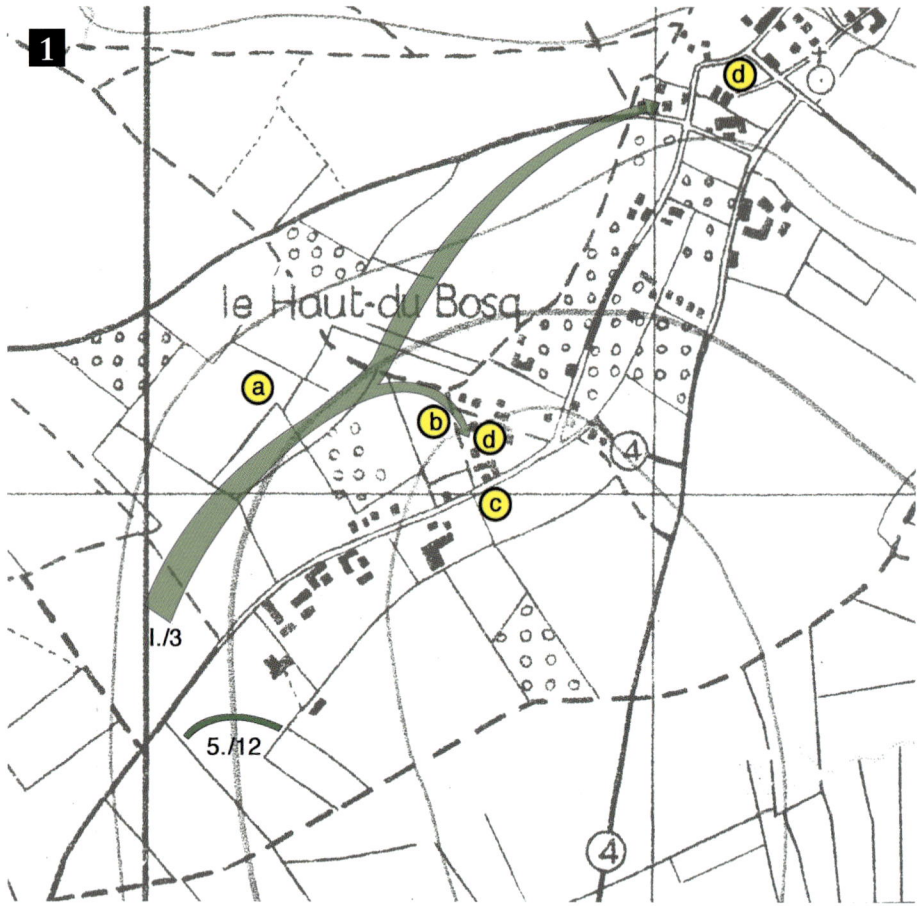

1. The presumed plan of attack by the seventeen Panther tanks from I./3 (a), with the position of C & D companies from 5 DCLI (b), 5 DCLI's CP (c), the battalion CP (d) and the water tower (e).

2. Looking north, the field on the left indicates the positions of C and D companies, 5 DCLI. To the right is the farm where the battalion's CP was located. (G.B.)

3. The field on the east of this small road, with the farm buildings on the right. Several tanks were destroyed in this meadow. (G.B.)

4. The main road from Grainville towards Cheux, crossing le Haut du Bosq. The water tower, located to the south-west of Cheux, is on the axis. The small road leading north towards the open ground (image 4) is on the left. The main farmhouse, with its magnificent gable, is clearly visible. The meadow where C and D companies were located is on the left. The meadow (image 5) behind the farmhouse, where the Panther tanks were destroyed, is located on the left, behind the building. (G.B.)

Cheux, 27 June to 4 July

This village would be a hub for the British offensive. Surrounded, ravaged and emptied of its population, the rebuilt centre is now unrecognisable. Here we will see the routes through which most of the battalions from VIII Corps had to travel through. It was almost impossible to find the correct locations and thanks must go to Monsieur Lajoie, who helped Erik Groult to find them.

1. This photograph by Sergeant Palmer was taken on 3 July and takes us to Cheux from the main Carpiquet-Fontenay road and Hill 83. We are heading towards Cheux from the north-west. The narrow road has been transformed into a quagmire by rainfall. Remember that the secondary roads at the time were not paved, which complicated the progress of the motorized columns considerably. (IWM B 6321)

2. The same location today. The small road is just as narrow, but is now paved. Saint-Manvieu is 2.4 km to the east (left). (EG/Heimdal)

3. This photograph by Major Stewart (taken 27 June) shows a Carrier from 10 HLI bringing wounded from the area around Grainville-sur-Odon. They had obviously been wounded in the assault on the position of 8./12 and SS-Ostuf. Siegel. This is the Field Ambulance at Glinel farm, north of the village. The 15th Division's insignia can be seen on the front of the Carrier. (IMW B 6037)

4. The farm today has remained intact. (E.G./Heimdal)

1. This photograph was taken on 4 July by Sergeant Midgeley and shows Tommies helping refugees to push their cart through the mud, along with the few possessions that they could save. On the left is the town hall at the time, which has since disappeared. The buildings towards the back still exist. Those on the right have disappeared, but can be seen in the following images. (IWM B 6342)

2. The same view toady. The houses at the bottom of rue Marchanville have survived. The barn on the right has been destroyed. (E.G./Heimdal)

Cheux (Calvados).   Juin-Juillet 1944 – La Mairie et l'Ecole des Garçons.

3. The corner of the street. A pavilion (far right) has replaced the town hall from 1944. The trees are in the same location as of those in 1944, the street having been slightly repositioned. (E.G./Heimdal)

4. The town hall in the summer of 1944. (Lajoie)

5. Detail of a map of Cheux in 1944, by Monsier Lajoie. Each photograph is shown on the map by its number.

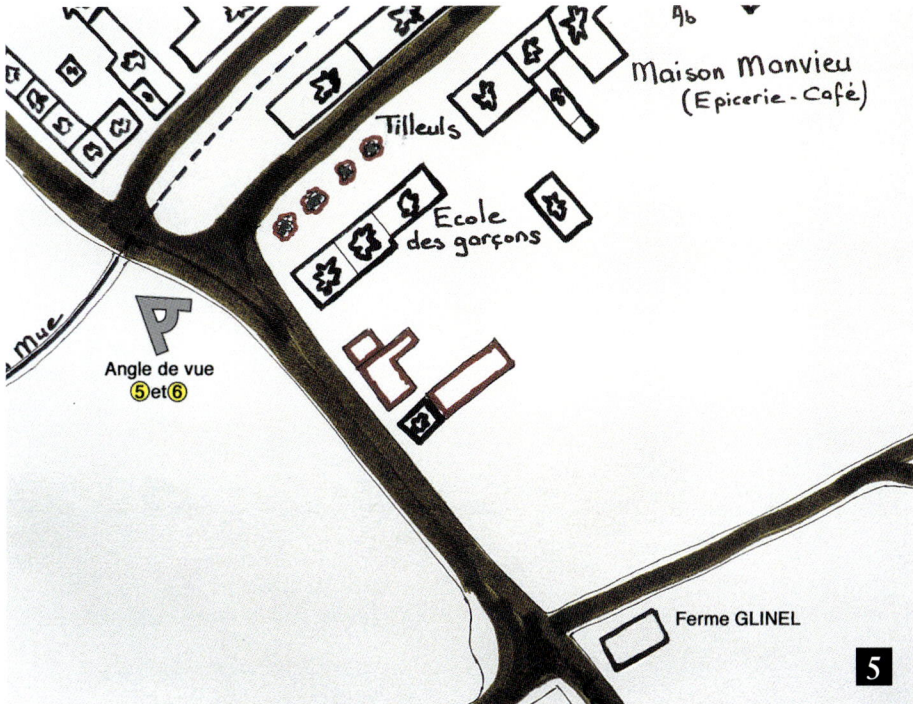

Cheux (2)

1. A report by Major Stewart dated 27 June showing a wounded man being transported from the front, probably to the Glinel farm. The location is once more rue Marchanville (image 5) and as previously noted, the streets are muddy due to the lack of paving. On the left is the barn (image 6) that has since been knocked down. In the background stand the ruined houses that can be seen in the following photographs. (IWM B 6036)

2 & 3. Moving along the street to rue Robert Courteheuse, where the ruined houses are already visible. The street has been transformed into a pond due to the intense rainfall. (IWM B 6638 and B 6144)

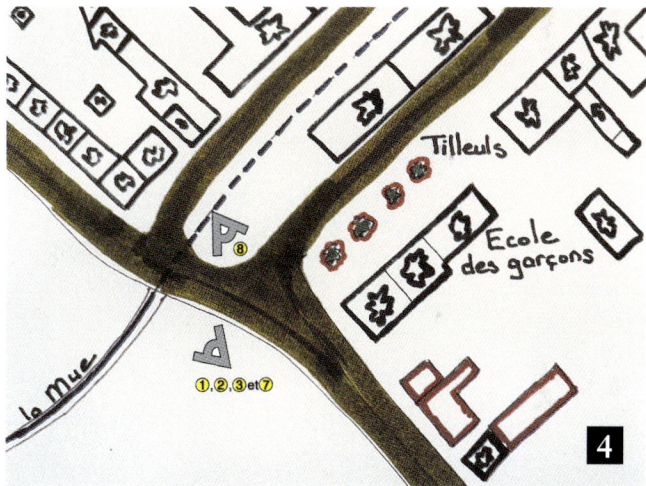

4. Detail of the map by M. Lajoie indicating the location of the buildings shown in these images.

5. A close-up of the destroyed houses. Note the wall bordering the street on the left. Of particular interest are the two German signs: *Schöps* is for the SS-Stubaf. of the same name who commanded the 2nd group of the *Hitlerjugend* artillery regiment (who was killed on the night of 25/26 June) and the position on the Salbey, while *Bremer 4* is for the 4th Company of the reconnaissance group. (IWM B 6322)

The same place today.
Only the remnants of
the walls reflect the area
as it was before 1944.
(E.G./Heimdal)

Turning slightly to the
left, one can see an intact
house and a new street
that has been built since
1944. (E.G./Heimdal)

In this other image taken
by Major Stewart on 27
June, a truck from 29th
Armoured Brigade (11th
Armoured Division) can
be seen coming from rue
Marchanville towards
rue Robert Courteheuse.
This picture was taken at
an angle similar that in
image 5. (IWM B 6039)

Cheux (3)

1. This photograph was taken by Sergeant Midgeley on 4 July and shows two women with their few possessions that have been saved from destruction. The original text stated that they were civilians returning to Cheux. The reality is the opposite: the British evacuated all civilians, who did not return until much later, often undergoing the further fighting. Some suffered in the fighting in the Falaise Pocket and were killed after being caught up in the battle. These civilians are clearly fleeing the battle and travelling through Cheux to find a safer location. (IWM B 6339)

2. The same place today: rue Robert Courteheuse (formerly the location of the market), opposite the present town hall. (E.G./Heimdal)

3. The same place today. (E.G./Heimdal)

1. One of the refugees from the first photograph, seen leaving here with her two sheep. The war brutally affected tens of thousands of Normandy civilians, killing around 20,000. Many subsequently lost everything. This image acts as a testimony to the drama suffered by the Norman population, and of which little is spoken of. The joy of liberation was often stifled by mourning and the stoic dignity of these civilians should not be forgotten. (IWM B 6344)

2. Planted in 1850 by Léonard Fortuné Lefrançois, the redwood served as a reference point for the returning inhabitants of Cheux, who found themselves lost in the middle of the ruins, unable recognise anything. (E.G./Heimdal)

3. Monsieur Lajoie, who helped to find the lost locations, indicates the old rue du Tripot (seen behind the Sherman tank, image 3), which has now been transformed into a short driveway. (E.G./Heimdal)

4. The old rue du Tripot. Compare this with the one in Image 6. (Lajoie)

5. On this detail of the map can be seen the locations described here, along with the redwood (denoted as 'sapin' (tree)).

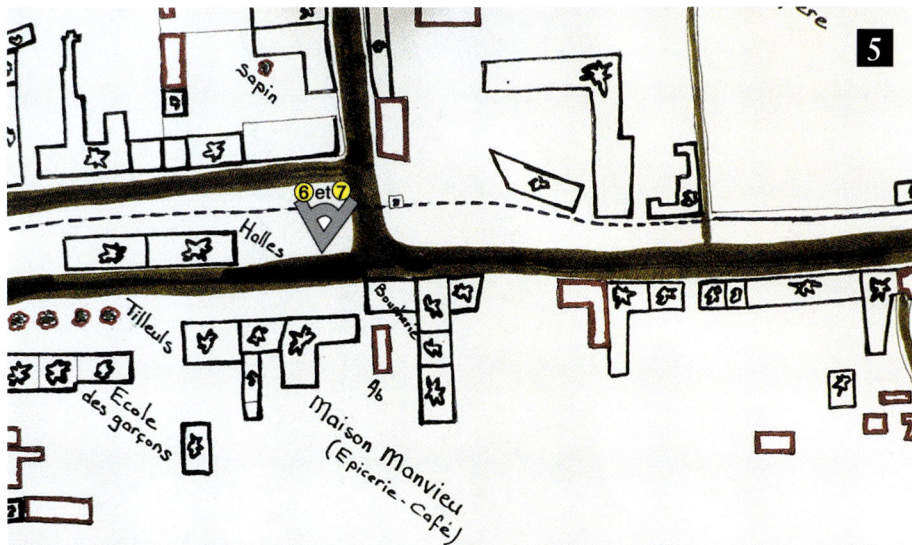

Cheux — Maison Cauvin

1 & 2. The commercial centre of the village, before and after the battle. Lajoie.)

Cheux (Calvados) — Juin-Juillet 1944 — Le Centre commerçant du Bou

Cheux (4)

1. This other picture by Sergeant Midgeley taken on 4 July shows the same woman with her two sheep, but on an unidentified street. (IWM B 6343)

2. Map of Cheux in 1944 showing the destroyed houses. The 'tree' and the church can help to find one's bearings. This map was drawn by M. Lajoie and the detailed maps presented on the previous pages are taken from this general plan. Please note: south is at the top.

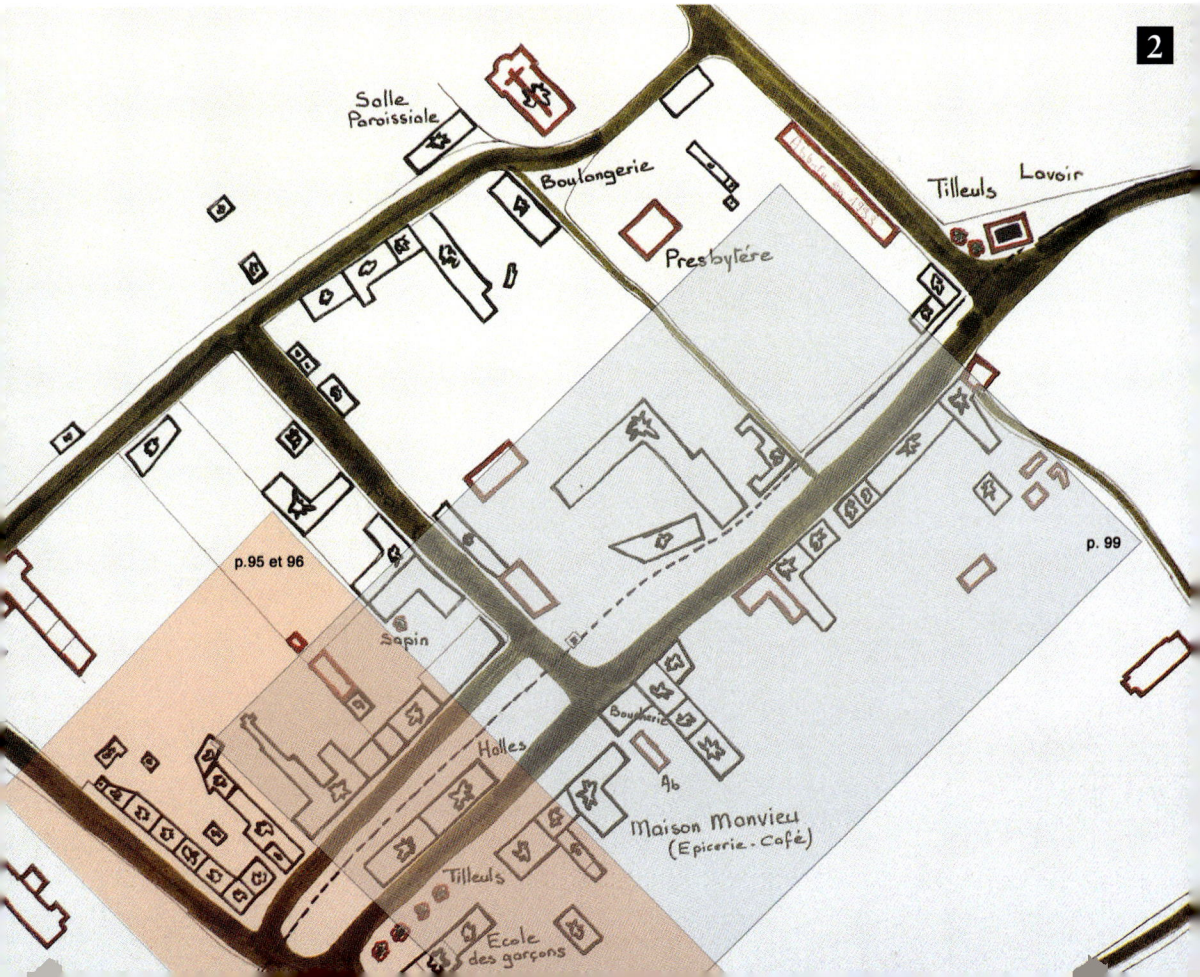

Cheux (Calvados). — Juin-Juillet 1944 — La Ferme du Calvaire.

1 & 2. The Calvaire farm, which appears to be relatively well-preserved, stands to the south-west of the village.. (E.G./Heimdal.)

3. The Calvaire farm after the battle. It was mainly the artillery barrage that ravaged the village: the fighting itself was mostly only short-lived skirmishes. (Cheux Town Hall)

4. A wing of the farm building that was renovated after the battle. (E.G./Heimdal)

5. Detail of the British Staff Map used in 1944. (Paich)

6. This monument in the centre of Cheux is to the units of the 43rd Wessex Division, but poppy wreaths have also been laid in memory of the 15th Scottish Division. (E.G./Heimdal)

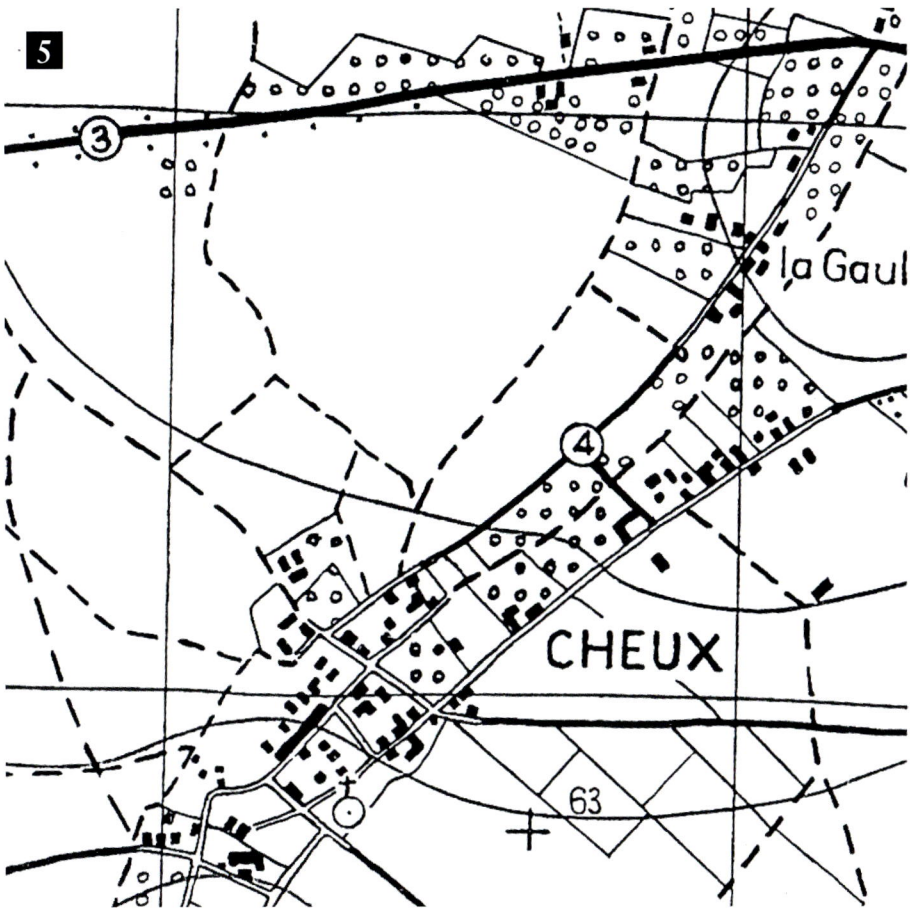

4

The Second Day – Tuesday 27 June

The 3ʳᵈ Company from SS-Panzergrenadier-Regiment 19 (SS-Panzer-Division '*Hohenstaufen*'), which was made up of very young soldiers, march towards the Normandy Front, initially to launch a counter-attack in the Balleroy sector. However, the evolving situation would mean they were redirected towards the Odon Sector. (HF / Heimdal)

The *Hohenstaufen* insignia was designed by Herbert Fürbringer as part of a competition. In his initial idea, the sword was directed downwards.

Hohenstaufen move towards the front

After moving quickly from the front in Galicia to France, 9. SS-Panzer-Division '*Hohenstaufen*' were forced to move slowly towards the Normandy Front due to the allied air threat. On Sunday, 25 June, 3rd Company, SS-Panzergrenadier-Regiment 19 (3./19), under the command of SS-Hauptsturmführer Bruno Kriz, was resting in the vast Forest of Gouffern, north-east of Argentan, along with other companies in the regiment. Little did they know that eight weeks later, this dense woodland would play a role in their breakout of what was to become known as the 'Falaise Pocket'. The men were resting a few kilometres from the front lines, enjoying the last moments of calm before the storm, and knowing that as soon as the next day dawned, they would have to reapply their camouflage and move towards the front. They resumed their march during the night of 25/26 June. The armoured elements of the division, along with Panzergreandier-Regiments 19 and 20, followed behind. The other units remained in the assembly area, ready to leave the following night.

The route had been scouted by both the reconnaissance elements of the Panzer Battalions and Regiment 19. The SS-Felgendarmerie-Kompanie '*Hohenstaufen*' (the unit's military police) was ordered to regulate the traffic to the Condé-sur-Noireau/Vire line. II-SS-Panzerkorps was ordered to continue marching during the night through the Longvilliers/Saint-Martin-Don/ Tinchebray/Thury-Harcourt sectors, with the '*Frundsberg*' Division on the right and the '*Hohenstaufen*' Division on the left. The forward line of *Hohenstaufen*'s assembly area passed through Montamy/Le Tourneur/Saint-Martin-Don (north-east of the Vire), while the rear line passed through Condé-sur-Noireau/La Bazoque/Tinchebray. The units advanced in the following order: SS-Panzergrenadier-Regiment 19,

1. SS-Haupsturmführer Bruno Kriz commanded 3./19. (HF/Heimdal.)

2. SS-Sturmmann Herbert Fürbringer was born on 20 February 1924 and later wrote the history of the division. He died in Switzerland on 22 April 1990. (HF/Heimdal)

3. During the night of 25/26 June, SS-Sturmmann Willi Haering was deep in his thoughts. (HF/Heimdal)

4. SS-GruppenführerWilhelm Bittrich commanded the *Hohenstaufen* and would soon take command of II. SS-Panzerkorps. (HF/Heimdal)

5. Camouflage was a matter of survival for this *Hohenstaufen* vehicle. (HF/Heimdal)

6. SS-ObersturmbannführerWalter Harzer. (DF)

SS-Flak-Abteilung (Anti-Aircraft) 9, SS-Panzer-Regiment 9's Staff and Command Company, and SS-Pionier-Bataillon 9 (without its 3rd Company). To the left of SS-Panzergrenadier-Regiment 19 advanced the bulk of the tank battalion (without 1st Battalion, 'Panther') and behind it SS-Panzergrenadier-Regiment 20 (minus 3rd Battalion), then SS-Panzer-Aufklärungs-Abteilung 9 and finally SS-Panzer-Nachrichten-Abteilung 9. Two groups (2nd and 3rd) of the artillery regiment were added to the two grenadier regiments. The division's commander, SS-Gruppenführer Wilhelm Bittrich and his 1st staff officer, SS-Obersturmbannführer Walter Harzer, kept an eye on the terrain ahead, warning the travelling units of any Allied aerial activity by listening to enemy radio conversations. For example, the following message was received on 25 June at 3.37 pm: 'Aerial engagement requested at 14.49 at a quarry where 1,000 Germans are currently stationed, south of Haut-Mesnil, 16 kilometres south of Caen.'

'That's where we have to go!'
During their night time advance on 25/26 June, when Operation Martlet had ended and Operation Epsom was about to begin, 3./19 had to take a small break following an aerial alert to see if the 'guys in the sky' were going to come back. In the darkness, a few abandoned houses were stood near the roadside and 20-year-old SS-Sturmann Herbert Fürbringer (who would later write the division's history), leaned against one of buildings, deep in his own thoughts. The artillery continued to thunder in the distance, as the horizon remained in constant flames and thousands of ghostly flashes of light blazed through the night. Another young corporal, SS-Sturmann Willi Haering, approached Fürbringer, saying what most of his comrades were thinking: 'That's where we have to go!' ('*Dorthin müssen wir!*'). Herbert Fürbringer said in his testimony:

> Such words fell very heavily into the depths of each one of us, and we could feel them crush our chests, as breathing became harder and our hearts beat faster. The men from 3rd Company, Regiment19 felt, for the first time, the reality of the expression 'rolling fire'. It clearly showed the colossal superiority, in terms of equipment, of the enemy ahead. Death and desolation were waiting at the front and what appeared to the resting column to be just a gigantic stage was, in fact, a bloody reality only a few kilometers further ahead. Our minds turned involuntarily to those comrades who had to sit through this inferno of thousands of artillery shells. From here, the men were witnessing great British offensive.[1]

A few hours later, Major John How (see page xx) had the same reaction, thinking, "That's where we have to go!' The brazier that was the front line aroused fear among the combatants on both sides.

After their night of marching, the men of II. SS-Panzerkorps became 'men of the woods'; hiding during the day while waiting for the next short night. On 26 June the SS armoured corps had not yet been ordered towards the Odon sector, but to

---

1   H. Fürbringer, *9. SS-Panzer-Division 'Hohenstaufen'* (Heimdal, 1984).

the area around Balleroy Forest, where the planned counter-attack was to take place. The launch of Operation Epsom at dawn on 26 June meant that the armoured corps would be diverted from its objectives. Heeresgruppe B (Army Group B) had instructed Panzergruppe West to engage between the Drôme (Balleroy) and the Seine, with the start of the combat scheduled for 28 June at 5 pm. However, on the evening of 26 June, the commander-in-chief of 7. Army, Generaloberst Dollmann, disclosed the situation in all its seriousness to Generalfeldmarschall Rommel. He told him that how the Scots were in the process of overrunning the *Hitlerjugend* Division's entire right flank, and demanded that the planned counter-attack in the direction of Bayeux-Balleroy should be abandoned. II. SS-Panzerkorps would therefore have to change direction towards VIII Corps and counter-attack there, instead.

These modifications to the plan consequently gave 9. SS-Panzer-Division new sectors to attack, that of Neuilly/Le Locheur/Tournay, to the west of Evrecy, in an area that was heavily criss-crossed by hedges. The first elements were to engage on 28 June, with Missy/Noyers-Bocage as the first objective, then Mouen and Cheux as the second objective, followed by the airport at Carpiquet. The course of the Odon ensured the separation of the *Hohenstaufen's* sector and that of the *Frundsberg*. The two divisions were to advance northeast, hitting VIII Corps's flank

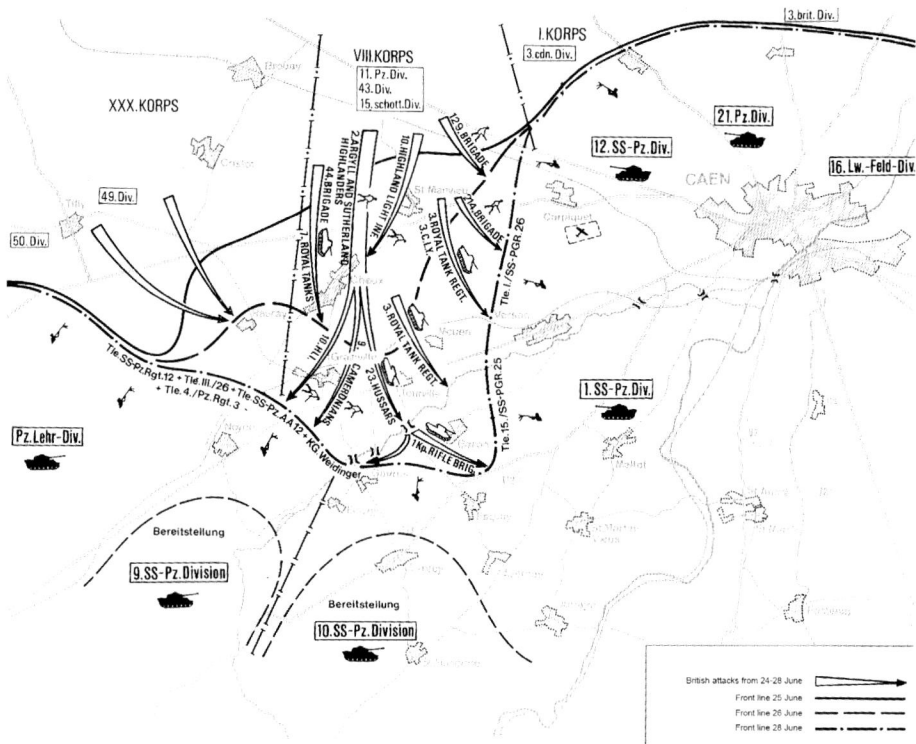

As the attack by VIII Corps advanced to the foot of Hill 112, the Panzer-Lehr-Division and, above all, 12. SS-Panzer-Division '*Hitlerjugend*', whose frontline was cracking, were reinforced: a regiment from the *Leibstandarte* (1. SS-Pz.-Div.) to the east, and the *Kampfgruppe Weidinger* to the west. II. SS-Panzerkorps also arrived with 9. SS-Panzer-Division '*Frundsberg*'. (H. Fürbringer/Heimdal)

near Caen, with the *Hohenstaufen* to the north of the Odon and the *Frundsberg* to the south of the valley (see map). The latter division was to attack from Gavrus, towards the head of the British offensive. And so the two armored divisions were now redirected to the Odon Front to face VIII Corps, but would not reach it until the 28th, at best. Montgomery had to act fast!

The Odon must be crossed!

At 11 pm on the previous day, the 15th Scottish Division had received its objectives for the second day of the offensive. Its commanders believed, correctly, that the enemy was down to its last reserves and on 27 June the division would finally have to cross the Odon: an objective that it should have achieved by noon on 26 June. The 227th Brigade were to seize Grainville-sur-Odon, a task entrusted to the 10 HLI, supported by C Squadron, 7th RTR (who, as we shall see, were to come up against Hans Siegel's four panzers). The battalion would then have to seize the Odon crossing, near Gavrus and Tourmauville, as quickly as possible. Advancing past the positions of 2 Gordon, the brigade's 3rd Battalion, 2 Argyll & Sutherland Highlanders, joined by other tanks from the 31st Tank Brigade, would attack east (southeast of Cheux) and cross the Odon to the south of Tourville. The 11th Armoured Division would support the brigade's attack with its 29th Armored Brigade (Fife & Forfar and 23 Hussars) and advance with the 159th Infantry Brigade over the Orne and form bridgeheads as soon as the tank battalions had crossed the Odon. The first two brigades from 15th Division, who had been fighting the day before, had to be relieved. The 46th Highland Brigade (west) could not be relieved as planned by the 214th Brigade (43rd Wessex Division), and so its 7 Seaforth stayed on the line. The 5 Duke of Cornwall's Light Infantry (5 DCLI) were able to relieve the Cameronians at 5 am. On the other hand, the 44th Lowland Brigade were relived during the night and headed to le Mesnil-Patry, where it was held in reserve due to the amount of losses it had suffered, especially those from 6th Battalion Royal Scots Fusiliers. The rotations between the units were consequently completed almost as planned, meaning that fresh units were able to join the front line.

To the west, the 49th Infantry Division were ordered to proceed with the attack, mainly with 70th Infantry Brigade, and with Noyers-Bocage as its objective. The attack would be conducted in four phases: 1. Taking of Rauray. 2. Taking of Brettevillette. 3. Occupation of Hill 124, 2 kilometres north-west of Noyers. 4. Taking of Noyers. The attack would be supported by a tank battalion (Sherwood Rangers Yeomanry) from 8th Armoured Brigade, supported by four field regiments, four middle regiments, one heavy regiment, meaning a total of nine artillery groups altogether.

Opposite, the positions of the *Hitlerjugend* had been disrupted during the previous day's activities, and they were now clinging on to a few defensive pockets, relying mainly on panzers, with thirty Panzer IVs and seventeen Panzer Vs (Panther) in working order. The heavy tank battalion (s.SS-Panzer-Abteilung 101) had eighteen Tiger Is in working order. Most of the available heavy Pak (anti-tank) guns were in the SS-Panzergrenadier-Regiment 25's sector, to the north-west and north of Caen (according to H. Meyer). In the second line, mainly south of the Odon, further support was provided by General Pickert's Flak-Sturm-Regiment 2 and

1. This photograph was taken on 27 June by Sergeant Leeson and shows Churchill tanks from 31st Army Tank Brigade travelling from Norrey-en-Bessin, whose magnificent Gothic church had been badly damaged. They are heading for Bretteville-l'Orgueilleuse, probably to act as relief. The state of the road reflects the heavy rain that had fallen in the past few hours. (IWM B 6054)

2. This image was taken the day before, at the beginning of the offensive, by Sergeant Laing and shows a machine that will have no opportunity to be used, due to the absence of the Luftwaffe in this area of the front. It is a self-propelled Bofors vehicle, made by mounting a 40 mm Bofors anti-aircraft gun on a Morris C9B chassis, and belonged to the 15th Scottish Division's 119 Light Anti-Aircraft Regiment. The division's insignia can be seen painted on the back of the vehicle. (IWM B 6004)

Flak-Sturm-Regiment 4. The regiments' 8.8 cm guns were primarily used in aerial and ground combat from camouflaged positions and could be easily spotted from a great distance, such as in an anti-tank combat. From a short distance, they did not have the means to defend themselves against tanks for a long period of time.

Although Montgomery's offensive had been delayed, the *Hitlerjugend* Division had been unable to reorganize effectively after the attacks on 25 and 26 June, with only one Panther tank battalion acting as reinforcements (I./3).

The second day of the offensive thus dawned on a battlefield where the troops had spent a 'wet and miserable' night; the heavy rains having transformed it into a beautiful nightmare. The British soldiers first had to dig their individual foxholes in order to avoid the intermittent German mortar fire, before then having to try and sleep under the persistent rain, although the moisture and mortar shells made it almost impossible. At dawn, they would have to be content with cold sausages and a loamy, tea-like beverage. The night wasn't any more comfortable for the soldiers in the tanks. They had had to head behind the front lines to fill up with fuel and ammunition and as this had taken three hours, they had all had a very short night.

Fighting on the Salbey

For Hans Siegel, in position with his four Panzer IVs from 8./12, the end of the night was more tranquil. Around 4 am, he headed out to make contact with his neighbour on the left; there had been no one on the right since the gunners

Photograph taken of the road coming from Cheux and leading to Grainville. The hedge in the foreground, on the left, marks the field where Hans Siegel would position his Panzer IV during the course of the morning and is where his tank would be destroyed by a shell coming from the east (left of the picture). Further to the right can be seen the large hedge behind which the Panzer IVs of 8./12 were positioned. (G.B.)

retreated. After 300 meters he came across the first sentries, covered by a canvas tent and asleep in the bushes. It was the same story in the battalion CP: everyone was exhausted and asleep. On the way back, he tried to wake the men by warning them of a possible attack. At around 4.30 am on 27 June, the second say of the offensive, he came back into the view of the field where his panzers were. Suddenly, enemy shells began their 'harvest':

> They screamed passed over our trees, falling behind us. Landing too far away, to our delight! But the water-soaked ground engulfed them, lifting up columns of mud and stone that formed a macabre curtain. They didn't explode, but were engulfed in sort of 'flop'! From a distance, I could see that the panzers wanted to escape the deluge of shells and, suddenly, they started to disengage one after the other. I ran towards them, but they moved away from the hedge and would soon appear in the enemy's sights. What stupidity! However, they saw me and realised I was signalling them to stop. The lead tank had thought that I was not coming back and so the crew had made the decision to escape the artillery fire. The other panzers had followed suit and moved backwards, but I immediately sent them back to their positions. It was happening, the enemy attack had begun. The British infantry were advancing from the high ground south of Cheux, accompanied by tanks slightly behind them.

The attack that Hans Siegel saw was by 10th Battalion The Highland Light Infantry (10 HLI). From its starting point at Cheux, the Scottish battalion had marched south, with Grainville-sur-Odon as its objective. Hans Siegel's four Panzer IVs were in the way. Isolated, without any infantry, they now found themselves facing four infantry companies. However, they were well-hidden behind the hedge and had four guns and their machine guns on board. The Jocks' (HLI 10) attack was due to be launched at 6.30 am, but had to be delayed as the Churchill tanks from C Squadron, 7th RTR, who were to act as their support, had not yet reached the starting base. B Company, 10 HLI, had set off at 7.30 am, but was unable to reach its starting line after coming under mortar fire. As it finally reached the ridge overlooking the Salbey, the silhouettes of the infantry could be seen advancing towards the hedge in front of the stream.

Hans Siegel describes the scene:

> We let the attack come to us. I gave the order that only the on-board machine guns were to fire so as not to betray the presence of the panzers. The British infantrymen were anxious and fired at the ground in front of them to steady their nerves. We let them come into point blank range. I gave the order to open fire and we fired [at them] with our four machine guns. We were experienced and, as expected, they panicked and ran back towards the rear before falling down once more under our bullets. We opened fire with our guns when the tanks arrived with the second wave, and were successful once more, without suffering any losses on our side. The crews of the destroyed tanks fled their vehicles, which were either burning or had exploded, while the rest of them turned around and heaedd back towards the high ground with the infantry.

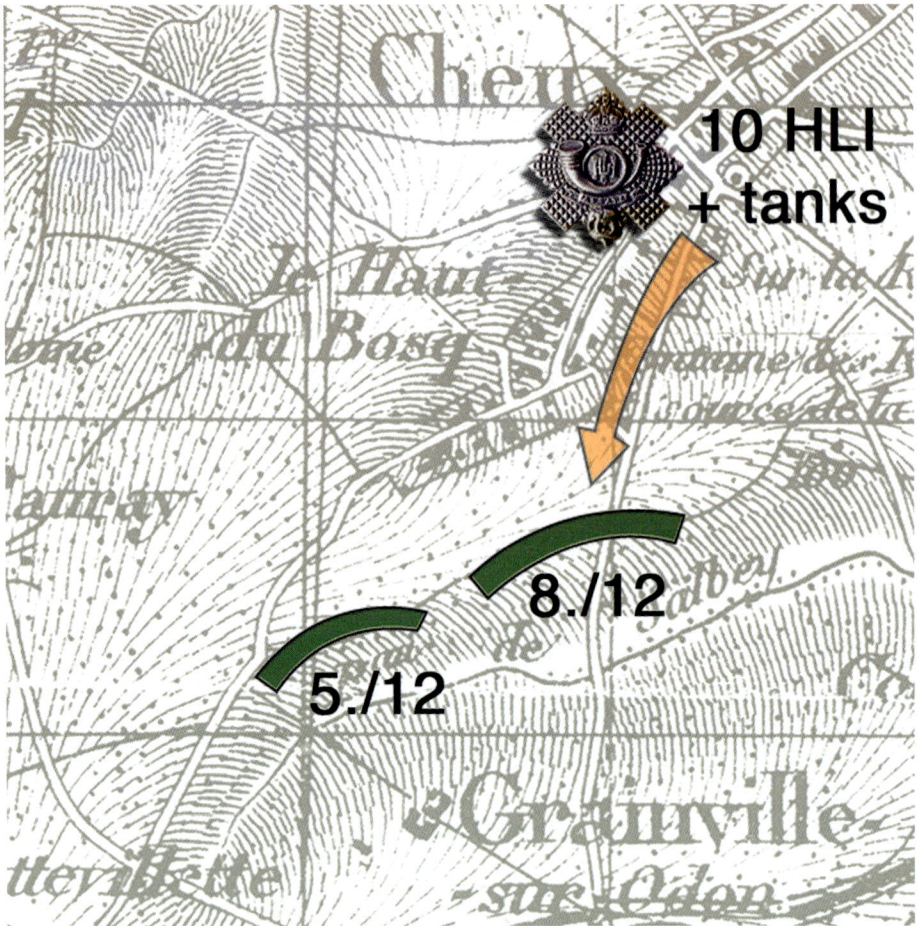

Map showing the attack by 10 HLI and elements of 7th RTR against the four panzers from 8./12. (Heimdal)

In fact, B Company, HLI 10, had just been trounced and was overtaken by D Company, before the latter was blocked in turn. At 8.30 am, companies A and D were at the starting base, joined by tanks from C Squadron, 7th RTR, which had suffered heavy losses from the four 7.5cm KwK's fire. C Company attempted an outflanking maneuver on the right, but fell in the midst of the tanks' fire.

The British patrol during the night had left three dead, including two next to the panzer and one on the road. It had reported false information, saying that it had found 'Tigers', but had actually overestimated the strength of this small group. This was why, as the colonel who commanded British artillery told Hans Siegel in 1973, the guns had fired for so long; they believed they were attacking infantrymen, when in reality, there were none. The sun had now risen and Hans Siegel asked for reinforcements and ammunition. The attack was now directed to the right (east), towards Colleville. Any danger would come from there and so Hans Siegel was forced to pull his panzer out of its shelter and position it in the field to the right. This meant that he was covering this direction (east) and was able to observe any possible change of movement. It was now about 9.30 am.

Since dawn, the Sherman tanks of the Fife and Forfar had also been attacking from the east of Cheux, and were also heading south to exploit a breakthrough achieved by the Jocks and Churchill tanks. A Squadron led the way as it advanced downhill towards a wood. There were two troops there (four tanks including one Firefly per troop), with Freddie Craig's troop on the right. After passing the ridge, three Sherman tanks were immediately destroyed, but not by Hans Siegel, who, as we shall see, was not paying enough attention. Instead, they were probably destroyed by Tiger tanks from s.SS-Panzer-Abteilung 101. The testimony of SS-Hauptsturmführer Rolf Möbius, commander of 1st Company, tells us that they were probably destroyed by SS-Untersturmführer Amselgruber:

> I lost my panzers one after the other under the enemy's fire. There were only three of us left, and one of the tanks had lost its cannon. I prevented a British breakthrough myself by destroying six tanks from a sunken road. Alongside me, a panzer (that of SS-Untersturmführer Amselgruber) was still attacking an armoured column and destroyed three tanks. I had problems loading my gun and was destroyed by ten tanks. I evacuated, Amselgruber had already done so.

The battalion's Tiger tanks were engaged in small groups, without infantry. They inflicted losses but also suffered in their attempts to contain the assault. However, following their own losses, the Sherman tanks from A Squadron, Fife and Forfar, would soon take their revenge.

Once more, Hans Siegel describes the scene:

> Through the binoculars we could see an astonishing collection of infantrymen, who put down their heavy backpacks and sat down. They were about 1,200 metres away. The panzer on the left fired a shot that was a direct hit. There were flames and explosions. Human bodies were thrown into the air, their arms and legs spinning like windmills, before falling to the ground like stones. We thought they were sappers armed with explosives intending to blow up our panzers. Shortly afterwards, the expected attack resumed, but this time more to the right. This third attack suffered the same fate as the other two, as we allowed it to get close once more before crushing it. There were now a dozen tanks burning on the ground. The sun was heating up in the sky. I spotted a tank (probably a Sherman from the Fife and Forfar) about the same level as me, on the right. It was difficult to see its turret through the branches and the episcope. At the time I thought that he had not seen us and that it posed no threat, not to mention that the shells would lose their accuracy through the branches. It was now about 10.30 am and the fourth wave was already on the attack, but this time there seemed to be more tanks. The situation was the same but, during a frontal duel with the tanks, a tank shell suddenly landed on my right and I was immediately surrounded by flames. The hatch was quickly opened; the gunner, on fire, got out on the left and the loader on the right. I wanted to exit from the top

of the turret, but I was caught-up by my radio wire. I got out behind the loader on the right, but found myself face to face with the radio and lost consciousness for a few seconds amid the flames. I managed to jump free and was finally out in the open. I still had the radio wire around me as I had been unable to remove it due to my helmet. I was hanging from the panzer, the wire choking me, as the bursts of machine guns fired at the vehicle. I freed myself by breaking the wire in a final desperate effort (the wire was as thick as a finger).

I found the crew in the sunken road where the night's events had taken place. The only man missing was the driver, SS-Sturmann Schleweis, who remained in the burning panzer, no doubt injured or killed by the impact. His hatch was open, so he could have gotten out. The gunner was on the ground and was on fire. The crewmen, themselves also partly burnt, covered him with their own bodies to extinguish the flames. He had no leather outfit (like the rest of the crew) and was only wearing a camouflage lattice because he had been sent to replace the previous gunner who had been sent back. The leather outfits, taken from the Italian Navy, had been Max Wünsche's idea, as he knew the kind of protection such a garment could provide. The gunner would later die in hospital from his wounds. Like the others, I didn't suffer immediate burns to my face and hands. The enemy attack was in progress and there was no question of us staying there. The three other panzers had seen nothing of the drama that had just taken place and were still in action. I was in the midst of them, powerless, but I observed with joy and relief that the tank leaders, all non-commissioned officers, were fighting courageously and were accurate with their shots; almost every one reached its target. They were well-camouflaged behind their natural protection, and only the flames as the shells left the gun barrels betrayed their location. Just then, the turret of a panzer opened up and a head looked out. The face was unrecognizable, blackened by powder, marked by fatigue and frightened at the sight of its leader, who now looked more like a baked potato than a man. After handing over command to the oldest tank commander, a corporal, I brought the wounded back to the CP at Grainville in Sturmbannführer Schöps' VW-Kübelwagen. The commander, Max Wünsche, patted me on the shoulder and the nurses gave us morphine.

A Panther company from 2. Panzer-Division came to relieve the few panzers from 8th Company around noon, with the actual relief taking place at 2 pm. Hans Siegel explained to the company captain where to position his tanks. The latter, condescendingly, neglected all of the cautionary advice, preferring to advance towards Cheux and consequently lost around seven Panthers in a short space of time. For his decisive actions at le Mesnil-Patry on 11 June, and by the Salbey on 27 June, Hans Siegel received the Knight's Cross of the Iron Cross on 23 August 1944. He states that: 'At le Mesnil-Patry, I had success because I was more attentive than my opponents, but here [on the Salbey] I was wrong to ignore the tank that came up on my right. I then forgot about it and so this time it was I who was inattentive. In war, the quickest man wins.'

1. The insignia of 2. Panzer-Division was a trident, and was painted on the vehicles of this armoured division. (Heimdal)

2. Metal box found on the battlefield area, bearing the trident of 2. Panzer-Division. (Heimdal)

Le Haut du Bosq: the failure of the Panthers from I./3

The *Hitlerjugend* Division, supported by Tiger tanks, also received reinforcements from the 2. Panzer-Division, whose recruits mainly came from Austria. Its commander, Generalleutnant von Lüttwitz, received an order the day before to put the Panzer-Regiment 3's Panther tank battalion (1./3), at the *Hitlerjugend* Division's disposal in order to launch a counter-attack on Cheux. The unit was located in the area east of Saint-Lô, between Caumont-L'Eventé and Villers-Bocage, but the battalion would be unable to conduct a coordinated attack with the *Hitlerjugend* Division as their CP was in Verson, on the other end of the front line. As the division's former Chief of Staff, Hubert Meyer, asserts, on its way to the front the battalion took orders from the Panzer-Lehr-Division's CP, which did not have as an exact view of the situation on the Odon Front. The battalion was made up of four companies of seventeen Panther tanks each. But was it fully committed? According to the testimony of Hans Siegel, British historians believe that only a single company of seventeen Panther tanks was engaged, and Hubert Meyer also seems to follow this minimalist view. In the 7th Army's report, and in its war diaries, there was talk of putting a battalion into the front line, and in its divisional orders for 27 and 28 June, the Panzer-Lehr-Division only mentions the arrival of a company from I./3.

The British only had six tanks in the area, with others to the south of Cheux attacking along the road leading from Rauray to le Haut du Bosq and who were terribly exposed because they had no accompanying infantry. According to a 'top secret' report on 14 July 1944 addressed to Generalleutnant von Lüttwitz, which was seized on 26 July by the US Army, the head of this unit reported that: 'It was no longer a question of using panzers in a traditional way, as had been the case in Russia. In Normandy they could only be used as infantry support. The enemy's anti-tank weapons had to be neutralised before launching an attack because the terrain favoured short-range anti-tank weapons, and each individual panzer needed infantry protection.'

Prior to this attack by the Panther tanks from 1./3, the units at le Haut du Bosq had been relieved. The 46th Highland Brigade could not be relieved as planned while they were in the area around Cheux (see above), however, the Duke of Cornwall's Light Infantry (5 DCLI) came to relieve the Cameronians, who needed to 'lick their wounds' following the losses suffered on the previous day. The 5 DCLI had set off at 2 am and Major George Taylor, second in command of the 1st Worcester (who were in position at Cheux) wished Lieutenant Colonel Atherton (commander of 5 DCLI) good luck when he saw him. The latter had replied, 'I'll need it George'. Private Denis Coulsen remembers that the men were still wet and had little appetite for their breakfast. They set off at the sound of the whistle, accompanied by Churchill tanks from 7th RTR. As they descended a grassy slope, they came under fire from several directions; their officer was hit and would not be seen again. They were unable to advance further and soon came under the artillery fire. It was the first time that they had experienced such fire and panic made the men turn around. However, they did return after admiring the countenance of their colonel, who was standing in his scout-car, observing the terrain with his binoculars, his attitude denoting a mixture of anguish and fury. In turn, Private John Tilsen said the reserve company then drove down the slope, passing by the smoking carcasses of the Churchills, as the ambulances and medics picked up the wounded. It was a tough introduction to warfare for the 5 DCLI.

DCLI cap badge.

Fabric shoulder badge worn by the 5 DCLI. From top to bottom is the name (DCLI) and then formation badge of the 43rd Wessex Division. The red band indicates that this battalion belongs to the division's first brigade (Senior Brigade).

Lieutenant Colonel Atherton had the greatest difficulty in getting his companies back on the road behind the reserve company, although after this initial shock, this novice unit would go on to become one of the most efficient units in the British Army. The 5 DCLI finally arrived at its objective, le Haut du Bosq, at about 11 am, only to find that the Cameronians, a battalion that they were supposed to relieve, had already left! The Germans were already in the hamlet, which stretched out along an area to the south-west of Cheux, and the Allies now had to take it back. The men of the 'Fifth' (5 DCLI) began to dig their positions while all the while looking for snipers.

The 5 DCLI was not on the front line at le Haut du Bosq, but simply had to hold the sector in case of a German counter-attack. Captain Johnson (second in command in Major Fry's D Company) and Corporal Rohan returned to D Company's CP bringing a sniper with them. 5 DCLI's CP was located in a large farmhouse at the corner of the main road, while the company command was located in an orchard north-east of this CP. Companies C and D (further north) were positioned in a field to the west of the road that led to the farmhouse (see map). For Captain Johnson, it was a peaceful time, almost like a training exercise near Folkestone. He had fresh eggs, as did Corporal Ronan, and life seemed rather grand. Suddenly, a cloud of dust accompanied by a rattle of caterpillars enveloped the area. At around 9.30 am, six Panther tanks (no more) from 1./3 arrived across the fields to the east of Rauray and emerged in the middle of le Haut du Bosq via a sunken road, right in the middle of the 5th DCLI's position, but with no accompanying infantry.

Captain Johnson saw the six magnificent tanks with their curious camouflage and was astonished when he recognised the German black crosses on the vehicles. The leading Panther tank opened fire on a battery of four 17-pound anti-tank guns that had just arrived. The other five panzers invaded the field where C Company's CP stood (west of the farmhouse), almost trampling on the heads of the infantrymen in their foxholes. Meanwhile, Major Fry and his second (Captain Johnson) killed two German motorcyclists on the road. Continuing their infernal firing in the midst of 5 DCLI's position, the Panther tanks destroyed another two 6-pound anti-tank guns, killing or injuring most of their crew. They also attacked C Company's carriers and the transport trucks, which were soon engulfed in flames. However, as the powerful panzers had no accompanying infantry, they were very vulnerable to the British infantrymen. The British soldiers organized themselves with a few teams equipped with PIATs (from C Company's three platoons), 6-pound anti-tank guns and at least one 17-pound anti-tank gun. After their initial surprise, the panzers were then eliminated one after the other. The first was hit three times by PIAT bombs; the PIAT teams were then reinforced by PIATs from nearby D Company. The Panther turned back, its crew in shock, and joined the road leading north of Cheux. Two DCLI 6-pound anti-tank guns began to fire, with a target less than 50 metres in front them. One of the two guns hit the side of one of the Panther tanks, but the two guns were destroyed and the battalion commander, Lieutenant Colonel Atherton, who had replaced a wounded artilleryman, was killed. One of the Panthers was destroyed by a PIAT from C Company, and a second was quickly destroyed by Sergeant Hicks. Two others tried to flee, but one of them was destroyed by Captain Blackwell. The fourth toppled into a ditch in its haste to escape. Finally, the fifth tank was in flames after being hit by an anti-tank gun (probably the 17-pounder), meaning that of the six panzers engaged, all but one were destroyed. Despite the painful loss of Lieutenant Colonel Atherton, and a total of twenty killed and injured for 5 DCLI, it was the first victory for a unit from 43rd Wessex Division over Panther tanks. Of the twenty-five crew members from the five destroyed Panther tanks, nine were killed and four taken prisoner, meaning twelve were still missing. However, what had become of the sixth panzer?

Never mind the fact that the company had seventeen panzers in total and only six had been sent in to le Haut du Bosq.

While six Panther tanks were plunging into le Haut du Bosq to attack Cheux from the south, another part of the company was continuing directly on Cheux itself, where it came upon the rear of 10 HLI. Consequently, 6-pound anti-tank guns, which had been pointing south from Cheux (and towards Hans Siegel's 8./12), were quickly redirected 180° against this new threat. A battle would now take place between these anti-tank guns and the Panther tanks. In between the fire stood the CP and Aid Post of 10 HLI, and as the shells from the Panthers hit the tops of the walls, the debris fell onto the wounded below. The medics had to take the injured to shelter on their stretchers, using the walls as protection. Smouldering carcasses were left behind, with numbers varying from four to five according to different testimonies. The Jocks from 10 HLI were very bitter when they discovered the Sherman tanks on the roads nearby, their hatches closed in fear of snipers as they waited for orders on the radio. As far as they were concerned, the sound of the fighting seemed to come from a different sector. As H. G. Martin (*The Fifteenth Scottish Division*, 1948) recalls, 'Cheux's roads seemed full of our tanks, closed and deaf to our calls.'

This adds up to a total of nine to ten Panther tanks from I./3 destroyed: a good portion of the engines from a company of seventeen panzers. British historians consider this company to be the same as the one that was coming to relieve Hans Siegel, but it remains a mystery. In the testimony given by Hans Siegel, he referred to the relief of his 8./12 by a Panther company from 2. Panzer-Division, who had lost seven Panthers near Cheux. The relief had started around noon and had finished by about 2 pm. In another testimony, Hans Siegel recalls that a captain from the Panther tank battalion came to see him at 9 am, telling him that he had arrived from Saint-Lô with his company during the night. The crews of its seventeen Panther tanks were resting a little further to the west (near the positions of the Panzer IVs from 5./12, south-west of le Haut du Bosq, according to a report by SS-Untersturmführer Kändler).[2]

As the captain had pointed out to Siegel, his company were tasked with restoring the situation south of Cheux by launching an attack. Siegel had observed that the British had massed on the right, to the south-east of Cheux, in order to break into Tourville, and consequently thought that common sense dictated the Panther tanks should take up position to the right of his panzers, and would thus able to attack the enemy's flanks as it advanced towards the south. However, this went against the company commander's orders, who was unaware of the situation at that particular time and had consequently decided to attack along the road leading from le Haut du Bosq to Cheux, counting on the support of the infantry who were engaged there.

In trying to reconstruct the chronology of what happened, here is what could be concluded: Only one company from the battalion was able to arrive during the night and took up its position near 5./12. The captain headed to Hans Siegel's position, which was nearby, to the east. He arrived at 9 am and announced that

---

2   H. Meyer, p.285

At the start of the commune of Cheux, the large hamlet of le Haut du Bosq stretches out along the road. At the beginning of the road, on the north side, is the chateau that housed the CP of SS-Ostubaf. Wilhelm Mohnke (SS-Pz.- Gren.-Rgt 26). (G.B.)

Almost opposite, on the south side, stands a farm, north of 5./12's position, according to the testimonies of SS-Ustuf. Willi Kändler. (G.B.)

he had come to relieve 8./12. He then left and in spite of Hans Siegel's advice, left his position near 5./12 to attack from the east of Rauray, at 9.30 am, alongside le Haut du Bosq in the north. Six of the company's tanks turned off towards le Haut du Bosq around 11.30 am, and only one escaped the massacre. The others continued on to Cheux, where they would still lose three (or four) Panther tanks. The nine or ten survivors joined Hans Siegel at his position, where they finally relieved the survivors of 8./12 at around 2 pm.

Le Haut du Bosq sector

Hans Siegel's Panzer IV was destroyed by a Sherman tank from Fife and Forfar. But before noon, the HLI's attack had been halted in the face of the stubborn defence by the same Hans Siegel. The surviving tanks from 7th RTR fell back to their bases, announcing the destruction of three panzers, but not those of Hans Siegel. These could have been panzers in a position further to the west, where comrades of Hans Siegel were also blocking the Allied attack, in particular, the Panzer IVs from 5th Company (5./12), commanded by SS-Obersturmführer Helmut Bando. SS-Untersturmführer Willi Kändler, the commander of the company's 3rd section has provided a valuable testimony allowing us to understand the fighting that took place in this sector. His section was on the right side of the road that led from

Cheux to Noyers-Bocage, passing by le Haut du Bosq, and on about the same level as Siegel's panzers:

My field was bordered by a sunken road that ran east-north-east, where a well-constructed CP was located *[according to Hubert Meyer, it could be the CP evacuated by the 2nd artillery group and now occupied by the staff of an infantry battalion, maybe that of SS-Sturmbannführer Siebken's II./26]*. My company commander, SS-Obersturmführer Bando, was also there. With our panzers in the front line, we were exposed to intensive fire from anti-tank guns and other armoured vehicles. Following a hit, I received a few bits of shrapnel in my head, but while I was able to stay where I was, my gunner had been seriously injured and had to be evacuated. Bando, my company commander, did not arrive nearby until 11 am. He told me my objective was an enemy machine gun in front of us, on the right-hand side of the road, and ordered me to destroy it. Upon leaving, and only a few metres from my panzer, this machine gun hit my commander in the back of the head with a burst of bullets and killed him. I reported Bando's death to Porsch and Kunze, the other two sections leaders.

On the way back, I noticed that my panzer had been hit again and was now destroyed *[probably by a Churchill tank from 7th RTR, C Squadron]*, although it had already been pulled back from its position. Wichman's panzer came towards me and I climbed on board shortly after. My new gunner was Willi Schnittfinke, from Cologne, and the loader was Jansen, from Essen. While there had been five panzers from my section along the hedge in the morning, our small group had been reduced to three, commanded by Jürgens and Biback as well as myself.

The anti-tank fire against our hedge grew heavier and heavier. It was clear that the enemy intended to hit our camouflaged tanks through systematic

1. The section's tank commander. Note the mix of outfits: the standard officer jacket on the left and the camouflage 'pea' jacket on the right, although both men are wearing leather trousers. (G.B.)

2. Members of the crew from SS-Ustuf. Kändler's 3rd section, 5./12, who from 27 June operated in Panzer IV 535. From left to right: Ustuf. Kändler (tank commander and head of section), -? - Sturmmann Willi Schnittfinke (gunner), - an Uscha. (probably from the workshop company), - a replacement driver. Note the numerous white rings painted on the gun barrel testifying to the many victories (one per ring) obtained by this panzer. (G.B.)

3. SS-Sturmmann Willi Schnittfinke, became the gunner for 3rd section's tank commander on 27 June. He would achieve several victories near Cheux and on Hill 112. (G.B.)

fire. To avoid losing these last three panzers I brought them into a hollow on the back slope of the meadow, where they were protected from direct fire. I posted some soldiers in the front line to keep a look out and to inform me immediately should anything happen.

Note that following the destruction of his own panzer, a company commander or section chief who was more senior and generally more experienced, took charge of a subordinate commander's panzer. This was the case in this situation, where Wichmann (a sergeant) entrusted his panzer and the rest of its crew to Kändler (a second lieutenant). Wichmann was then kept in reserve, capable of replacing a tank commander who might be killed or wounded.

4. SS-Ustuf. Karl-Heinz Porsch commanded 5./SS-Pz.-Rgt. 12 following the death of SS-Ostuf. Bando. He, in turn, was killed on 8 August 1944, north of Falaise. (G.B.)

Rauray

As VIII Corps tried to break through at Grainville and towards the Odon, on the right wing of the offensive, the 49th West Riding Division resumed the attack on Rauray with its 70th Infantry Brigade, supported by tanks. Before dawn, the Hallamshire Battalion (146 Brigade) set out once more to establish positions south of the Bois de Tessel, while 11th Battalion, The Durham Light Infantry (11 DLI), held the positions it had achieved the night before on the east bank of the Bordel, on the plateau to the west of Rauray. The 4 Lincoln (146 Brigade) and the Tyne Scots (70 Brigade) advanced between these two salients in the morning and cleared the central area around the Grand Farm (north of Tessel, bordering the Bordel stream). Thus, 11 DLI (70 Brigade) was less exposed on its right flank and advanced at noon to attack Rauray.

The area on each side of the northern boundary of Rauray was defended by III./26, commanded by SS-Sturmbannführer Olboeter, who had positioned there the remains of his battalion of grenadiers, supported by elements from 13./26, 15./26 and 16./26, along with a platoon from 1st Company, HJ Engineer Battalion. Support was provided by the HJ Division's 2. Panzer-Kompanie, as well as Panzer IVs from 6./12 and a section from 9./12. It was the only remaining force on the left flank of the *Hitlerjugend*'s front line: the reconnaissance group (Gerd Bremer) having left the area on the previous night in order to reinforce the threatened positions north of Mondrainville, to the east. Moreover, apart from 2./12, the 1st battalion of panzers (I./12) had left for Grainville, south-east of Rauray, which was another area under threat.

A Company, 11 DLI, had started its attack at 8 am, advancing from the southeast corner of the present-day British military cemetery towards a row of trees. Faced with German resistance, only six survivors remained from the first two sections (seventy men in total) after just twenty minutes. The whole battalion then attacked towards noon, as we have already seen, and suffered heavy casualties under the German cross-fire. There were losses on both sides and a truce was held from 12-2 pm to collect the wounded. Oberscharführer Hans Georg Kesslau fought with 10./26, one of the four companies of grenadiers from III./26: 'We watched the British medics, with a Red Cross on their chests and backs, as they carried their wounded and dead to the ambulances on our right. Immediately after the end of the truce, the attack resumed and SS-Sturmann Walter Frobel, who had given me the order regarding the truce, was wounded.'

The infantrymen from 11 DLI were supported by Sherman tanks from the Sherwood Rangers Yeomanry (SRY) who came up against the Panther tanks from 2./12. SS-Unterscharführer Süsse, who had already lost a panzer the day before (but had luckily been able to escape, along with his crew), went back into battle on this day with another Panther. He first destroyed three of the Sherwood Ranger's Shermans, before being wounded when his Panther tank was destroyed. This was clearly Panther Ausf. A '204', which was set on fire near the crossroads, north of the chateau at Rauray, as it was the only Panther wreck photographed by the British in this area. However, the German defensive line could not resist for long, and in the course of the afternoon SS-Sturmbannführer Olboeter's *Kampfgruppe* retreated in a line north of Brettevillette, and 70th Brigade would not continue its attack after the capture of Rauray. The war diary of 49th Division noted the following for this day: 'Today we took Rauray, which the enemy had defended for almost two days. Its infantry and tanks had defended every inch of ground against all attacks, to the north and east of the locality.'

The following from Hans Georg Kesslau's account completes our knowledge of the day's struggle surrounding Max Wünsche's former CP:

On 27 June, command of the company (10./26) fell to two non-commissioned officers and twenty men. In the evening I was called to *SS-Sturmbannführer* Olboeter's CP, where he told me to guard the CP with a few men, because it was not known if contact with the other companies still existed. I went down there with two comrades and about 200 metres in front of the CP we

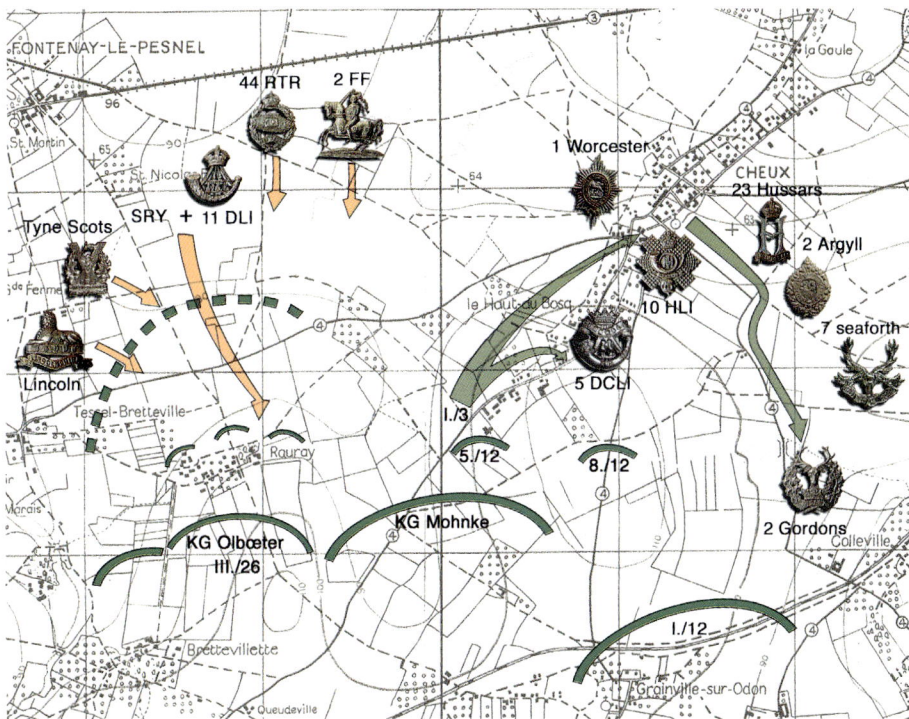

Map showing the action that took place during Operation Epsom on the morning of 27 June. On the left, we see the attack by 11 DLI, backed by the Sherman Rangers Yeomanry (SRY) tanks, following support on the right wing by the Tyneside Scottish and 5 Lincoln. Rauray was finally taken, but the attack would not advance further. In the centre, two companies (each reduced to a few tanks) of Panzer IVs from 5./12 and particularly 8./12, block the attack by the HLI, which was to reach as far as Grainville and then the bridge at Gavrus The counter-attack by a Panther tank company from 1./3 at le Haut du Bosq and Cheux resulted in the loss of a good number of these powerful panzers. Apart from 2./12, who were providing support in Rauray, the rest of the Panther tanks from I./12 were in the Grainville sector. In spite of the losses suffered the previous day, the weak point in the German line lay to the east, in the area around Colleville and Tourville, which was held only by SS-Stubaf Bremer's reconnaissance group, as well as a few tanks from SS-Pz.-Rgt. 12. It is in this sector that the 2 Argylls advanced, from Cheux to Colleville, before finally reaching the bridge at Tourmauville. (L.K./Heimdal)

The British military cemetery at Rauray is an oasis of greenery surrounded by fields, and is where the attack by 11 DLI started in the morning of 27 June. The cemetery contains both British and German graves. (G.B.)

captured three Englishmen who had no idea where their own lines were. During their interrogation, they stated that they believed the area had been occupied by their own troops for some time. I was injured as I retreated to the new position, and was taken over by an SPW from our battalion. *SS-Sturmbannführer* Olboeter took his leave of the wounded with a handshake before we left for the aid station at Missy.

The 'polar bears' finally took Rauray but progressed no further. They suspended their attack against *Kampfgruppe* Olboeter and consequently had not advanced beyond Phase 1.

Le Haut du Bosq: the afternoon

We now return to 5./12 at le Haut du Bosq, during the afternoon of 27 June, while on the left flank, to the west, the German front was bending in the area around Rauray under the advance of the 49th Infantry Division. SS-Untersturmführer Willi Kändler, head of the 3rd section, 5./12, had placed look outs to keep an eye on the artillery:

In the early afternoon, one of these men knocked on my panzer and told me that to the right of the farm in front of us, three Sherman tanks had arrived, at a distance of 600 metres. The crews had come out and were on top of their tanks. I slipped down on foot, along with the other two commanders and the three gunners, to the look-out point. We confirmed what they had reported and saw that the crews were wandering around carelessly on top of their tanks. I gave the order: 'Biback, you take the right tank, Jürgens, the one on the left and I'll take the middle one. Try to advance quietly to the high ground near the hedge. Shoot at the same time, destroy each of your tanks and return immediately to your shelter!'

Biback would stay trapped in the sunken road as the bottom of his panzer was stuck on a tree stump, but Jürgens pulled away from me on the left. I was therefore left to me to try and shoot Biback's Sherman. In the meantime, Jürgens arrived and immediately struck 'his' tank with a direct hit. The three Sherman tanks burned. We had not yet reached our shelter before terrible fire from several invisible tank guns headed in our direction from each side of the farm.

At the end of the afternoon, three panzers emerged to the right of the sunken road. I thought they were our reinforcements, but they were actually looking for 8th Company. I told them the rough direction, not knowing the exact location.

These 'reinforcements' were only the panzers from 8th Company that had been hastily restored by the workshop. However, they would contribute significantly to a subsequent success.

In the afternoon of 27 June, near the crossroads north of Rauray, infantrymen from 11 DLI rest following the hard fighting they had just suffered in order to finally take the 'cornerstone of the German front'. They are in position to the south-west of the crossroads, near the wreck of the Panther tank and in the background can be seen the burning Sherman previously seen on page XX. Note the regiment's name on the soldier's shoulder, 'Durham LI', the 49th Division's polar bear, and the stripes indicating 3rd Brigade. (IWM B 6044)

Colleville: the Argylls advance

The day before (26 June), the 15th Scottish Division's reserve brigade, the 227th Highland Brigade, had arrived to provide reinforcements. Two of its battalions were subsequently engaged: the 2 Gordons to the east, (up to Colleville and the railway line), and the 10 HLI to the south of Cheux, facing 8./12. However, the third battalion, the 2nd Battalion The Argyll & Sutherland Highlanders, was still waiting, bored and uncomfortable, in the pouring rain south of le Mesnil-Patry. The battalion had been totally reconstituted after being annihilated in Singapore when it came up against the Japanese offensive. Under the command of Lieutenant Colonel Tweedie, this new Highland Battalion was now expecting to prove itself in this new offensive. Their night had been hard, just as it had for everyone in the midst of the mud and rain, but then it was breakfast time, the famous breakfast that is so dear to British hearts. Lieutenant Colonel Tweedie arrived back from a meeting at 227 Brigade headquarters and told the men that they had to be ready to leave immediately. Breakfast was abandoned in quick haste, but soon the waiting began again, as it always seems to do in the British Army, hence the old adage: 'hurry up and wait'.

Tweedie had received his orders at 5.30 am: he must head for Colleville, which was held by 2 Gordons, cross the railway, and re-join the main road (from Caen to Villers-Bocage) at Tourville-sur-Odon. But for now, he had to cross through

At the start of Operation Epsom, a group of soldiers from the 2nd Battalion The Argyll and Sutherland Highlanders (227 Brigade), preceded by their piper, head for the front. This photograph was taken by Sergeant Laing. (IWM B 5988)

Cheux using the narrow roads, with companies A and B at the front, followed by companies C and D. H-hour was scheduled for 7.30 and the battalion was to be supported by tanks from the 23rd Hussars. However, their problems soon began as they arrived at Cheux from the north: the village was already cluttered with rubble and vehicles, and the battalion was forced to move forward through the chaos. Tweedie had been instructed keep the 'Gothic church' (it is actually Romanesque) on his left, and so looked for any 'Gothic fragment' with which to identify it. In reality, the building was in ruins and one would have been hard pressed to find any such indication. Progress through the village was a nightmare. They were still coming under fire from the Germans and Corporal O'Hara from Carrier Platoon was shot in the back of the neck; he would die from his wound later that day. The streets were saturated with transport vehicles and anti-tank guns, and the battalion had to fight hard to make its way through. Shortly after the church they emerged onto the open ground via a narrow road that passed near Contour 100, where the hard fighting against 15./25 had taken place the day before. The plain descended slightly to cross the Salbey, and the battalion bypassed Hans Siegel's position, which was located a little further up on the right. The road rose slightly and the first farm at Colleville appeared, north of the railway and 2 Gordons' positions. The Argylls were then confronted with the remnants of the previous day's fighting, including the corpses of the Gordons along the road. Before reaching the railway line, the Argylls passed by the blackened corpse of a liaison officer lying next to his motorcycle.

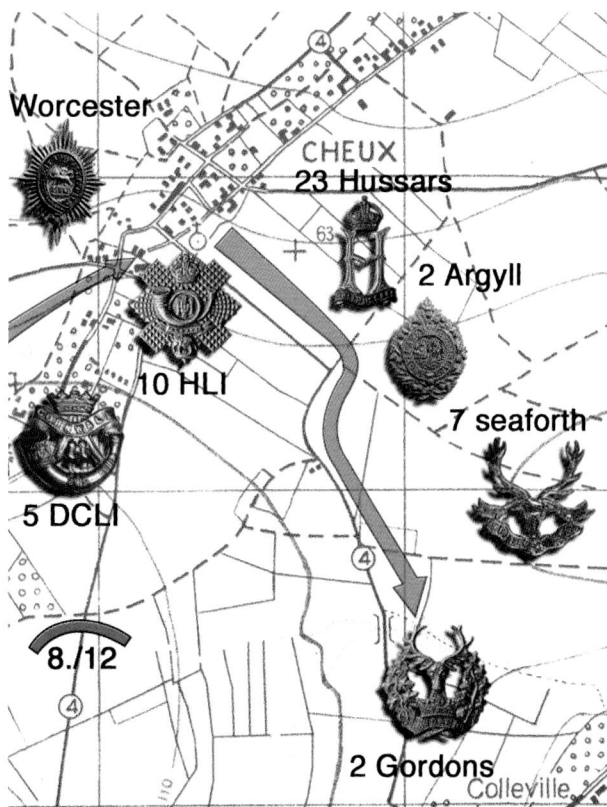

Map showing the Argylls' advance, from Cheux to Colleville, where they crossed the Gordons' positions and then the railway. They first advanced through open fields before encountering the *bocage* after the railway. (LK/Heimdal)

1. After passing through the devastated and crowded centre of Cheux, the Argylls passed by the town's large church of Saint-Vigor. The church is Romanesque and dates from the beginning of the twelfth century. Only the chapels east of the transept are Gothic. Cheux had once been an important area and was the main administrator for the surrounding fifteen parishes. There was a Tuesday market founded in the twelfth century by one of William the Conqueror's sons, Robert Courteheuse. The principal officers of the King of France's army lodged at Cheux in 1450, when the Comte de Dunois came to lay siege before the city of Caen against the English, who then in 1944, would use it as a crossroads for their offensive. (G.B.)

2. The Argylls left Cheux and headed east, through open fields, before turning south towards Colleville and Tourville. A little farther ahead and slightly to the right is the slight incline that the British called Ring Contour 100, which was where heavy fighting took place on 26 June against 15./25. The position was held by 7 Seaforth. (G.B.)

3. The road continues south. The hedge in the background marks the Salbey river, which was unguarded here, the Gordons having been there since the previous day. (G.B.)

4. The Salbey river (which is more like a large creek) where the Argylls crossed as they arrived at the Gordons' position, which was dotted with corpses. Hans Siegel's position was in the background, to the west.

They crossed B Company's (Gordons) lines, which were located just in front of the railway (the present A84 road) and near a large farm.

The only German forces they met in the area were elements from the HJ reconnaissance group (commanded by SS-Sturmbannführer Bremer), which had been hurriedly withdrawn from the Rauray area during the night to close the dangerous breach in the line. Only a few covering elements were to be found in Colleville, along with the first battery of Flak-Regiment 53 (Flak-Sturmregiment 4). In addition, only isolated soldiers had established defensive positions in the vicinity. SS-Sturmbannführer Bremer had sent a reconnaissance patrol up to the crossing north of Tourville to monitor the area, under the command of SS-Oberscharführer August Zinssmeister.

Fighting between the Germans and the Argylls now began. Corporal Campbell was in charge of one of the 6-pound anti-tank guns:

Suddenly 100 yards (about 90m) away, a tank appeared side-on in a gateway; this was my first German. He hadn't seen us and fired at something else. We fired one of the brand new 6-pound discarding sabot rounds into his side. With the first shot nothing seemed to happen, so I grabbed second and I saw a spurt of flames come out from between the bogey wheels. Then I saw a bloke jumping out of the turret. We fired a third shot and the whole thing blew up, knocking me over.

This is how August Zinssmeister described the fighting from his side:

Dead and wounded Tommies were lying at the railway crossing. They were members of an assault squad caught by their own artillery fire. A heavy artillery barrage was raining on Mondrainville and our sector again. The whole area was full of smoke. We wanted to repair a flat tyre on the 8-wheeler on the southern fringe of Tourville, but the artillery fire drove us to the other hill [on the other side of the Odon valley] at Baron. The tyre was completely ripped and useless. Back to Tourville. We encountered a section of our riflemen withdrawing along our path from the railway. A counter-attack with panzers and motorcycle riflemen failed and Tommy was able to get into the village to our flank. We fired everything we had at close range, with devastating effect. The Tommies hammered us with heavy artillery. I drove to the CP, south of Mondrainville, to report. We were reinforced by the *Flanderka* scouting party, and returned for another counter-attack along the northern edge of town. The bushes and hedges were teeming with British infantry and the fire fight continued without pause. One of the wheels on my 8-wheeler '121' was blown away by a hit and I bailed out and moved over to '122' which had pulled up in the meantime. The English infantry managed to advance further through the hedges and we came under anti-tank fire. We returned to the main road, continuing to fire on the Tommies, who, in the fog, tried to jump over the road. We inflicted heavy losses on them until a period of quiet set in.

SS-Untersturmführer Flanderka ordered me to drive to Mouen and make contact there with our own panzers and assault guns, I drove up and down among the Tommies for a short while, firing. Then I ordered: 'Let's go, step

Colleville: this crossroads leads towards Mouen (on the left) and Tourville (straight ahead), and was the road the Argylls took as they advanced through the middle of several German patrols. (G.B.)

on it!' We came face to face with a Sherman tank. I looked down its muzzle as Dey shouted: "Sergeant, is that a German?" The gunner sent a salvo of anti-tank shells across its bow and we were surprised when we saw its crate disappear behind a house. Then we took off. While I was reporting to Flanderka, six Shermans pushed out from behind the house and rattled down the street. It was twelve noon. A group of armoured cars was trying to make its way to us in Tourville. As they turned, one of them was hit on the road and caught fire. We raced past them along the embankment to the south of Grainville, to report there. On my own, I sent three Panthers out against those beasts in Tourville. The battalion issued new orders for 1st and 2nd companies: go to the divisional staff and defend it! The panzers were refuelled then we set out via Bougy and Gavrus. There we once more found Tommies advancing and fired on them until calm set in, then we drove on.[3]

On their side, the Argylls came under fire from a 'Spandau' (MG 42), which swept the railway as they crossed it, killing one man and wounding several others. The machine gun was silenced by a 2-inch mortar shell from 12th Platoon that was covering the crossing while the other two sections, 10th and 11th Platoons, crossed the railway. In Colleville, the landscape changed radically, as the view was limited by the numerous hedges. From there, the main road lead to Tourville and stretched for nearly 2 kilometres with hedges on either side. According to some testimonies, the journey went practically unopposed.[4] However, according to others, the Argylls and the 23rd Hussars lost an enormous amount of time fighting in Colleville.[5] This latter opinion is corroborated by the testimony of August Zinssmeister and especially by the delay in reaching the RN175 main road, which was reached at about 3 pm: seven hours after passing through Cheux. Despite the delays and the fighting, this was a great success. The railway was finally crossed and the main road had been reached; the Odon Valley was near!

---

3   Ibid., p.285-6.

4   I. Daglish, Operation Epsom, p. 87.

5   T. Saunders, Operation Epsom, p.112.

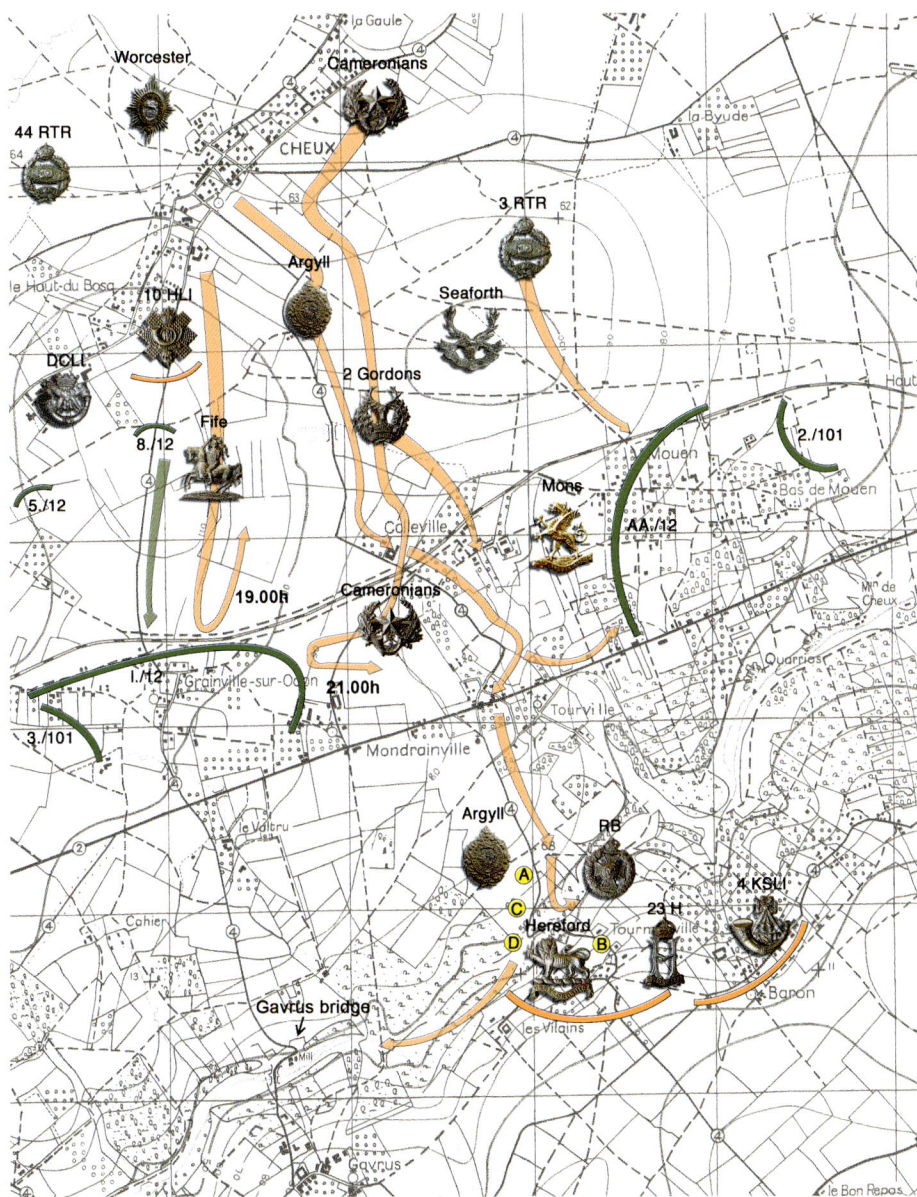

The 'Scottish Corridor'. On this day, 2 Argyll left Cheux and crossed the Odon using the bridge at Tourmauville, while the HLI was struggling against 8./12. Behind 2 Argyll (positioned in the bridgehead with its A, B, C and D companies), the 29th Armoured Division rushed through the corridor with 1 Hereford, 4 KSLI and 23 Hussars and positioned themselves for the night south of the Odon. To the east, the Mons positioned themselves to take Mouen, an area defended, among others, by Tiger tanks from 2./101. To the west, around 7 pm, the Fife and Forfar stalled at Grainville, which was defended by Panther tanks from 12./12. The Cameronians were also stopped at around 9 pm. (L. Krispin/Heimdal)

As the Argylls arrived on the main road, any threats from patrols from 12. SS-Panzer-Division were quickly eliminated. However, while attempting to advance westward along the road towards Mondrainville, 11th Platoon was confronted by an armoured reconnaissance unit, which blocked their progress and forced them to hide in a wheat field. Private Peter Bocock, from B Company, remembers the effects of the 'Spandau' machine gun as it pulverised the wheat ears over their helmets and they were ordered to pull back through the hedges. They used their machetes to open a way through the thick groves, but Bocock was hit in the legs and was taken over to an ambulance jeep at the Colleville crossing. There, on his stretcher, he saw the caterpillars of the Sherman tanks crushing the corpses of the Gordons who remained on the railway tracks.

They had to move westwards along the main road, to Mondrainville, in order to reach the small road that led down into the Odon Valley and the bridge at Tourmauville, where B Company was still trapped. An anti-tank section arrived from Cheux, under the command of Captain Muirhead, who directed the fire himself. Suddenly someone shouted, 'A German tank!' An anti-tank gun was directed at it and one of the new Sabot shells was loaded, but there were cows positioned between the barrel of gun and the panzer and they didn't know whether to wait or fire through the animals. However, the panzer fired along the road and directed its turret towards the anti-tank gun before firing again. The blast of the explosion caused panic and the anti-tank gun returned fire, but was too close. The loader was injured and the anti-tank gun fired again. A long flame came out of the panzer before another shot completed the task. The tank commander leapt out of the turret and then the driver followed after a third shot; the two men were on fire. There was an explosion and the panzer's turret was blown off. Although reports would describe the panzer as a Tiger, it was, in fact, a Panzer IV.

The bridge at Tourmauville

Lieutenant Colonel Tweedie now had to continue forward and descend into the Odon Valley. They were still at risk from a German counter-attack, which would then be able to take control of the main road. A Company were to defend the battalion's CP at Tourville, while B Company covered the main road from the west. C Company, under the command of Major Hugh Fyfe, was ordered to take the bridge over the Odon and the first two sections reached the intact bridge at around 5 pm. The bridge itself had been protected by a Flak battery, the second battery of Flak-Regiment 53, positioned near the bridge on the north shore, near the bridge itself. However, it had now changed position along with the rest of the regiment, although an anti-tank gun was still located near the bridge. When the Argylls arrived, the gun remained inactive and there was nothing to stop the British soldiers from crossing the bridge. C Company and a section of carriers descended road to the bridge, while Major Graham's' D Company provided covering fire from the plateau that overlooked the steep slope. By 5.15 pm C Company were crossing the bridge, which was neither mined nor guarded. It was quite an achievement as the advanced element of the Argylls penetrated into open terrain, without opposition, but they were still terribly vulnerable because the road provided no significant protection on its flanks, and so they remained at the mercy of a counter-attack.

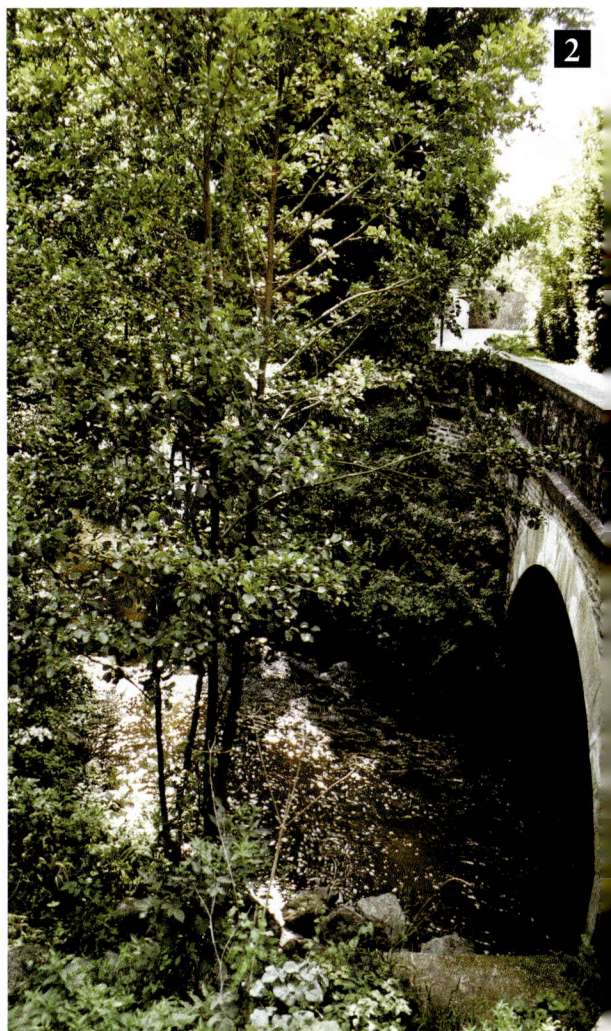

1. The Odon Valley showing the bridge at Tourmauville. On the left, the road comes from Tourville (to the north). Caen is in the background. This aerial photograph was taken several years ago. On 27 June, the 2nd Argyll reached this bridge at around 5 pm then proceeded to form a bridgehead on the southern bank. (Dufresne/H.Meyer).

2. The solid stone bridge at Tourmauville spans the Odon and was a real lifeline for the 'Scottish Corridor'. It managed to support the passage of hundreds of armoured vehicles, in both directions, without weakening. (G.B.)

Major Fyfe's C Company was then joined by Major Graham's D Company and other members from B Company. The Argylls advanced around 200 metres along the southern bank in order to establish a defensive perimeter on this side of the river. The anti-tank section then provided reinforcements with its 6-pound guns, as the remarkable news reached the staff at VIII Corps. General Roberts reacted immediately: he was finally able to engage his tanks. The 23rd Hussars were already following behind the Argylls (its Sherman tanks were currently in Tourville), and behind them, in turn, were the half-tracks from 8 Rifle Brigade. However, the rumble of the tanks alerted the Germans who now emerged on the main road at Tourville, and very quickly destroyed two Sherman tanks and three carriers, one after the other. An M10 anti-tank gun from H Troop, 81st Antitank Regiment arrived and opened fire on any panzer or other armoured vehicle that it could see to the west, and after six shots had been fired, the calm returned once more. Later on, a Panther tank took up position on the side of the road, at Mouen, 1 kilometre to the east of Tourville, before proceeding to drive down it, eventually reaching the bridge as one or two tanks were in the process of crossing it. Brigadier Hilton (Commander Royal Artillery) from 15th Scottish Division had arrived, bringing with him a 17-pound anti-tank gun, but the Panther was faster.

Meanwhile, the Gordons arrived at Tourville where they relieved the elements of the Argylls who still remained there. Lieutenant Colonel John Tweedie arrived at Tourmauville bridge with A Company and his CP, and eagerly awaited reinforcements from 11th Armoured Division. An officer from the division arrived and timidly asked whether or not the bridge would hold under the weight of the tanks. Tweedie became angry, saying that if the 29 Armoured Brigade didn't want the bridge, then he would pull back and blow it up! At 18.07 pm, a reconnaissance group from the division reported that the bridge was 'wide and capable enough of supporting all types of vehicles'. The 23rd Hussars were ordered to proceed immediately and its C Squadron was already underway, preceded by a section from H Company, 8 RB. According to the 11th Armoured Division, the squadron arrived at 6.45 pm followed by B Squadron with part of the battalion's CP later arriving at 7.25 pm. According to the Argylls, however, they only arrived at around 10 pm. H Company, 8 RB, commanded by Major Mackenzie, also descended cautiously towards the valley, still concerned that elements of the *Hitlerjugend* would attack their tanks with *Panzerfausts*, but no casualties were suffered.

The commanders of 11th Armoured Division were champing at the bit now that they had launched its tanks, and enthusiastically anticipated the success that was sure to come. For example, the division's HQ announced at 9.45 pm that 159 Brigade were crossing the Odon (which was not yet the case) and that at 11.20 pm, the 23rd Hussars has already engaged two squadrons south of the Odon towards Hill 112, facing the enemy's tanks. It was all completely premature. Only the infantry from 2 Argylls were able to establish a small defensive perimeter along the ridge of the plateau, south of the wooded slope that overlooked the Odon. During the evening, while companies B and D from the Argylls joined C Company in defending this perimeter, which was about 200 metres wide, near Baron, Lieutenant Colonel John Tweedie sent two heavy patrols to the bridge at Gavrus. They took the bridge, announcing their success via the radio. As they pulled back, A Company held the bridge at Tourmauville (whose code name was "Quags"), and its surroundings.

But the arrival of the armoured vehicles was not easy: the road down into the valley was narrow, relatively steep, and with a very steep turn, yet their appearance was 'magnificent' for the infantrymen confined in the wooded valley. Finally, the stone bridge would be strong enough to withstand the weight of the tanks, although it was the terrain that was problematic, and the caterpillar tracks from the tanks and various armoured vehicles struggled. Captain Kenny (Quartermaster) had arrived first to watch the progress over the difficult terrain, and when the corps commander of 23rd Hussars, Colonel Harding, arrived, his own Sherman tank slipped after the road had been gradually worn away by the heavy and intense traffic. The next day, engineers (2 Platoon, 282 (Welsh) Field Company, RE)

Panoramic views of the large bend at the Tourmauville bridge. The old Tailleboscq mill can be seen on the left. (G.B.)

An example of the dense vegetation in the Odon valley. This photograph was taken slightly downstream of the bridge at Tourmauville, on the southern bank. (G.B.)

worked to establish a second direct crossing, east of the original bridge, but the new crossing would not be ready until 11 July.

For the time being, Major General Roberts continued to pile on the pressure; elements from his division must cross the river and advance forward as quickly as possible. He ordered Brigadier Sandie, the commander of 159 Brigade (motorized infantry), to be on his starting line at 9.30 pm, with progress to continue until nightfall. Looking at the traffic jams and general chaotic advance, Sandie believed the mission to be impossible, but an order is an order and he had to throw himself into the fray. His lack of enthusiasm would lead him to be sacked the next morning and he was replaced by Colonel Churcher from the Herefords. You had to follow orders, in spite of the bad conditions, and the two leading battalions, the 1 Herefords on the right and the 4 King's Shropshire Light Infantry (KSLI), on the left, crossed the Odon at nightfall. The 3 Monmouths (3 Mons) were placed in reserve, in a defensive position, on the north side of the valley.

To Grainville and Mondrainville

The narrow 'Scottish Corridor' leading to the south shore of Odon was not yet secure. At the end of the afternoon, the 23rd Hussars had sent a troop (four tanks) from A Squadron towards Mouen, to silence a panzer that had become very dangerous. But the four Sherman tanks came under fire from a variety of sources and only a single tank came back safe and sound. Throughout their advance along the unpaved roads leading to the bridge at Tourmanville, thousands of vehicles were subjected to anti-tank fire, which only helped to erode the narrow roads.

Two Panther tanks appeared between Tourville and Mondrainville. The one at the front advanced to put himself in full view, only to be destroyed by an anti-tank

Two Panther tanks appeared between Tourville and Mondrainville; the one at the front was destroyed by a single shell. This Panther D obviously belonged to the *Hitlerjugend* Division, I./12.

gun, while the other quickly escaped. The wreckage of the type D Panther would remain on the road and was to be examined by many passing British soldiers. It was probably from 2nd Company, SS-Panzer-Regiment 12, a unit that possessed a few such engines. The Panzer had been destroyed by a single shell fired by Sergeant Brand and his team. Albert Grandais published the testimony of a civilian, M. Lelarge, who had witnessed all the action from his attic, a few yards away:

> I saw four or five British soldiers collapse onto the road as they tried to cross it. I think the gunfire came from a German sniper hidden in an apple tree. At one point, the firing ceased. No doubt he was trying to save himself, unless he had been killed in his turn. Then I saw a big tank coming from Mouen. It stopped at the bottom of Tourville and fired several shells in the direction of Cheux. Suddenly I saw it wrapped in thick black smoke.[6]

To the west, effort was also made to loosen the vice around Mondrainville and Grainville. To the north of the latter, the 10 HLI's continuous assaults were exhausted in the face of Hans Siegel's position and at the end of the day the Highland battalion had to abandon its objective. However, a battalion of tanks engaged in this sector, the Fife and Forfar, decided to go it alone and try its own luck. It advanced without infantry support and, by chance, found that the three surviving Panzer IVs from 8./12 had left their position to refuel and reload. But where were the surviving Panther tanks from I./3 and the panzers sent in to reinforce 8./12? Advancing cautiously, the Sherman tanks finally reached the railway to the south of the Salbey, near Grainville, and could see the village rooftops. Steel Brownlie's

---

6   A. Grandais, Bataille du Calvados, p.139.

The location today (E.G./Heimdal)

Sherman tank opened fire on the camouflaged vehicles just over 3 kilometres ahead. Kenneth Matheson's reconnaissance section went to inspect the village with its Stuart tanks, but a Panther tank was lying in wait on a path beside Grainville church. It fired a shell at the first Stuart, which nevertheless managed to retreat, along with the rest of the group.

The 9th Cameronians infantry reorganized to the north of Cheux, in order to follow the route of the 2 Argyll to Colleville. They crossed the railway before advancing through the fields between the railway and the main road, up to the hill at Mondrainville, supported by Churchill tanks from B Squadron, 9th RTR. Some of the infantrymen even climbed on to the tanks for the ride, and they arrived at the northern edge of Grainville around 7.30 pm, where they made contact with the forward positions of the Fife and Forfar. Captain Leggat-Smith's D Company, (Cameronians) attempted to advance through Grainville with six tanks, which were quickly destroyed, leaving the infantrymen alone. The battalion commander, Lieutenant Colonel Villiers, convinced his leader, Brigadier Barber, to suspend the attack until the next morning. However, Captain Leggat-Smith, who was still isolated in Grainville with his company, knew nothing about the suspended attack. Lieutenant Colonel Villiers headed into Grainville, under fire, and found Leggat-Smith near the church, and ordered him to pull back for the night. The tanks returned to their bases, while the infantry dug their foxholes, but at midnight, Captain Leggat-Smith returned to Grainville with the chaplain and four medics to fetch the missing soldiers from D Company. Leggat-Smith asked for reinforcements, but Lieutenant Colonel Villiers was soundly asleep: the reinforcements didn't come and Grainville wasn't taken.

During the night, the trucks of 159th Brigade were to head for the south bank of the Odon, starting from the main road. It was 9.30 pm and the battalions were still in the area around Colleville, but anxiety was growing in the ranks. Night was approaching and the leader of 1 Hereford was worried that he would not arrive on

The church at Grainville-sur-Odon. On 27 June a Panther tank was hiding in the nearby road and the Stuart tanks from the Fife and Forfar's reconnaissance section were pushed back by the Panther's fire. (G.B.)

time at the plateau south of the Odon in order to take up his planned position on the right (west), at Tourmauville. The 4 King's Shropshire Light Infantry (4 KLSI) were to be positioned on the left (east) at Baron and the 3 Monmouthshire (Mons) were to remain in reserve. Those were the orders. At nightfall, D Company, 4 KSLI took the lead. On the other side of the river, it turned left and moved into position around the Baron chateau, the closest point to Hill 112. In the rear, the traffic jams had reached fever-pitch; a broken-down Sherman was now blocking the bridge and the drivers of the various vehicles had great difficulty staying awake. The two battalions at the front would not be installed in their positions until 2 am, but the 3 Monmouths would remain stuck north of the main road through the night, in the rain.

At the end of the day, the *Hitlerjugend* recorded the following losses: three killed, nine wounded and twenty-one missing for the staff of Regiment 26; eleven killed, seven wounded and two missing from I. /26; two killed, three wounded and four missing from II./26; eight killed, twenty-three wounded and one missing from III. /26 (Olboeter); one killed and two wounded for the Engineer Battalion; two killed and thirteen wounded for the reconnaissance group (Bremer); fourteen killed and twenty-five wounded from SS-Panzer-Regiment 12; three killed, twenty-four wounded and ten missing from the artillery regiment. The total losses amounted to forty-four killed, 109 wounded and thirty-eight missing (191 men). These were much lower than those of VIII Corps, which amounted to 666 men, including sixty-five killed, 303 wounded and 298 missing. However, the corps had increased its manpower to 66,000 men.

This photograph by Sergeant Laing shows foot soldiers from the 7th Seaforth Highlanders (46th Highland Brigade, 15th Scottish Division) advancing through a wheat field towards a hedge that might be hiding formidable German machine guns which the British called 'Spandaus'. This Highland battalion had fought against 15./25 on 26 June and would resume its attack on 27 June. This picture illustrates the nature of the fighting during Operation Epsom, which was mainly carried out by the infantry, with additional tank support. (IWM B 5999)

South of le Mesnil-Patry, 28 June

1. An attack is being planned. Officers from an armoured troop meet on a Churchill tank from 7th Royal Tank Regiment, 31st Tank Brigade. Seen here are Lieutenant Colonel Delacombe (in the helmet) commander of 8th Battalion The Royal Scots (8 RS), who were in action from the first day of the offensive, Lieutenant Colonel Gainsford (in the beret), commander of the 7th RTR), and Major Taylor from the 350th Artillery Regiment. (IWM-B6113)

2. This photo shows infantrymen from the 8th Royal Scots (44th Brigade, 15th Scottish Division) advancing along the tree-lined Fontenay-Carpiquet road, passing by vehicles from the 7th RTR. In the foreground is one of the unit's reconnaissance vehicles (No. 991 painted in white, with a white bar on a dark green background). It was a Scout Car Humber weighing 3,390 kg and measuring 3.83 m long and 2.12 m wide. It had a top speed of 90 km/h with a range of 320 km and was generally armed with one or two FM Bren guns, (two are seen here pointing towards the sky. (IWM – B6115)

3. The Fontenay-Carpiquet road today. The trees are about the same size having been cut down a few decades ago and replanted. (G.B.)

4. A close-up of the front of the Scout Car Humber. From right to left: the insignia of the 31st Army Tank Brigade formed of two triangles joined at the tip, in a dark green colour; - the black number 5 on a yellow background constitutes the Bridge classification Number denoting the vehicle's weight classification when crossing a bridge (for example, a Sherman tank carries the number 30); - the number 991 between two white bars on a dark green background denotes the 7th RTR, which belongs to the brigade. (Erik Groult/Heimdal.)

5

Brigade Headquarters — **990**

991 — 7th Battalion Royal Tank Regiment

992 — 9th Battalion Royal Tank Regiment

993 — 141st RAC

6

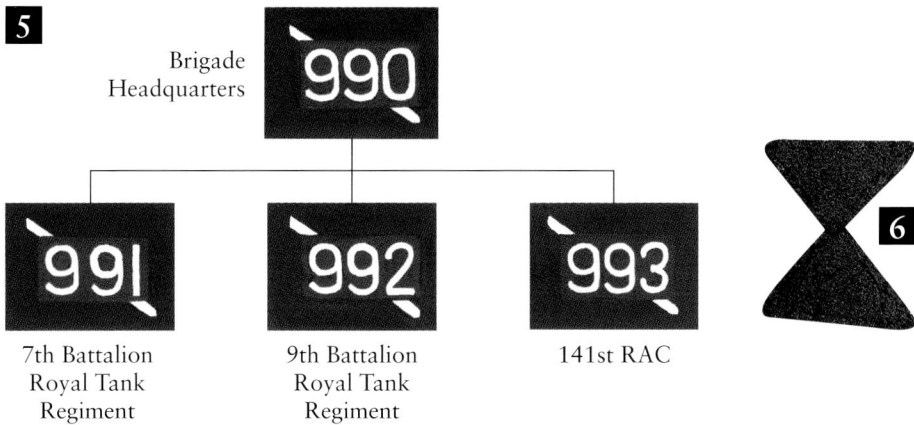

5. The 31st Army Tank Brigade, created on 15 January 1941 and commanded by Brigadier G.S. Knight, was an independent tank brigade that was sent to support the 15th Scottish Division during Operation Epsom. It was equipped with Churchill tanks, including special Crocodile tanks (flamethrowers) that were grouped with the brigade's 3rd Battalion, the 141st RAC. On the first day of the offensive, 26 June, the brigade's 1st Battalion, the 7th RTR, provided support for the 46th Highland Brigade with its C Squadron (for the 9 Cameronians) and its B Squadron (for the 2 Glasgow Highlanders). The 2nd Battalion, 9th RTR, supported the 44th Lowland Brigade, although its B Squadron supported the 8 Royal Scots. The 141st RAC, which had special flamethrower tanks, only had its A Squadron within the brigade, having reinforced the other two battalions by dispersing its resources for specific missions (Troops 4 and 5 providing support for the 9th RTR). Some of these tanks saw action in Saint-Manvieu against I./26's CP.

6. Fabric insignia of the 31st Army Tank Brigade worn by the men of this great unit on the top of the left sleeve.

7. This other image from the same report shows Churchill tanks in support along the Fontenay-Carpiquet road, which acted as a rear offensive line. In the foreground is an anti-tank gun (6-pounder), which was used by men from the 8th Battalion Royal Scots, as indicated by the original caption and by the number '55' painted on the helmet of the man on the left. The situation presented here is no longer that of the beginning of the offensive. Throughout 26 June, the 44th and 46th Brigades were progressively relieved, mainly by the 227th Brigade, which was further relieved at the end of the day by C Squadron, 7th RTR (for the 10th HLI) and by C Squadron, 9th RTR (for the 2 Gordons). This meant that by 28 June, a defensive line containing elements from the 7th RTR and the Royal Scots were in the area behind the main front line, which was at risk from a counter-attack by II. SS-Panzerkorps. (IWM – B6117)

7

Rauray, 28 June (1)

1. On this day, the 49th West Riding Division and 70th Brigade attacked from Rauray in the direction of Brettevillette, in the south-west, before being pushed back by *Kampgruppe Olboeter* (HJ) and then by *Kampfgruppe Weidinger* (Das Reich). Here, infantry from one of the brigade's three battalions, the DLI, are seen heading up to the front. The trees at the back, on the left, stand in front of the chateau at Rauray, where the CP of SS-Pz.-Rgt. 12 was located until the evening of 26 June. (IWM B 6160)

2. The advance continues. *Kampfgruppe Olboeter* was further ahead, while in the foreground lays the corpse of a grenadier from the *Hitlerjugend*. On the right, a motorcycle liaison officer is in position near the bank, but he has left his bike on the other side of the road. The bike displays the number '67', denoting the first infantry battalion of the Junior Infantry Brigade, ie, for the 49th Division, the 11th Royal Scots Fusiliers of the 147th Infantry Brigade. That he is a liaison officer might explain his presence to his DLI comrades. In background, on the left, is a destroyed Tiger tank, and on the right, a house that will also serve as a landmark later on. (IWM B6161)

3. The infantry advance towards the crossroads opposite the chateau. The last soldier passes by another corpse. (IWM B6135)

4. The same locations today are relatively well-preserved. (E.G/Heimdal)

5 & 6. These relics from the battle were recently found in the area where the liaison officer was positioned. (E.G./Heimdal)

Rauray, 28 June (2)

1 & 2. Two British infantrymen bring back a German prisoner, a simple SS soldier, who would have been flushed out from behind the destroyed Tiger tank. (IWM B 6136 and 6157)

3. Sherman tanks move towards the front in response to the counter-attack. (IWM – B6156)

4. A British soldier passes by the corpse of a young *Hitlerjugend* soldier, who had created significant casualties for the 49th Division's infantry. (IWM B6141)

5. Another captured Waffen-SS soldier is brought towards the rear by men from the 10 DLI. (IWM)

Rauray, 28 June (3)

1. A Bren Carrier from the 2/Kensingtons, the machine gun battalion, denoted by the number '64' in white letters on a black background, from the 49th Division, passes in front of the destroyed Tiger I near the chateau. The façade of the house facing the chateau has been damaged by shelling and the access staircase destroyed to allow the tanks to pass by. The gable of the farm building on the south-west corner of the road has also been hit by a shell, destroying most of the building which was then rebuilt after the fighting. (IWM B6137)

2. The same location today. The staircase has been rebuilt but the façade of the house is still marked by the shell impacts. The gable of the rebuilt farm building has since disappeared. (E.G./Heimdal)

3. Sergeant Christie took this new photograph in Rauray on 28 June. It shows Sergeant N. Durbin of the 2nd Princess Louise's Kensingtons Regiment using an ingenious system to direct the fire of the soldier crouching on his left. He may well just be pretending to point towards the target for Sergeant Christie, as the men appear to be having difficulty keeping a straight face. (IWM)

4. The same location today. (E.G./Heimdal)

5. A Bren Carrier from the 2/Kensingtons, bearing the number '64' and the polar bear, preparing to pass in front of the house seen in image 1. Notice the sign claiming 'Attention, the enemy is watching', which was placed in front of the entrance to the CP of SS-Pz.-Rgt. 12. (IWM)

6. In the same place, looking to the right, a steel monster stands in front of two infantrymen from 70th Brigade. It is a Tiger I type E from 3rd Company bearing the number '334'. It was commanded by SS-Oscha. Rolf von Westernhagen, who had painted the name 'Alfred Günther' and a knight's cross on the side of the Tiger, in memory of his friend who was killed in Evrecy on the night of June 14-15, although the inscriptions are not visible here. The tank is in a curious position, with its back to the enemy and stuck in the chateau's hedge, no doubt pushed there by another tank. (IWM B 6140)

Rauray, 28 June (4)

1. A few metres further ahead, at the crossroads, looking west towards Tessel, from where armoured vehicles are arriving. Here we see a Bren Carrier from the Polar Bear Division and a formidable TD. (IWM - B 6158)

2. The same location today, the 'rebuilders' clearly did not have the talent of their predecessors... (G.B.)

3. Another burned-out Tiger I type E, a few kilometres to the east. This one belonged to 2nd Company (see the position of the insignia) and was not found in the area around Rauray. This company was in action further to the east, in the sector around Mouen. (IWM B 6155)

4 & 5. Two views of the park and the chateau at Rauray, which had acted as Max Wünsche's CP. (IWM B6217 and 6214)

6. The chateau at Rauray today. (G.B.)

Counter-attack by SS-Panzergrenadier-Regiment 1 LAH at Mouen, 28 June 1944

1. SS-Obersturmbannführer Albert Frey commanded one of the *Leibstandarte*'s grenadier (motorized infantry), the SS-Pz.-Gren.-Rgt. 1. He is seen here on 28 June giving his orders for the counter-attack on Mouen. (Munin)

2. Born on 16 February 1913, Albert Frey was given command of a section in the *Leibstandarte* on 12 March 1938. In 1940 he commanded 9th Company, LAH, participating in all campaigns. In the USSR, in 1941, he was given command of a battalion and was awarded the German Gold Cross on 17 November 1941, and then the Knight's Cross of the Iron Cross on 3 March 1943, following his actions in the recapture of Charkow. After Fritz Witt's departure for the *Hitlerjugend* Division, Albert Frey took command of the SS-Panzergrenadier-Regiment 1 in March 1943. In this picture he was still a SS-Sturmbannführer and was promoted to SS-Obersturmbannführer on 1 July 1943 and participated in Operation *Zitadelle* (Kursk). This valuable military leader received his oak leaves on 20 December 1943 (the 359th soldier to do so) and continued to see action with the LAH before surrendering to the US Army in May 1945. (G.B.)

3. Preparing for the attack in the Venoix sector. (Munin)

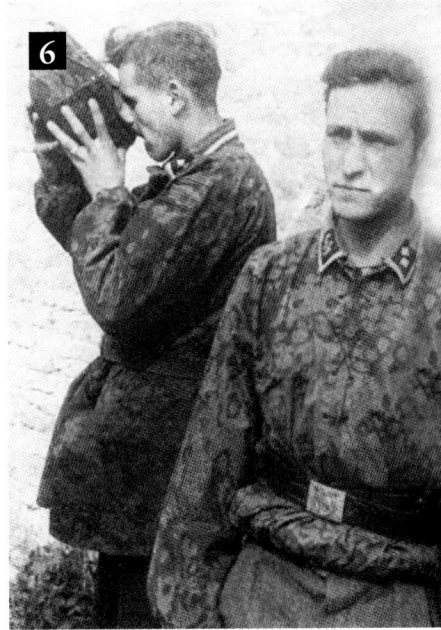

4. Advancing along the main Caen - Villers-Bocage road, with a camouflaged Kübelwagen seen in the foreground, protected by a tank Tiger. (Munin)

5. Two grenadiers from SS-Panzergrenadier-Regiment 1 advance cautiously while watching for the bigger dangers that come from the sky. (Munin)

6. Non-commissioned officers from 3./1 take a break. The SS-sUnterscharführer (left) uses his helmet to take a drink, despite its leather trim. The Oberscharführer (right) has rolled-up his camouflage jacket under his belt. The company was advancing north of the national road to take Mouen. (Munin)

1. This vehicle has been transformed into a moving bush in light of this aerial threat. (Munin)

2 & 3. Grenadiers from a company in the LAH advance through the thick *bocage*, between the railway line and the Odon valley; typical of the terrain found in the area around Mouen. They are carrying a lot of equipment, including ammunition boxes and Panzerfaustes. (Munin)

The Third Day – Wednesday 28 June

The panzers of the *Hitlerjugend* fall back to Hill 112...

While the *Leibstandarte* was going to try and cut the 'Scottish Corridor', the serious Allied threat against Hill 112 forced the *Hitlerjugend* to pull back several of its panzer companies to this sector. The redeployment was facilitated by the intervention of the *Kampfgruppe* Weidinger. By dawn on this new day of the offensive, the British bridgehead south of the Odon was still weak and so the race began. 12. SS-Panzer-Division were determined to do whatever it took to prevent VIII Corps from taking Hill 112 and thus break through to the Orne, hence the counter-attacks by *Kampfgruppe* Weidinger and thea *Leibstandarte* regiment's aim of cutting off and encircling the bridgehead. SS-Panzer-Regiment 12 pulled back its 5th and 8th companies from their positions south of Cheux (8./12) and south of the Haut du Bosq (5./12), as well as those companies engaged in the Mondrainville/ Tessel sector, supported by the *Kampfgruppe* Weidinger. A Panther tank company soon arrived on the east side of Hill 113, 2 kilometres west of Esquay, with the aim of covering the ground to the north. Its presence was confirmed by British sentries, who spotted five Panther tanks between 7.50 am and 4.30 pm. Another Panther company from SS-Panzer-Regiment 12 was engaged west of Verson, on either side of the main road, to support the *Leibstandarte*'s attack.

Panzer IV No.538 from 5./12, commanded by SS-Uscha. Willi Kretzschmar, seen here in Esquay-Notre-Dame on 28 June. It had arrived to block the British advance at Hill 112. The section head, SS-Ustuf. Willi Kändler, is in the motorcyclist's coat, on the right. Next to him wearing a leather jacket is Willi Kretzschmar. (W. Kretzschmar/Heimdal)

The church at Esquay-Notre-Dame, restored after the war. (E.G./Heimdal)

According to the report by SS-Oberscharführer Willy Kretzschmar, 5th Company (5./12, commanded by SS-Untersturmführer Porsch) arrived at Esquay, near Hill 112, at around 8 am. SS-Untersturmführer Willi Kändler, the head of section, describes the company's transfer from le Haut du Bosq to Esquay:

The whole of 5th Company, now led by *SS-Untersturmführer* Porsch in the point Panzer, had only around ten armoured fighting vehicles left. I had orders, the gun pointing at six o'clock, to secure the rear as *[I was]* the last panzer and to pay special attention to the paths and roads from the east. We kept watch intensely, sometimes believing we had spotted tank targets. We fired a few shells in that direction but could not make out any details. I do not remember crossing the Odon, but we probably crossed it in the early morning between le Valtru and Gavrus, and in any case, we reached the centre of Esquay without any problem, where we stayed for around half an hour. Completely exhausted from the intensive days and nights of fighting, I fell asleep on a grassy square amidst a group of houses, opposite a church. I was woken by a member of my panzer crew: 'They've already gone!' By this time it was probably around 9 am. We immediately set out with our panzer and spotted the others about 200 metres ahead of us, swinging to the right from Esquay, advancing on the hill. We also headed to the right and then turned into a small wood, three-quarters of the way up on the right. I then advanced around 100 metres and suddenly saw the brown uniforms of the

Tommies. We received heavy fire and suffered casualties, and were constantly under fire from the anti-tank guns. We were pushed back behind a hedge at the foot of Hill 112 and hid ourselves behind some rolling terrain, around 1km east of the hill. Rocket launchers were already set up there, ready to leave. I was exhausted and fell asleep.

… 29th Armoured Brigade arrive

While the panzers were positioning themselves around Hill 112, armoured vehicles from 11th Armoured Division were also heading there. The23rd Hussars were at the front and for the time being, were on their own. The first two days of the offense had been frustrating for this armoured division, as its commander General Pip Roberts, noted: 'Cooperation between the Scotsmen and the 11th Armoured Division was not very close; they rather went their separate ways.'[1] Moreover, some officers from 159 Infantry Brigade (see I. Daglish, p. 119) questioned the lack of coordination between tanks and infantry, and the fact that senior generals did not realise the effectiveness of this cooperation. But even if there were shortcomings in the British command, the nature of the land dictated its orders. The bridgehead was very narrow and the villages they had to pass through were criss-crossed by small lanes (particularly Cheux), which formed the basis for the subsequent confusion and traffic jams. In addition, the complicated system of rotation between the units only added to the mess. The battalion in the front line had to find a way to let the reserve battalion through along the narrow roads, where it was often difficult to pass each other, especially when the reserve unit was not pulling back at the same time. Just one battalion meant dozens of vehicles, but a brigade meant hundreds. Considering the small size of the bridgehead, it was a miracle that the offensive did not fall into total chaos, while south of the Odon, the crossing over the narrow valley was even smaller and thus even more difficult.

At dawn, two squadrons from the 23rd Hussars and two infantry battalions from 159 Brigade (11th Armoured Division) were still fanned out around Baron. The 23rd Hussars would later be followed by the other tank battalions from 29th Armoured Brigade and this powerful armoured force was ready to head towards its objective; the Orne. The terrain ahead was now clearer, with wheat fields leading down to the valley. A gentle slope led up imperceptibly towards Hill 112, providing an exceptional viewpoint as far as Caen in the north-east and Mont Pinçon to the south-west. The open hill was crossed by the *Chemin Haussé*, an old Roman road leading to the village of Vieux, which had been the small regional capital in the Gallo-Roman era. The terrain in this area was highly strategic and would remain the premier objective for the fighting in the weeks to come; the battle for Hill 112 would begin today!

The British tanks were certainly optimistic. The German front seemed to have exploded and for them (the British, this small valley reminded them of the Yorkshire Wolds; it was good tank country and an ideal ground for fox hunting! At 10.30 pm on the day before, the division's intelligence services provided more than encouraging information to General Roberts: 'Enemy losses for both infantry

---

1   Memoires of Pip Roberts, pp. 164

The church and chateau at Baron-sur-Odon. The 4th King's Shropshire Light Infantry were positioned here, near the chateau, by the end of 27 June and were still there early the next morning. (E.G./Heimdal)

and armoured vehicles have been elevated during the last two days, and the resources at his disposal do not appear strong enough to organise a defensive position between the Odon and Orne rivers.'

Squadrons B and C of the 23rd Hussars were at the front of the advance and spent the night south of the Odon. At 5.30 am, it received orders to resume progress once more. B Squadron advanced towards Hill 112, with C Squadron providing cover as A Squadron crossed the Odon via the bridge at Tourmauville. The lead two squadrons advanced cautiously at first, camouflaging themselves behind the houses in Baron, and then at the foot of the hill as they reached the old Roman road. But why exercise so much caution when German presence in this sector was only considered to be hypothetical? Time was precious, as the panzers of SS-Panzer-Regiment 12 were approaching from the west with the intention of surrounding Hill 112, as we know from the testimony of Willi Kändler. This was to be no a fox hunt, and an opportunity had already been lost.

The 23rd Hussars turned to the right, moving along the axis of the old Roman road and heading for Hill 112 (codename: Countess), with B Squadron to the right (west) and C Squadron to the left (east). Suddenly, they found themselves facing the Panzer IVs of 5./12: one tank was immobilized after its caterpillar tracks were hit by a 50 mm Pak shell, while Lieutenant Cochrane's tank was destroyed. The Germans also suffered the same fate: one tank destroyed and one damaged. The fighting itself took place over a 1 kilometre area (1,200 yards) and according to Ian Daglish, the time was 6 am and both Panzer IVs were declared to be Tigers. The testimony of Willi Kändler suggests it was obviously later than 6 am:

We were then reduced to four panzers. The commanders were: SS-Untersturmführers Porsch, Kunze and Kändler, and Hauptscharführer Müller. The other panzers were rendered unavailable after being destroyed in combat or for technical issues. Porsch, the company commander, wanted to attempt to take the 'Kastenwälden' and the hill summit for a second time, and so we attacked from our base in the valley straight at it. It was now midday. Very quickly my gunner, SS-Sturmann Willi Schnittfinke, told me that we had a technical problem with the gun's electrics. We had to stop and retreat behind the advancing three tanks in order to make repairs. It was a difficult situation for me. SS-Hauptcharführer Müller also remained behind Kunze and Porsch. In the lead tank, I heard Kunze's voice as he called out to the addressing the latecomers. His tank was destroyed 200 metres in front of the 'Kastenwäldchen'. The attack had failed and the three panzers returned to their starting points. The driver of Kunze's tank, SS-Sturmann Gröter, and his radio operator were able to evacuate the vehicle. Gröter was shaken and said, 'The shell fell between my legs'. (It is amazing that such details remain in my memory as I cared about the fate of my friend, Kunze). I intended to reach his panzer as soon as possible.

We can thus learn from this testimony that the destroyed Panzer IV was that of SS-Untersturmführer Helmut Kunze.

There were now the three remaining Panzer IVs from 5./12, five Panther tanks and artillery observers with some anti-tank guns. In the meantime, however, more reinforcements had arrived from other panzer companies in 2nd Battalion. At around noon, four Panzer IVs from 6./12, commanded by SS-Standartenoberjunker

SS-Uscha. Willi Kretzschmar's Panzer IV 538 (5./12) was hit during the first attack on Hill 112. Kretzschmar and corporals Schweinfest and Stephan are seen here observing the damage. The latter has just received the Iron Cross, 2nd Class. (W. Kretzschmar/Heimdal)

The Panzer IV belonging to SS-Ustuf. Helmut Kunze (section chief in 5./12) was destroyed in front of the 'Bois Carré' during the first attack. Helmut Kunze, seen here, was killed and found curled up on his seat. In this picture, he still has the rank of an SS-Standartenoberjunker (aspiring officer). (Heimdal)

(Officer Cadet) Kurt Mühlhaus, headed out to reconnoitre Hill 112, approaching it from the south-east. SS-Sturmann Heinz Nussbaumer was among the party and states that:

> The panzers were lined up in a meadow surrounded by hedges. The commanding officer told me to go take a look through the hedge. In the opposite hedge I saw enemy tanks, whose crews were basking in the sun. Enemy artillery continued to send scattered fire. I relayed my information back to the commander in panzer '648', who reported it in. At 5.15 pm, '648' was hit by a shell on the left corner of the front of the vehicle. The fire injured the drivert, the radio operator and the loader, but the tank did not burn and the company would bring it back to Germany.

This new testimony does present a few problems. The panzers in this particular area that were combat-ready numbered at least ten. As Ian Daglish reminds us, the presence of these panzers made the British believe that the Germans had numbers here in force and the men of the 23rd Hussars who were 'basking in the sun', were waiting for reinforcements. This was a grave error, because a strong attack would have likely resulted in a quick victory, after all, there were only these few panzers to fight.

However, if the British remained relatively inactive, then the Germans were even more so and could only stand guard with their meagre resources, as the British received their expected reinforcements. Seventeen-pound anti-tank guns from G Troop, 75th Antitank Regiment arrived and attempted to hit the Panzer IVs (still mistaken for Tigers), but without success due to their excellent camouflage. The two squadrons from the 23rd Hussars were now positioned a little further east, on the northern side of Hill 112, while the panzers were on the south-west side, in front of Esquay. Infantry reinforcements also arrived in the form of H Company, 8th Rifle Brigade. The infantrymen left their vehicles and dug themselves in the orchard, where the tanks were positioned. The weather had now improved and so the Hawker Typhoons could finally set off again in pursuit of the panzers, although the tanks were too well-camouflaged in the Bois Carré wood (*Kastenwäldchen* for the Germans). The British artillery sent up red smoke to mark the enemy targets, but the shots fell too short and a shell landed right in the middle of B Squadron, meaning the tank commanders quickly had to throw out yellow smoke canisters to identify themselves as 'friends'. In the rush, Colonel Harding's crew dropped a smoke canister in the turret of their tank, to the delight of the crews nearby, as the entire flank of Hill 112 became covered with yellow smoke.

Meanwhile, 29th Armoured Brigade continued to pass along the south bank of the Odon. At 6.30 am, 3rd RTR, accompanied by G Company, 8th RB, crossed the river, followed by Brigadier Roscoe's Tac HQ. The 2nd Fife and Forfar crossed at around 10.30 am and the two tank battalions proceeded to join the 23rd Hussars. The 3rd RTR headed east, but shortly after noon, a tank from A Squadron landed on a mine in Baron, and blocking the advance. After it had slowly resumed once more, the 3rd RTR took up its position east of the summit, to the left of the 23rd Hussars, while the 2nd Fife and Forfar positioned itself to the west, on the right of the 23rd Hussars, facing Esquay. Towards the middle of the day, the armoured brigade was finally complete on the northern slopes of Hill 112. Moreover, the 44th RTR (previously detached from the 4th Armoured Brigade and provisionally attached to the 29th Armoured Brigade), accompanied by B Company (8RB), was positioned to the west, ready to relieve the Fife & Forfar. And so by the middle of the day, the entire 29th Armoured Brigade, reinforced by a fourth battalion of tanks, was in position north of Hill 112, in an arc that ran from south of Gavrus to the north-eastern slopes of Hill 112. In total, there were around 200 tanks facing a dozen panzers.

Battle dress of an SS-Unterscharführer in a tank unit, typical of that worn during the hot summer days in 1944: black cap, shirt, camouflaged trousers (Erbsenmuster) with braces. (Private Collection)

However, the first clashes would already reveal the terrible fighting that was to take place on Hill 112 over the weeks to come. Apart from two wooded areas (an orchard to the north-east, on the British side, and the Bois Carré on the German side), the large hilltop was completely unobstructed, with the adversaries positioned on opposite sides. The tanks and anti-tank guns remained on the hillsides, watching their prey. Every armoured vehicle that appeared near the summit was silhouetted against the sky and faced certain destruction. The terrain surrounding Hill 112 should have facilitated the deployment of tanks in the hoped-for 'fox hunt'. The problem was that the two opponents had arrived

1. A Churchill tank looks out over the Hill 112 memorial site, recalling the terrible fighting by both tanks and infantry that took place here from 28 June 1944. (E.G./Heimdal)

2. The monument at Hill 112 dominates the battlefield. From here, the view of the surrounding area is exceptional and shows the importance of this strategic location. It marks the end of the Epsom offensive and was to become the objective for more hard fighting during long weeks to come; a true 'Norman Verdun'. (E.G./Heimdal)

almost at the same time. The Germans had arrived first, but lacking the resources to defend themselves, had at first set up an anti-tank barrage with Panther and Panzer IV tanks, as well as 88 mm guns. As the first element of surprise passed by, and realizing the treacherous nature of the terrain and ignorant of the Germans' actual numbers, which were hidden by the hill, the British initially decided to be prudent and wait for reinforcements. Meanwhile, the Germans did the same.

Colonel Harding attempted to force a route through with his two squadrons of Shermans from the 23rd Hussars, and B Squadron, commanded by Major Seymour, was the first to attempt to reach the top of the hill. The attack was unsuccessful, even though Colonel Harding directed the anti-tank fire himself. By 1.45 pm their ammunition was almost exhausted and they had to wait until nightfall to receive supplies, as the heavy trucks would otherwise be too exposed. The 3rd RTR also took on the assault, at around 3 pm, with tanks at the front followed by the half-tracks of G Company, 8th RB. Once again, the attack was a failure, and from 3.30 pm, the battalion was confined to its role of providing cover on the eastern flank, on the left of the hill. Following its losses, the 23rd Hussars retreated and were replaced in the centre by the 3rd RTR, which arrived to relieve it, and who were in turn relieved on the eastern flank by the Fife & Forfar, with the whole operation finishing at around 5 pm. As G.S.C. Bishop notes in his history of the 23rd Hussars: 'Numerically, we were overwhelmingly superior in tanks, but the position was a commanding one and the enemy, knowing its importance full well, had taken every step possible to deny it to us.'[2]

---

2   Bishop, *The History of the 23rd Hussars*, p.58

After regimental headquarters had arrived (HQ 23H), the British engaged infantry from H Company, 8 RB and, from 12.35 pm (1.35 pm for the Germans), three tank battalions (23rd Hussars, 3rd RTR, 2nd Fife and Forfar) from 29th Armoured Brigade, and the anti-tanks from G Troop (75th AT Rgt.). For their part, the Germans also strengthened their resources. In addition to the two meagre Panzers companies (5./12 and 6./12) already mentioned, Panther tanks, mainly from 2./12, also joined them (in his book, Hubert Meyer notes at the end of the day there would be thirty Panther (I./12) and Panzer IV (II./12) tanks. There were also the formidable 88 mm guns (from a Flak battery belonging to I./53) and probably a company of grenadiers. In addition, as the summit of Hill 112 was held by the Germans, their observers were able to pass on the coordinates of the British positions to the rocket launchers from 8th Werfer Brigade. Feldwebel Doorn used the field telephone to inform Hauptmann Gengl, commander of the 6th Battery, that 'the British are at the top of the hill. A Sherman tank has stopped just five metres from one of our observation posts. For God's sake don't ring – they'll hear it. We'll try and get back somehow. I do not know what has happened to Leutnant Wernike and Leutnant Nitschmann, I think they must have been overrun.' Feldwebel Doorn later went out to reconnoitre the area and would lose two men there.

The bulk of the offensive's armoured force was now blocked in front of this strategic point, and Brigadier Harvey's Tac HQ came under fire from anti-tank guns, near Esquay. His liaison officer, Lieutenant Rogers, was wounded in the face thanks to a *Nebelwerfer* rocket. In the face of this immobilized armoured force, the Germans continued to receive further reinforcements, as Willi Kändler's testimony reminds us:

Around 5 pm, we were reinforced by new panzers and moved from three to nine machines. In the late afternoon, our commander, Max Wünsche, came to our hedge and congratulated us on our fighting. He told us that thirty-six armoured vehicles had been counted in front of Hill 112. After we had pulled our panzers into the hedges, I agreed with Untersturmführer Porsch that I would establish contact on foot with our neighbour to the right, 6th Company, who were located in the hedges close by. On the way I encountered a *Schwimmwagen* from the battalion's reconnaissance group, with two men in it who had come down from the hill. They had seen a Panzer IV with its engine running and a dead soldier sitting in front of it. This had to be the panzer of Helmet Kunze. After reporting to Porsch, I drove immediately with the two *[men]* in the dark up the hill to the panzer. It really was Kunze's. In front of the panzer, the loader, Howe, was lying dead on his back, his big blue eyes open and blood on his face. Helmut Kunze sat dead in the commander's seat. The shell appeared to have hit him right in the back. On his left sat the dead gunner. The panzer's engine

Major W.H. Close commanded A Squadron, 3rd RTR. He was ordered to advance at all costs. (G.B.)

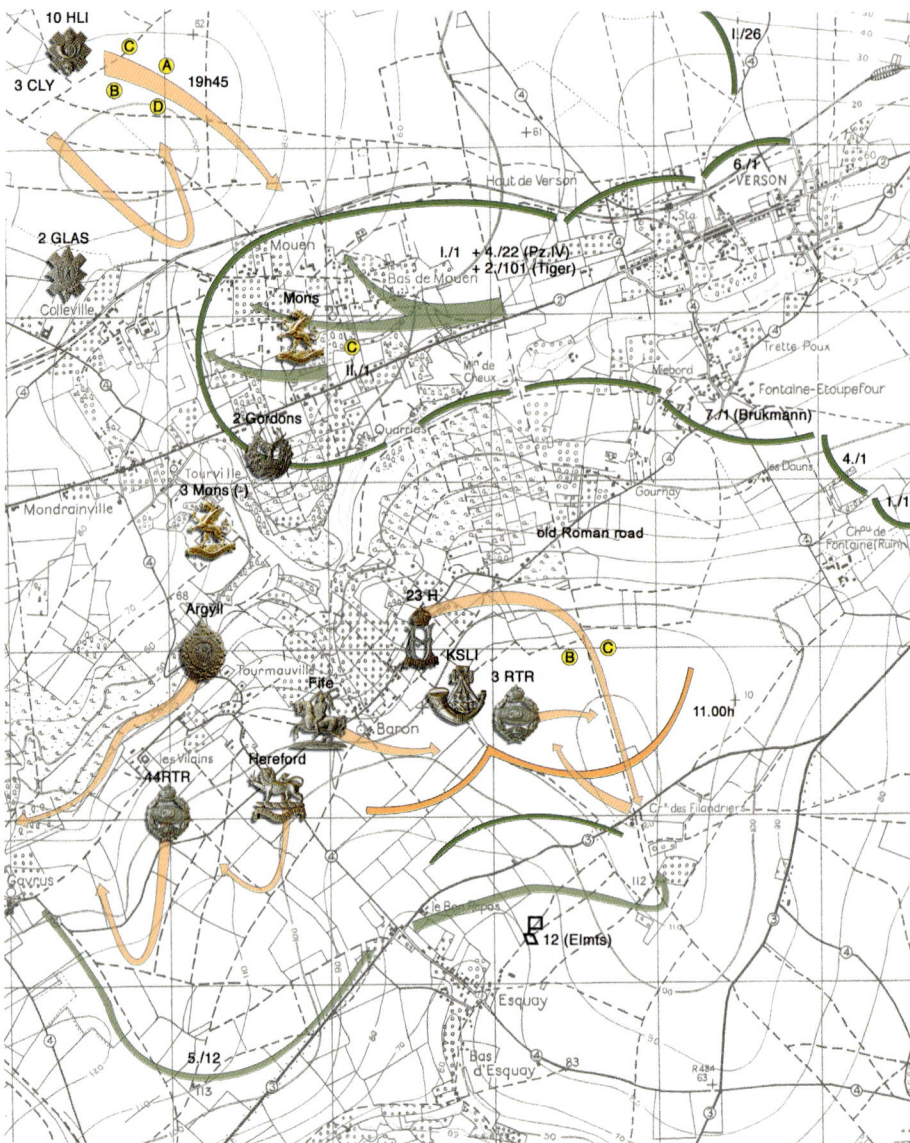

To the east of the offensive, SS-Pz.- Gren.-Rgt. 1, reinforced by 4./22, a Panzer IV company from 21. Panzer-Div., and Tiger tanks from 2./101, counter-attacked from Venoix and Verson towards Mouen, annihilating C Company (Mons) as they went. The 10 HLI, supported by 3 CLY tanks then counter-attacked at the end of the day. To the south, the 23 Hussars advanced towards Hill 112, but were met by panzers and first contact took place around 11 am. Despite reinforcements from the two other tank battalions, 3 RTR, Fife and Forfar, and even 44 RTR, the Armoured Brigade's offensive remained stuck in front of Hill 112. (L.K./Heimdal)

had been running since noon. I had the two scouts provide cover towards the enemy and I drove the panzer nearly up to our positions, but it ran out of fuel and stopped before we got there. Unterscharführer Heinz Berner, the leader of 6th Company's repair squad, pulled me the rest of the way to the hedge with his tractor. Our comrades, Kunze, Howe and the gunner, whose name I do not remember, were buried in the chateau's garden at Coultru, near that of the company commander Helmut Bando. The panzer, complete with a new turret, was back in action the following day.

Near Hill 112, the orchard became untenable for the tanks of Colonel Silvertop's 3rd RTR. Major William H. Close, who commanded its A Squadron, was ordered to advance at all costs. But Close knew it was hopeless when he saw the turret of his first tank damaged and the Sherman tank in flames. The actions of the day were over, and it was not even possible to establish precisely how many German tanks had destroyed. The war diary of 2nd Panther Company, SS-Panzer-Regiment 12, notes that, 'Striber destroyed a Churchill. Results: Twenty-one tanks have been destroyed by 2nd Company.' During the fighting, 29th Armoured Brigade had suffered seventeen killed, forty-eight wounded and two missing. The night before, it had fielded 165 Sherman and Stuart tanks and had been reinforced during the day by the 4th RTR. Forty Sherman tanks had been lost.[3]

Around 7.45 pm the shooting gradually stopped and by 10 pm, three newly arrived Tiger tanks were reported. The 3rd RTR pulled back for the night, retreating to the east of Baron. The spearhead of VIII Corps, the 29th Armoured Brigade, was stuck at a dead end; caught in a vice on three sides, with elements of the *Leibstandarte* appearing to the east (see below). Operation Epsom would now move from being offensive to defensive.

Verson and Mouen: the *Leibstandarte*'s counter-attack

From 17 June, 1. SS-Panzer-Division '*Leibstandarte* SS Adolf Hitler' (LSSAH) had arrived by rail from its garrison in Belgium, where it had undergone restructuring. Although western Belgium is relatively close to Normandy, as a result of the Allied air threat the elements of the LSSAH were forced to make a wide detour, landing at the railway stations of Reims, Soissons and Laon. Transport by road took much longer and for certain elements of the division would not be completed until 6 July. By 20 June the division's CP was located at Condé-sur-Iton, 4km east of Breteuil, in the Eure. Casualties had already been suffered along the way following attacks by Allied aircraft: five dead and thirteen wounded from II. SS-Panzergrenadier-Regiment 2 and five killed and twelve wounded from II. SS-Panzer-Artillerie-Regiment 1. On the night of 22-23 June, the first elements of the division arrived at the Forêt de Cinglais, south of Caen, near the Caen-Falaise road. This elite division, originally formed from Hitler's regiment of bodyguards (hence the name; *Leibstandarte* Adolf Hitler), had grown considerably from its original beginnings and had suffered heavy casualties on the Eastern Front. Following the major losses to the *Hitlerjugend* Division, the LSSAH suffered a further reduction in manpower as soldiers, as well as officers, were reassigned there, a situation only exacerbated by the losses suffered during the previous winter on the Russian Front. The 'restructured' division that arrived on the Normandy

---

3   T. Saunders, *Operation Epsom*, p.132.

Front was no longer the old *Leibstandarte*: the *Hitlerjugend* Division was now the superior division, thanks to many of its officers and the combativeness of its very young soldiers.

Sometime after 4 pm the previous day, the head of I. SS-Panzerkorps, SS-Obergruppenführer Dietrich, informed Generaloberst Dollmann (commander of 7th Army) of his intention to launch a counter-attack on both sides of the RN175 road (the main road from Villers-Bocage to Caen). The aim was to use one of the *Leibstandarte*'s two grenadier regiments, SS-Panzergrenadier-Regiment 1, commanded by SS-Obersturmbannführer Albert Frey, who would attack VIII Corps's flank on the east, while the *Kampfgruppe* Weidinger attacked from the south-west. VIII Corps would thus be caught in a pincer movement, as the Germans awaited the arrival of II. SS-Panzerkorps. The operation was initially planned to take place during the night, following the arrival of the staff of SS-Obersturmbannführer Frey (SS-Pz.-Gren.-Rgt 1.), SS-Hauptsturmführer Lotter (1st Battalion) and SS-Sturmbannführer Max Hansen (2nd Battalion). SS-Obersturmbannführer Weidenhaupt (3rd Battalion) was still assembling south of Caen, in the May-sur-Orne and Louvigny sector.

However, the attack would not take place during the night and was instead pushed back towards noon. It was to be conducted on both sides of the RN175, with 1st Battalion (Lotter) on the right and 2nd Battalion (Max Hansen) on the left, with Mouen as its objective. The main aim of the attack was to take out the British flanks on either side of Tourville and then to isolate its forces that had crossed the Odon.

SS-Obersturmbannführer Frey received his orders from SS-Oberführer Kurt Meyer, commander of the *Hitlerjugend*, and immediately pointed out that he would be unable to carry them out without the support of heavy weaponry, asking him instead to wait for the arrival of the LSSAH artillery. Kurt Meyer replied that the 12. SS-Panzer-Division would support the attack, with additional support provided by a Panzer IV company from 21. Panzer-Division.

However, before SS-Obersturmbannführer Frey's grenadiers had even left their starting point, British artillery fire was already raining down on them, including that of the Royal Navy's 380 mm heavy guns. As for the support he expected, Frey saw none arriving and would not meet a single liaison officer from the *Hitlerjugend* artillery. This meant that his men would have to face the British tanks and their machine guns alone. As 2nd Battalion advanced through Verson (7 km west of Caen), its commander, Max Hansen, was wounded for the ninth time.

Venoix was the regiment's assembly area and we will now follow the progress of a company from 1st Battalion (Lotter), as it advanced to the right, north of the RN175. The testimony is that of Private Reif (2nd Company, commanded by SS-Obersturmführer Rink), as his battalion progressed west of Verson, towards Mouen:

> We were up against well-established British trenches. We circumvented them by using sunken roads and captured our opponents in a quick attack. The British wore an emblem of a bull *[11th Armoured Division]*. Our group leader was wounded in this first attack. During the next attack on the left of the railway line, our group was hit by our own Werfers *[rocket launchers belonging to the 83rd Werfer Regiment]*. Previously abandoned positions

provided good protection. These shots from our own side were somewhat demoralising, but we didn't worry about our losses. We then proceeded to position ourselves along the railway line where we met the advanced lookouts from the Werfer battery, who were on the radio enthusiastically calling for the Werfer fire to continue.

The testimony of Gerhard Franz, the liaison officer with 3rd Company's (SS-Hauptsturmführer Maurer) Command Group (*Kompanietrupp*), on the right of 2./1, provides further insight into the attack of 1st Battalion:

> The right flank was wide open towards the airfield *[at Carpiquet]*. Three Panzer IVs *[4th Company, Panzer Regiment 22, 21. Panzer-Division, who acted as support]*, which we welcomed during our advance, could only roll in single file along the railway line because the terrain was divided up by hedges and visibility was thus reduced. One of the panzers *[the leading one, No. 412]* destroyed three British tanks at a short distance. They came out of a forest road on the left and tried to retreat by moving backwards. Our group, with SS-Unterscharführer Ziegenhart, was already at the top of the crossroads, which were protected from the railway by a hedge. Shrapnel from an enemy tank shell hit Ziegenhart in the head and stuck in his steel helmet. However, the British had to take shelter in a small ditch when their tanks exploded and we captured ten men with two machine guns. We then climbed onto the railway tracks and saw the Brits jumping forward over the rails. The advance of our Panzer IV was blocked by burning enemy tanks. They had to clear the railway embankment, but the hanging telephone wires were caught in their tracks.

According to Werner Kortenhaus, the radio operator in panzer No. 422, among the British dead he could hear a radio station playing dance music.

> Our attack stopped in the face of some strong resistance. After about an hour, in the midst of the enemy's positions, we found two deserters, one of whom had been wounded by a bullet in the buttocks. Then we suffered accurate artillery fire which was directed by an artillery observation plane. Our 4th Section (heavy), whose mortars were in the former British position, near the level-crossing keeper's house, suffered particularly heavy losses. The counter-attack came from the north as the artillery continued to take us to hand. Several tanks then arrived, firing non-stop as the infantry advanced between them in groups of ten to twelve men. After a few bursts, they veered off towards the southwest.[4]

Covered on its northern flank by 1st Battalion (Lotter), 2nd Battalion advanced south of the main road, taking Verson and managing to advance into Mouen. Two Panther tanks also supported this attack.

---

4   These two testimonies are taken from the official history of the *Leibstandarte*, Volume IV/1 by R. Lehmann and R. Tiemann, (Munin, 1986).

C Company, 3rd Monmouthshire, was in position at Mouen and would be crushed by the attack by SS-Pz.- Gren.-Rgt. 1.

In Mouen, 1st Battalion was confronted by an isolated company (C Company) from 3rd Monmouthshire (one of 11th Armoured Division's infantry battalions) and tanks from the 3rd Country of London Yeomanry (3 CLY), one of the tank battalions from 4th Armoured Brigade. Lieutenant Kendall, section chief with the 3 Monmouths, was in the process of consolidating his infantry's position, giving out his orders before sitting down near a ruined house to drink tea and consult his map. Shortly afterwards some of his men came running from the other end of the village, shouting that the Jerries were coming. Kendall barely had time to get up before the Germans were already upon them. Panzers and half-tracks fired their machine guns at them, as the men tried to escape and take cover in the buildings, which collapsed amidst the explosion of the shells. The Germans were all around them and the noise was terrible. Lieutenant Kendall tried to protect himself behind a wall but was hit; he played dead and remained there throughout the subsequent British bombardment, and was later discovered during a counter-attack by 10 HLI. Three days later, he arrived back in England where his leg was amputated. One of the soldiers in his company, Private Evans, remarks that the men were not properly buried, with many being killed or wounded by the shelling. When a light reconnaissance vehicle from 3 CLY arrived, Evans and his companions shouted at him to leave due to the German panzers. It remained and was consequently hit and caught fire.

C Company, 3 Mons, were overrun in Mouen by II./1. The company commander, Major Richards, and fourteen men managed to pull back, but twenty-three others were killed and the rest of the company was captured by the *Leibstandarte*'s battalion. Private Edwards was among the prisoners as they tried to take care of their wounded as best as they could, with one of them being carried on a door. Edwards remembered that the 'SS General' arrived and saw that his soldiers were taking cigarettes from the British prisoners. He became angry and pointed his finger at their shoulder badge displaying the bull of the 11th Armoured Division. He then said something else and the cigarettes were restored. His name was Kurt (in this case Kurt Meyer, commander of the HJ). Private Edwards, who witnessed the scene, noted, 'He was a gentleman'.

After taking Mouen, around 5 pm the fighting calmed down and allowed the men from 4./22 to open their tank hatches. The *Leibstandarte*'s next objective was Colleville. The 2nd Glasgow Highlanders (2 Glas H, 46 Brigade, 15th Division) held the village, as well as the vital road leading south to the bridge at Tourmauville. As we will now see, other elements of 2nd Battalion also infiltrated the Odon valley in an attempt to cut off the Scottish bridgehead. On 2nd Battalion's left flank, SS-Hauptsturmführer Bruckmann's 7th Company crossed Le Rosel, then advanced along the Odon valley and reached a place called La Bruyère, to the south of the Commune of Mouen, before reconnoitring the area towards Baron-sur-Odon shortly before nightfall. A powerful counter-attack was then carried out by the 10th Highland Light Infantry (227 Brigade), supported by tanks.

This attack was carried out in 'open formation' and began at 7.45 pm, with A Company on the left and D Company on the right, followed by C and B Companies respectively. The companies were flanked by Sherman tanks from the 3rd County of London Yeomanry (3 CLY). The Highlands infantry then moved forward through the wheat fields, which were strewn with a few bushes, shooting and 'shouting like madmen' as they advanced, according to Private Arkwright. As the men from the 10 HLI moved through the high corn away from Cheux, they were caught by machine gun fire as they arrived at the railway line. The unit's log notes that at 8.15 pm, the tanks were taken in hand by anti-tank guns on the left flank and a Sherman tank was destroyed. Machine gun fire coming from houses and the railway, crackled over the wheat fields. Companies A and B, as well as the battalion's staff, were nailed to the ground, unable to advance further. Five Panther tanks were destroyed, as well as three Shermans. On the right, companies D and B advanced to the right of the railway line, towards a wood. Before reaching it, they came under machine gun fire from Panther tanks that were hidden in an orchard. The commander of C Company was wounded and two of his subalterns were killed. Unable to advance, they had no choice but to pull back along a sunken road.

Private Arkwright had been on the right flank of this advance:

It was fantastic but terrible when we saw all the bodies of our friends and those of the Jerries in their camouflage outfits. Some had been killed, others were wounded. Some were opening fire or trying to flee. We gave no quarter and fired in all directions to gain maximum effect. We were completely fired up. When we reached their forward position, we came under fire and went to ground. I was completely worn out and sweaty. I stared at all those poor dead Jocks and feeling bad, I started screaming.

The Panzer IVs from 4./22 (21. Panzer Division) were also involved in this counter-attack by the Scots. Panzer 422 (whose radio operator, Werner Kortenhaus, provides a testimony of the engagement) was hit on the turret, causing it to jam. What's more, due to the damage to the skirts (*Schürzen*), the gun could no longer be manoeuvred, and so the panzer had to leave the field and head for a sunken road where they could be removed. Returning to its position, Panzer 422 was once again hit by shells, which ripped along its armour leaving dark blues traces. Unteroffizier Weinz's Panzer 413 had a broken caterpillar track and thanks to the protection of the SS grenadiers, was able to fix it before moving back into line. The commander of Panzer 421, Unteroffizier Eichler, was in the turret and had his head blown off by a shell. The crew then had to pull back with the commander's body still in the turret. Feldwebel Korflur's Panzer 425 was suddenly grappling with the British tanks, which fired smoke bombs to restrict his vision so that only the shadows of the tanks wer discernible. As it changed direction, the engine suffered damage. Nearby, the SS grenadiers were engaged in close combat with the Scots. Soon, the panzer came under fire from Mouen and after being hit by two shells, it caught fire. Luckily, the crew managed to evacuate, even though some of them were wounded. Finally, Stabsfeldwebel Niewöhner's Panzer 434 was also put out of action, while Panzers 413, 421, and 422 with a damaged caterpillar, were also damaged. During this engagement, 4./22 had lost its eleventh and twelfth tanks, including those in Mouen. There were now only five damaged Panzer IVs to be fixed at the company's repair site, which was set up near Cagny, east of Caen.[5]

The counter-attack had forced the Germans to be on the defensive, and fierce fighting would take place throughout the night in this sector. However, the 10 HLI were unable to advance further and would have to dig in for the night, with their new position only a few hundred meters from where it had started from.

Elements of 2nd Battalion would pull back during the night and occupy a defensive line from Maltot to Eterville, with outposts at Fontaine-Etoupefour. In addition, the anti-tank section of the regiment's 13th (heavy) Company positioned its guns along the road leading from Bretteville-sur-Odon to Carpiquet. SS-Obersturmbannführer Frey's regimental CP was at Bretteville-sur-Odon, meaning II./1 held the following defensive line: railway line/crossing (north of Mouen) - western Mouen - Mouen quarry - Le Moulin Gournay (commune of Fontaine-Etoupefour). The regiment's attack had begun well, as it took Verson then Mouen, annihilating a British company in the process. But after this good start, the regiment was only able to put into position two battalions, with few heavy weapons, which were reinforced by a few tanks. It would now simply mark time, having pushed deep into the eastern flank of the British bridgehead. An attack as effective as this to the west, would have completely cut off and surrounded the bridgehead south of the Odon. On this day, the *Leibstandarte* had seriously threatened Montgomery's offensive.

Grainville and le Valtru

Having learned that Grainville had been abandoned by the Germans, Lieutenant Colonel Villiers decided to take the village at dawn. He sent B Company, 9 Cameronians to provide support and launched companies C and D to attack the flanks, supported by B Squadron, 9th RTR. However, this first attack was pushed back by German artillery. A second attack was planned at 11 am, but this time it would be a frontal attack, preceded by a ten-minute artillery barrage. It began at 12.15 pm and was successful; the Cameronians took up positions in the village, but, as shall be seen later, soon came under a German counter-attack.

In addition, Brigadier Barber sent in his two other battalions from 46th Highland Brigade to reinforce VIII Corps' flanks. The 2nd Glasgow Highlanders consequently left the sector around Cheux to join that of Mondrainville, where it stood in reserve before being sent in to Colleville to block the attack by SS-Panzergrenadier-Regiment 1. The 7th Seaforth Highlanders, in position on the Ring Contour 100, north of the railway, headed back to Colleville before advancing on the hamlet of Valtru (along the road leading to the bridge at Gavrus), in order to control it.

The bridge at Gavrus was also held by VIII Corps and at the end of the previous day Lieutenant Colonel Tweedie had sent patrols in its direction, who had reported back that the bridge was clear. New patrols from A Company (Lieutenant Desmond Morris) and B Company (Lieutenant Bill Edwards) were now dispatched and at 2 pm they sent radio messages signalling that not all the gangways and the Gavrus

---

5   See J.-C. Perrigault, *21st Panzer Division*, p.339

bridge were defended. The 2nd Argyll, whose presence was no longer necessary at the bridgehead in Tourmauville, was immediately ordered to leave for Gavrus, with Major Hugh Fyfe's C Company in the lead. While clashes took place south of Tourmauville, a route via a forest road passed unnoticed by the Germans, who were nevertheless nearby. The road itself looked out over the valley, along the edge of a ridge towards Gavrus. Progression through the forest was extremely difficult; the Lloyd Carriers even had to tow the 6-pound anti-tank guns along the forest road, which were then used to hold and defend the Gavrus bridge.

The *Kamfgruppe* Weidinger counter-attacks

While the 11th Armoured Division remained stuck in front of Hill 112 and SS-Panzergrenadier-Regiment 1 were dug in up to Mouen, on VIII Corps' eastern flank, at Colleville, another attack tried to push into its western flank in order to cut it in two. The road network was in the Germans' favour because it lay mainly on an east-west line, with two main axes cutting off the offensive, while the British only had a network of largely unpaved roads.

To the west, the 49th Division's 'polar bears' would re-launch their offensive at dawn by firing an artillery barrage at 6.50 am, followed by an attack by the Tyne Scots on Brettevillette. After the barrage, the attack had reached its objective one hour later. Meanwhile, 11 DLI were attacking south from Rauray to Ring Contour 110, which was then taken. The Tyne Scots then proceeded to come under counter-attacks from III./26, which would soon be reinforced by the *Kampfgruppe* Weidinger.

At 9 pm on 26 June 26, Feldmarschall Rommel authorised the 7th Army to engage a battalion of panzers from 2. Panzer-Division (which, as we have seen, were partly engaged on 27 June, at Cheux), and two battalions from 2. SS-Panzer-Division 'Das Reich', in a counter-attack. This division was ordered to form a *Kampfgruppe* in the afternoon of 26 June. It was made up of the staff from SS-Panzergrenadier-Regiment 4 '*Der Führer*', with the regiment's 13th, 14th, 15th and 16th companies mounted on half-tracked vehicles, as well as the regiment's 1st Battalion (I. / DF) and 1st Battalion, SS-Panzergrenadier-Regiment 3 '*Deutschland*' (I. / D). The *Kampfgruppe*, under the command of SS-Obersturmbannführer Otto Weidinger, arrived at Jurques

SS equipment found in Baron-sur-Odon, in 1987. (Private Collection)

towards midnight on 26 June. From there, it joined the Panzer-Lehr-Division and reached the area south of Monts-en-Bessin at dawn on 27 June. Weidinger was informed of the situation at the Panzer-Lehr-Division's CP at Monts-en-Bessin. The head of the division, Bayerlein, believed that a daytime attack was not possible. The *Kampfgruppe* Weidinger (two reinforced battalions), was placed under the command of the PLD, and on the night of 27-28 June, joined Regiment 26 (*Kampfgruppe* Mohnke). It was to be reinforced by a company of Panther tanks from I./3, but its progression was spotted by British planes.

The counter attack by KG Weidinger was launched in the middle of the day, with Mondrainville as its objective. I./*Deutschland* counterattacked at Brettevillette, while the Tyneside Scottish, supported by Shermans from B Squadron, 4th/7th Dragoon Guards, also attacked the hamlet. At 11.30 am, the shock was brutal, and the fighting made all the more confusing as the area was surrounded by *bocage*. The Tyneside Scottish had to retreat after suffering heavy losses: 126 men, which was the equivalent of a company. Under the subsequent artillery barrage, I./D also suffered heavy losses and was unable to progress further (it was only a reinforced battalion, equivalent in resources to the Tyneside Scottish).

Born on 27 May 1914, SS-Obersturmbannführer Otto Weidinger was an officer and section chief in the *Standarte Deutschland*'s 3rd Battalion from 1936. He showed his great qualities as an officer during the Polish campaign and was a tactical expert. He took command of SS-Panzergrenadier-Regiment '*Deutschland*' in July 1943. He obtained the Knight's Cross of the Iron Cross on 21 April 1944, the oak leaves on 27 December 1944 and the swords on 6 May 1945, the 150th soldier to do so. (Heimdal)

The counter-attacks by *Kampfgruppe* Weidinger on Brettevillette, Grainville and le Valtru. (L.K./Heimdal)

Further to the south, I./*Der Führer*, supported by Panther tanks, attacked Grainville which had just been occupied by the 9 Cameronians; something SS-Obersturmbannführer Weidinger was unaware of. He wanted to continue on towards the hamlet of le Valtru and cut off all access to the bridge at Gavrus. The 9 Cameronians were supported by B Squadron, 9th RTR, but the Churchill tanks had great difficulty navigating through the *bocage*, where the fighting was more penetrating through the vegetation, rather than a frontal assault. Lieutenant Teddy Mott's Churchill was hit and caught fire. He managed to escape, but his leg was torn off and he subsequently had to have the other amputated as well. The 9 Cameronians and the tanks managed to hold the eastern part of Grainville against the attacks by I./DF. Further south, I./DF was counter-attacked by the 7 Seaforth, which prevented it from reaching le Valtru. In difficult terrain and with limited resources, not to mention the British artillery fire, the KG Weidinger was unlikely to succeed in its counter-attack, and only managed to stop VIII Corps to the east of Brettevillette and in front of Grainville.

On this day (28 June), the *Hitlerjugend* recorded the following losses: I./26 suffered 4 killed and 7 wounded; II./26 had 1 killed, 2 wounded and 2 missing; III./26 had 1 killed and 4 wounded; 2 killed in the Engineer Battalion; 4 killed and 8 injured for the reconnaissance group; 7 killed and 17 wounded for SS-Panzer-Regiment 12; 3 killed and 16 wounded for the artillery regiment. These losses amounted to 22 killed, 54 wounded and 2 missing, meaning 78 men in total. These were relatively light when compared to those of VIII Corps, although those from other units, such as elements from Panzer Regiment 22, SS-Panzergrenadier-Regiment 1 and KG Weidinger must also be added. Losses among VIII Corps actually reached 311 men, including 68 killed, 221 wounded and 22 missing. However, its manpower was increased to 3,514 officers and 65,000 men.

Eterville sector, 29 June

This report by Sergeant Laing shows men from the 8 Rifle Brigade (11th Armoured Division) south-east of the bridgehead near Eterville, north of Hill 112.

1. L/Corporal Albert Ellis, from Staines, and driver Reg Girling, from Dalston, are preparing a meal on a gas-stove. Reg Girling is opening a Compo Ration box, which was designed to provide a day's worth of food for fourteen men. (IWM B 6186)

2. Men from a mechanized company from 8 Rifle Brigade are seen taking a rest from digging a trench. They have just been given letters and newspapers brought by one of the trucks used to transport water to the front lines. Behind them is an American half-track M5, which could carry thirteen men. (IWM B 6194)

3. Prisoners are taken to the rear. These men are Flak gun crew members and Waffen-SS soldiers. (IWM B 6189)

4. Germans captured in the area are waiting to be taken to a gathering centre. The corporal seated in the foreground, on the left, belongs to one of the Flak regiments from III./Sturm- Flak-Korps. The one sitting on the right is a Waffen-SS soldier. The number 54 (white on a red background) on the right-hand side of the tank denotes the Armoured Brigade's Motor Battalion, the 8 Rifle Brigade. (IWM B6188)

6

The Fourth Day – Thursday 29 June

MK II helmet from Army Dental Corps, 43rd Wessex Division.

The *Leibstandarte* must be pushed back

Following the successes of SS-Obersturmbannführer Frey's regiment the day before, its new position deep in the British flank was a major threat, and so it had to be pushed back. Two brigades from 43rd Wessex Division, 214 Brigade and then 129 Brigade, were to be launched in a counter-attack and lined up three battalions: 4th Battalion The Somerset Light Infantry, and 4th and 5th Battalions The Wiltshire Regiment. These were fresh units, while the Wessex Division now had to protect VIII Corps' entire eastern flank. The counter-attack would be launched at dawn.

After the HLI's failure the night before, Brigadier Essame's 214 Brigade had been ordered to counter-attack, hoping to retake Mouen in a night time offensive. Brigadier Essame had gone to reconnoitre Colleville, on the heels of the HLI, and had witnessed its failures and losses. In a terrain divided by hedges, and in the middle of a disorganized HLI, a counter-attack would only have increased confusion and so the project was suspended. Brigadier Essame had set up his headquarters at 3.30 am, near Gaule, in the light of a storm lamp. His brigade was to be engaged on 129 Brigade's left flank and would attack first, then providing cover for the latter's subsequent attack.

214 Brigade retake Mouen

For the preliminary attack, Brigadier Essame aligned one of his three battalions from 214 Brigade, 1 Worcesters, with companies B (on the right) and C (on the left), followed by D and A. They were positioned due south, north of the railway, then Mouen. The decision and set-up were made so quickly that the Commanding Officer of 1 Worcesters, Lieutenant Colonel Harrison, and Major Alexander did not have time to reconnoitre the area. H Hour was set for 8 am, with Mouen to be taken by 9 am. Despite this, the attack had been meticulously planned on the map, in coordination with the artillery. The latter opened a 30-minute barrage of explosive shells and smoke bombs on the railway line, which was considered sufficient time for an advance in open terrain. The barrage would then move towards the main road for four minutes and would be supported by 4.2-inch mortar fire from the 7th Somerset Light Infantry (another of the brigade's battalions), which would fire phosphorus smoke bombs, primarily on the Bas de Mouen. Meanwhile, machine guns would fire at the Carpiquet airfield to pin down elements from the HJ Division, and make them believe that another attack was possible.

Lieutenant Colonel Harrison directed his two leading companies via the electric pylons, with each company advancing on either side of this line; B on the right and C on the left. A Company would follow behind and guard the flank. The attack started on time and the companies advanced in perfect order through the corn, as if on a training exercise. During the advance, the Worcesters came under shrapnel fire, but the losses remained minimal and the 'open formation' was maintained. Blinded by the artificial fog, the Germans could not discern the real meaning of the attack and, believing it to come along the same axis as the evening before, opened fire in the wrong direction. A few shots coming from the railway were quickly suppressed before the *bocage* began; the network of roads, houses and farms scattered among it, often behind large walls, slowing the previously rapid advance. However, the Worcesters followed the artillery barrage as closely as possible and arrived at Mouen while the grenadiers of the *Leibstandarte* were still seeking shelter from the artillery fire. Fighting now took place against the SS grenadiers, as well as a number of panzers which had been camouflaged in the sunken roads. The Worcesters were only armed with PIATs, which were not particularly effective anti-tank weapons. Weighing 16 kilograms, the PIAT (Projector Infantry Anti-Tank) worked effectively at 100 metres against a tank and 250 metres against a house or a small building. It was the British equivalent of the German *Panzerfaust*. In this instance, the *bocage* around Mouen worked in their favour and the Worcesters reported that they had destroyed a Tiger tank by firing at its side, although it is difficult to say which Tiger could have been destroyed here. As SS-Hauptsturmführer Rolf Möbius (commander of 1./s.SS-Panzer-Abteilung 101) recalls for 29 June, 'There would never be a massive engagement of Tigers because our panzers had been dispatched everywhere. I speak from my point of view. It's easy to understand if I say that I only saw the command post twice because my vehicle could be anywhere, at anytime.'[1] However, we know that at the time 2./101 was engaged in the Mouen sector, whereas 3./101 was at Rauray. In his book, Patrick Agte gives an example of 'self-sacrifce' by a German tanker operator, probably located in the Mouen sector, Lance Corporal Erlander:

> … a small, blonde Alsatian who drove SS-Untersturmführer Hantusch's tank in 2nd Company. When Hantusch's Tiger was hit in the running gear and immobilised, Erlander wanted to leave the tank to repair the damage. Hantusch forbade him to get out under enemy fire. Erlander nevertheless climbed out and tried to restore the Tiger's mobility. The tank was hit again; nothing was found of the courageous driver. The crew of the platoon commander's tank were able to follow the drama over the radio. It and the company commander's tank were equipped with the Fu. 800 radio, which also allowed them to monitor radio traffic from superior units to the battalion and company. The radios also picked up music programmes ('Lilli Marleen', German folk concert at 10 pm). The remaining tanks were equipped with the Fu. 500 radio set.[2]

1   Agte, Patrick, *Michael Wittman and the and the Panzer Commanders of the Leibstandarte*, p.305

2   Ibid.

1 Worcesters.

7 Somerset LI.

At 11 am, the Worcesters reached their objective shortly before the Caen/Villers-Bocage main road. The village of Mouen presented a spectacle of wartime devastation; the whole area was strewn with destroyed objects, as well as the corpses of soldiers from the Monmouths and the HLI, who had been killed the day before. In contrast, due to the speed and effectiveness of their attack, the Worcesters suffered relatively few casualties. Montgomery praised this success, calling it 'the finest single action of the war'. The 7 Somerset LI then advanced behind them through Mouen and continued the attack to the main road without significant losses. Following the success of the Worcesters and the entire 214 Brigade, the conditions were ready for 129 Brigade's attack.

129 Brigade, which had been engaged at Manvieu, was initially relieved by 2 Guards Brigade, before moving to the right of 214 Brigade. It was supported by a squadron from the Grays and advanced with two battalions at the front; the 5 Wiltshire to the right and the 4 Somerset Light Infantry (4 SLI) to the left. The advance began in the open ground

On 29 June Rifleman Reg Oates, from Walthamstow, and Rifleman James Woodward, from Tottenham, are seen preparing to fire a PIAT. This weapon had less power and was less efficient than the German *Panzerfaust*, however, its short-range combat abilities meant that it was more useful in the *bocage*, near Mouen. This photograph by Sergeant Laing was actually taken south-west of Caen. (IWM)

up to the railway. From there, it was hit by mortar fire coming from Colleville, on the right, before entering the *bocage* landscape, west of Mouen. The front of the brigade reached the main road, lined with houses, after being hit by mortar fire up to this point. It then descended into the Odon valley through wooded and sloping ground. However, there was no bridge, although at this point the Odon was more of a powerful stream than a small river. Even so, the Carriers and anti-tank guns were unable to cross. The sappers of 5 Wiltshire set to work immediately to establish a crossing, using branches and earth. Meanwhile, on the right, the 4 SLI faced more difficult terrain. The ground here was wooded, rocky, and even steeper, and in a few days' time, this idyllic place would come to be called 'Death Valley'.

The gains made by the *Leibstandarte* were consequently reduced to almost nothing, as the tip of the breakthrough was submerged under the barrage of 43rd Wessex Division's two brigades. Around noon, 6./1 fell back to Verson and 7./1 to Fontaine-Etoupefour, even though SS grenadiers continued to reconnoitre the wooded Odon valley. A British attack was pushed back south of Fontaine-Etoupefour, but SS-Obertsturmbannführer Frey's regiment no longer posed any real threat to VIII Corps.

The Hohenstaufen attack

The day's attack was planned for 6 am, but delays in the units' advance towards the front meant that it was postponed, and actually pushed back to 2 pm because of enemy aerial activity. Time was needed in order to carry out sufficient reconnaissance, and 9. SS-Panzer-Division *Hohenstaufen* (5th Company) first had to protect itself from aerial attacks before continuing its route towards Estry. It came under further attack near Le Mesnil as the Allied fighters plunged into reconnaissance vehicles and delayed their progress towards the front line.

Furthermore, during this critical phase SS-Obergruppenführer Hausser had left his role as commander of II. SS-Panzerkorps to take over that of the 7th Army following the death of Generaloberst Dollmann the day before. Indeed, it was almost a game of 'musical chairs': SS-Gruppenführer Bittrich took over command of II.SS-Panzerkorps, replacing SS-Obergruppenführer Rise, and SS-Standartenführer Müller, who had commanded SS-Panzergrenadier-Regiment 20, now took command of the *Hohenstaufen*.

At 11 am, II. SS-Panzerkorps reported to *Panzergruppe* West that it would be in position by noon. One of the *Hohenstaufen*'s two grenadier regiments, SS-Panzergrenadier-Regiment 19, was only in position by 10 am, while SS-Panzergrenadier-Regiment 20 was

SS-Obergruppenführer Paul Hausser left his command of II. SS-Panzerkorps to take up that of the 7th Army following the death (heart attack or suicide?) of Generaloberst Dollmann at 10 am the previous day. Dollman's death shook the entire German chain of command at a critical juncture.

not in position until 12.15 pm. At 12.45, the corps reported its situation, stating that it could not attack without the support of the Panzer-Lehr-Division on its left flank, and at 1.15 pm, it announced that it would be unable to launch the counter-attack until 2.30 pm.

The attack was to be launched to the west of the corridor, primarily on the west-east axis of the RN175 road. The objective was to cut off VIII Corps by joining SS-Panzergrenadier-Regiment 1 and surrounding the advanced elements in the Allied bridgehead, which were mainly those of the 11th Armoured Division. The main attack would be led by SS-Panzergrenadier-Regiment 19 (SS-Obersturmbannführer Zollhöfer), supported on its left flank by the other infantry regiment, SS-Panzergrenadier-Regiment 20 and the *Kampfgruppe* Weidinger. However, General O'Connor had reinforced the corridor's flank, which had now been entrusted entirely to the 15th Scottish Division, supported on its right flank (in the Rauray sector), by the 49th West Riding Division. The fight would be tough, with the *Hohenstaufen* offensive unlikely to succeed in the *bocage* terrain, against superior forces and under the threat of allied artillery.

On the right wing of the offensive, on the south side, were two battalions from the 19th Regiment: I./19 (Hagenlocher) on the left (at Grainville), and

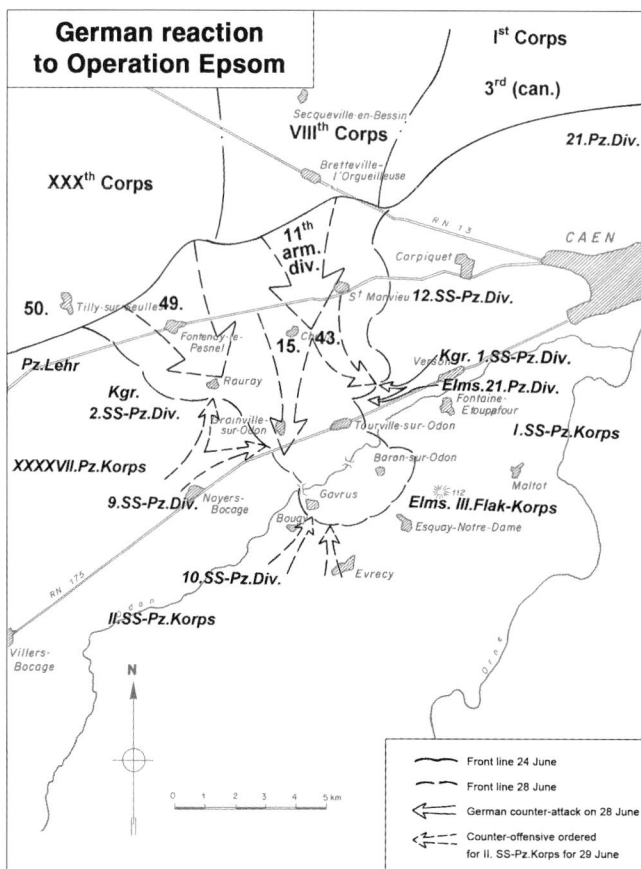

Too late! On 29 June, following the arrival of KG Weidinger and SS-Pz.- Gren.-Rgt. 1 the previous day, II. SS-Panzerkorps was now lined up with two armoured divisions. The Epsom offensive was caught in a steel vice and suspended. (Heimdal)

II./19 (SS-Hauptsturmführer Recke) on the right (attacking le Valtru and the RN175 road), which were to attack at 2 pm. On the right, II./19 were up against the 7 Seaforth Highlanders whose C Company were blocking the way on the RN175, in front of le Valtru. Two Panzer IVs led the attack and destroyed two anti-tank guns. C Company was overwhelmed and the remaining men headed for le Valtru, where they reported the death of their company commander, Major Telfer. Lieutenant Woodall and Captain Hendry were also killed. The latter, from A Company, died of his injuries after trying to stop the panzers with a PIAT. Approximately 200 grenadiers advanced on le Valtru, but artillery support was ordered by 7 Seaforth and the accurate fire from the guns of the 531 Field Battery RA stopped the grenadiers' attack. The German artillery replied with its own fire, thus allowing II./19 to resume its attack. This time it advanced with four Panzers IVs at the front, who advanced beyond the Grainville/Gavrus crossroads road, followed by a company of grenadiers. The carrier of 7 Seaforth's second in command, Major Johnson, was hit by a panzer shell, which crushed his leg. The Panzer IVs arrived at Mondrainville, in the middle of the 46 Brigade's reserve battalion, the 2 Glasgow Highlanders (Lieutenant Colonel Grant), supported by Churchill tanks. Lieutenant Colonel Grant led the fight back, putting anti-tank guns in to the battery and guiding their fire from one to the other, successfully destroying the four Panzer IVs. Corporal Cunningham distinguished himself by twice firing on a Panzer IV with a PIAT, with the second shot hitting the rear of the panzer. The four

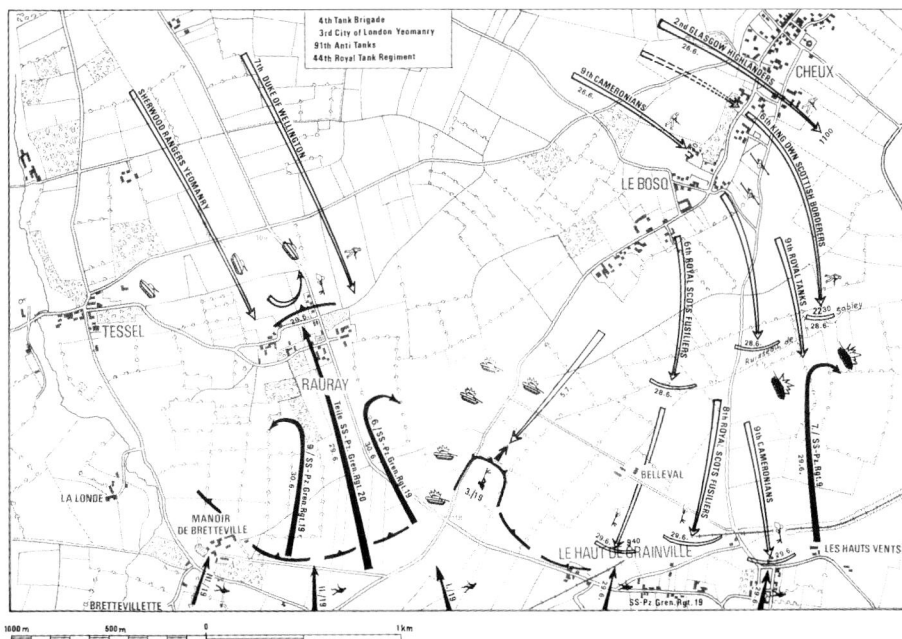

Herbert Fürbringer, who published a history of the *Hohenstaufen*, used this map to show the division's attacks on 29 and 30 June (and beyond), in the area around Rauray and Grainville. It shows the recapture of Rauray, as well as Grainville, with the support of StuGs from 7./9, which has been largely ignored by British sources. (H.F./Heimdal)

panzers burned for a long time; a testimony to the success of the 2 Glasgow Highlanders, while Lieutenant Colonel Grant would be decorated with the DSO for this action. The offensive on the RN175 road was consequently stopped, but the battalion had lost two company commanders and its leader, who was also wounded in the leg.

Five hundred metres to the north, the 19th Regiment's other battalion, I./19, advanced over the fields with Grainville as its target. The village was firmly held by the 9 Cameronians after the failure of KG Weidinger's attack the previous day, and the battalion had already suffered thirty casualties during the morning following German mortar fire. The battalion's companies were positioned defensively as follows: from north to south, companies A, C and D, with B Company held in reserve. The 9 Cameronians could follow the evolution of the attack against the 7 Seaforth, to the south, by listening to the sound of the battle and after 4 pm, I./19 arrived in the area around the chateau, south-west of the village, without being detected. C Company was surrounded and I./19 were able to reach the company CP in the village. The carrier carrying the battalion commander, Lieutenant Colonel Villiers, hit a British mine. Unconscious, he was evacuated from the area

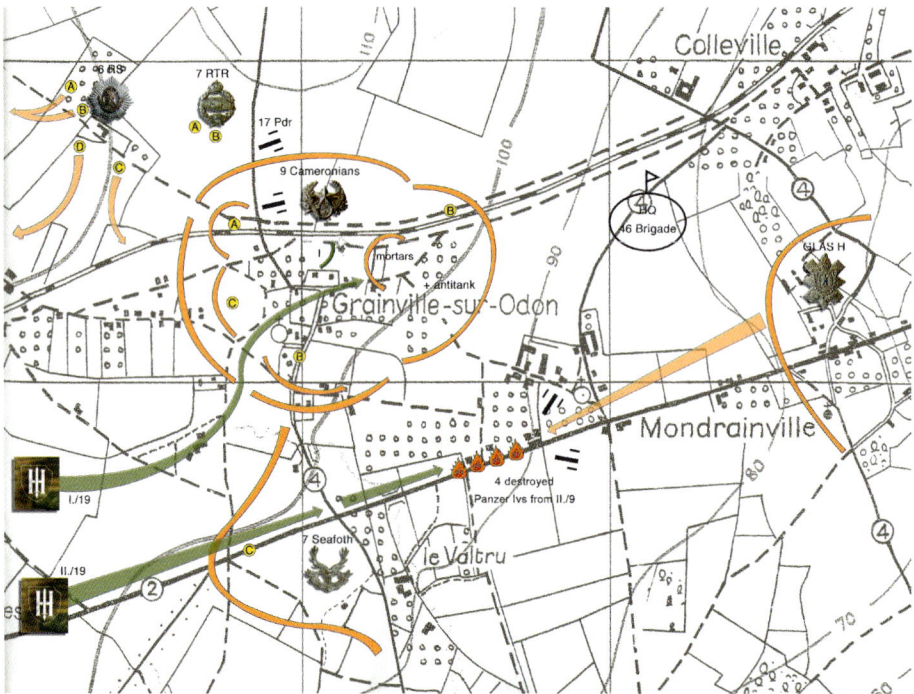

II./19 attacked along the RN175 road towards Mondrainville, starting at 2.30 pm. Its first attack overwhelmed C Company, 7 Seaforth, but was stopped by artillery fire. The second, led by four Panzer IVs, headed for Mondrainville, where the panzers were destroyed by the Glasgow Highlanders. Later, I./19 attacked Grainville, overwhelming the Cameronians' C Company and breaking through as far as the centre of the village, which would remain in the hands of Lieutenant Colonel Villiers' men. The 8th Royal Scots had settled north of the railway the night before and would be attacked by another battalion from the *Hohenstaufen*. (L.K./Heimdal)

and would return to the CP an hour later. The battle was intense, as elements of I./19 managed to infiltrate beyond Grainville and reach the positions of the Glasgow Highlanders. With his three battalions arranged in a triangle, Brigadier Barber's 46 Highland Brigade buckled under the strain. However, their pain was eased after the 43rd Wessex Division took over the eastern flank and the 15th Scottish Division were able to send reinforcements, including the 10 HLI, the 2 Gordons, as well as tanks from the RTR, which were deployed at 8 pm. At the end of the day (11 pm), Brigadier Barber would announce that he had been able to hold all of his positions.

On the left flank, in the area around Brettevillette and Rauray, the attack was carried out by I./ 20, supported by KG Weidinger, against 49 Division's 70 Brigade. The latter had planned to return to the attack on Brettevillette but, faced with the German offensive, the plan was canceled. The German attack, which was also supported by Panther tanks, allowed them to retake Ring Contour 110 and the entire sector south of Rauray. And from there, the *Hohenstaufen Kampfgruppe* continued its advance eastwards, where it would be confronted by another brigade from the 15th Scottish Division; Brigadier Money's 44 Lowland Brigade.

Indeed, until now, the 'Scottish Corridor' had only been supplied by a thin umbilical cord: the narrow road from Cheux, to Colleville, then Tourville. 44 Brigade's mission was to open a second axis, which was made possible by the departure of 8./12 and the capture of Grainville. This second axis would start from the Fontenay/Carpiquet road, and head due south to le Haut du Bosq, before crossing the Salbey, at Hans Siegel's former position (now known as MK IV Woods), to Grainville and the RN175 road. At 5 am the previous day, 8th Battalion The Royal Scots (8 RS), commanded by Lieutenant Colonel Delacombe, prepared to advance towards Grainville, aiming to link up with the Cameronians and secure the new axis. Delacombe advanced with A and B Companies at the front, and B Squadron, 7 RTR, advancing on the left. The 6 KOSB had already positioned itself at le Haut du Bosq, meaning it controlled the crossroads here. The 8 RS eventually set off at around 6 pm and crossed the Salbey before 8.50 pm. It then positioned itself north of Grainville, along with the Churchill tanks of the 7 RTR, where it would spend the night. On this day (29 June), near the railway, it would be confronted by the *Hohenstaufen* and was taken aback by I./20's attack. C Company moved into position along the railway and the 8 RS urgently requested reinforcements from the KOSB at 2 pm. It had been overthrown by the attack of I./19's two companies and was in utter confusion as the 6 RSF supplied reinforcements. The I./20 engaged its SPW flamethrowers and D Company (8 RS) was overwhelmed, retreating back to the chateau at Belleval. The well-trained Germans had broken the British positions with a minimum of resources and casualties, but were then quickly blocked by a curtain of artillery fire: a common feature of the attacks by II. SS-Panzerkorps in this sector. At the end of the day, the *Hohenstaufen* was stopped after having driven a wedge through the British front line between Rauray and Grainville. The Royals of the 8 RS and the 6 RSF were exhausted and, after suffering a number of casualties, were withdrawn from the front and replaced in this area by the brigade's 3rd Battalion; the KOSB.

This general map of operations on 29 June shows the offensive by 9. SS-Panzer-Division *Hohenstaufen* to the west, south of Rauray, on Grainville. The British counter-attack was launched to the east in order to push back SS-Panzergrenadier-Regiment 1 at Venoix and the attack by 10. SS-Panzer-Division '*Frundsberg*', south of the Odon (the bridgehead that had been largely evacuated by VIII Corps), marked the end of Operation Epsom. (L.K./Heimdal)

Insignia of the Frundsberg

The *Frundsberg* at Hill 113

While the *Hohenstaufen* attacked around Grainville, north of the Odon, 10. SS-Panzer-Division '*Frundsberg*', command by SS-Oberführer Heinz Harmel, attacked south of the valley. However, the Germans faced the same problems as the British had done in terms of conveying their units to the front using difficult road networks: the inevitable traffic congestion. The different units were unable to arrive at the lines according to the plan, and Allied aircraft only complicated the situation further, although tree-lined roads favoured the advance of certain units. As the testimony of Monsieur Poissonnier, at Esquay-Notre-Dame, reminds us:

In the morning, I saw some German tanks camouflaged under trees. They seemed to have come from the direction of Avenay, a natural approach that is served by shaded sunken roads. A plane had certainly spotted them because, a few moments later, we came under terrible allied artillery fire. I saw tanks hit by the shells, and soldiers jumping out of the wreckages completely terrified. One of them was seriously wounded in the head and was supported by two comrades. On the doorstop of our house, from which we were driven out earlier, four Germans lay in a pool of blood. Another soldier had been killed in front of our pigsty and I looked at his identity tags: he was eighteen.[3]

Madame Lebreton also witnessed the intensity of the battle from her farm, situated behind Esquay church, at the foot of Hill 112, and her testimony completes that of Monsieur Poissonnier:

> German tanks had been hit. I heard the unfortunate men screaming inside. We fled that day without taking the slightest thing [with us]. At the bottom of Esquay, we came across other German armoured vehicles, as well as a herd of cows that had been gathered together by the German soldiers.[4]

The battle for Hill 112 resumed early in the morning. At 8 am, supported by the 3rd RTR and by a heavy artillery barrage, H Company, 8th Rifle Brigade, once again marched on the Bois Carré, reinforced by three additional infantry sections and heavy machine-guns. German resistance was spirited, but 'by prudent struggle and intelligent maneuvering, slow but firm progress was made.' The small wood was taken and secured in the early afternoon by the 2 Fife and Forfar, which took up position on the eastern slope of the hill. The area would remain in British hands throughout the course of the afternoon, but the arrival of elements from the *Frundsberg* will call everything into question.

The division's attack had first been planned for dawn and then postponed towards noon, as with the *Hohenstaufen*, before it was postponed again until early afternoon. Unfortunately, transmitting the orders was difficult because of the dispersion of units, and the successive postponements could not be reported to all of them. This meant that some elements were put into action in the morning, as had originally been planned, actions that we have seen through the testimonies of Monsieur Poissonnier and Madame Lebreton. Panzers from the *Frundsberg* attacked the area early in the morning, as the testimony of SS-Obersturmführer

Born on 22 February 1906 in Königsberg, SS-Stubaf. Leo-Hermann Reinhold commanded II./SS-Pz.-Rgt. 10. He would receive the Knight's Cross of the Iron Cross on 16 October 1944.

Born on 2 December 1921 in Teschen, in the Sudetenland, SS-Ostuf. Franz Riedel commanded 7./10. He was awarded the Knight's Cross of the Iron Cross on 28 March 1945.

---

3   A. Grandais, *La Bataille du Calvados*, p.184

4   Ibid.

Franz Riedel, commander of 7th Company recalls. The company was equipped with seventeen *Sturmgeschütze* (assault guns) and was followed by Panzer IVs from 5th and 6th companies:

> On 29 June 1944, I received the following order: 'Attack Hill 113 at 07.00 hours and after that Gavrus.' Our forming up zone was situated near Evrecy. My company was to take point and 5th and 6th companies were to be to the right and left rear. I was not informed of that the attack had been postponed until 10.00 due to a delay in the arrival of the panzer grenadiers. All the others were apparently warned on time, but not me. Consequently, I launched my attack at the prescribed hour and my panzers rolled towards my objective, Hill 113 *[south-west of Hill 112]*. At the same time, an English armoured unit *[44 RTR]* with a great number of Shermans advanced across our front. In the blink of an eye, we fired and eleven of these Shermans burned on the hillside. My point tank, commanded by Ewald Menzel, destroyed five of the enemy tanks. We only lost one tank, which unfortunately was that of SS-Untersturm*fü*hrer Hilpert, head of 1st section. He was seriously wounded and the driver, a corporal was killed. As the English were unable to reorganise after the shock of our surprise, we immediately advanced upon them and pursued by us, they rapidly retreated. Our pursuit would have been even more effective had the English not surrounded themselves by smoke. To follow them would have been fatal. At this point I saw a motorcycle sidecar coming towards my tank at top speed. In it was Sturmbann*fü*hrer Leo Rehinhold, who loudly demanded, 'What is the meaning of this farting about?' As the smoke cleared, he saw the burning Shermans and said, more quietly, 'What have you done with these?' After we had explained what had happened, his face lit up at the significance of my success.

The attack by 7./10 was met with the full force of the 44th RTR, which tried to force itself along the road from Esquay to Evrecy. Three tanks from C Squadron, 44 RTR, were destroyed and two others seriously damaged. Several self-propelled guns were also destroyed.

This morning counter-attack shook the point of the British spearhead, although Hill 112 was not recaptured by the Germans in the ensuing confusion, but instead was taken by the 3 RTR. The hill was then peppered by the German artillery and the *Nebelwerfer*, as Major Noel Bell (commander of G Company, 8 RB) recalls:

> Shelling and mortaring commenced, varying in pitch from time to time. Bren Carriers were literally blown off the ground, but there were no direct hits. Our mortars, working with those of H Company, put down a steady stream of fire. Sergeant Hollands continued to operate the mortars until wound by shrapnel. Naish, leaning against a bank above his slit trench, was holding the wireless headphones in his hand, the better to hear any approaching shells, when there was an explosion nearby: shrapnel tore through the Bakelite, leaving only the metal band in his hand.

The tanks pull back behind the Odon

During the night of 28-29 June, the British High Command had discovered some disturbing information; Hill 112 would be rigorously contested by anti-tank guns; a *Kampfgruppe* from the *Das Reich* had arrived to threaten VIII Corps' western flank, while a *Kampfgruppe* from the LAH would threaten its eastern flank. More seriously, however, ULTRA had decoded messages announcing the arrival of II. SS-Panzerkorps in the area. To keep the news secret, it was to go no lower than the commander of the British Second Army, General Dempsey. Aerial reconnaissance also provided valuable information and so in order not let it slip about the decoded messages, it was enough to say that the discovery been supplied through this means. Dempsey conveyed the news to the head of VIII Corps, O'Connor, on the night of 28-29 June, advising him to pull the bridgehead back south of the Odon. This would mean the end of Operation Epsom; only twenty-four hours after the bridgehead had been established! O'Connor was disappointed about suspending an operation in which he had hoped to distinguish himself, and consequently hesitated. At 10 am on 29 June, in a meeting that took place at 15th Scottish Division's HQ, General Roberts learned that the Orne was no longer his objective for the time being. The 43rd Wessex Division would have to strengthen the east side of the offensive, while the 15th Scottish Division would be on the west side (due to the 49th Division's failure), and the 11th Armoured Division would remain at point. Any offensive was currently suspended and present positions had to be maintained. Apparently, the Germans were launching their biggest offensive since the Allied landing.

Major Noel Bell in Germany in 1945 and 1994. On 18 July 1944 he was in commanded of G Company, 8th Rifle Brigade, 11th Armoured Division. (G.B.)

Further to the west, the *Frundsberg*'s counter-attack finally began at 2.30 pm, while the 11th Armoured Division had just taken Hill 112. SS-Panzergrenadier-Regiment 21, one of the *Frundsberg*'s two infantry regiments left Bougy to attack Gavrus, where fierce fighting for the village would take place. Supported by panzers, the Germans finally entered the vicinity after an hour of fighting and SS-Panzergrenadier-Regiment 21 even managed to push the Argylls down into the Odon valley. The assault was supported by the *Sturmgeschütze* guns of 7./10 and 8./10, who provided supporting fire from the area around Hill 113. Following a withdrawal, the 2 Argylls clung to the edge of the plateau by taking cover in the woods and setting up anti-tank guns. Under Allied artillery fire, the position of the grenadiers became difficult to maintain as they tried to support the troops who were threatened with being surrounded. However, SS-Panzergrenadier-Regiment 21 continued its attack towards Baron and the bridge at Tourmauville. At 5.55 pm, 1 Hereford reported the enemy had infiltrated its lines, and five minutes later announced that its company on the right wing had been overrun. At 6.15 pm, 1 Hereford reported that it was holding its position and that the enemy was beginning

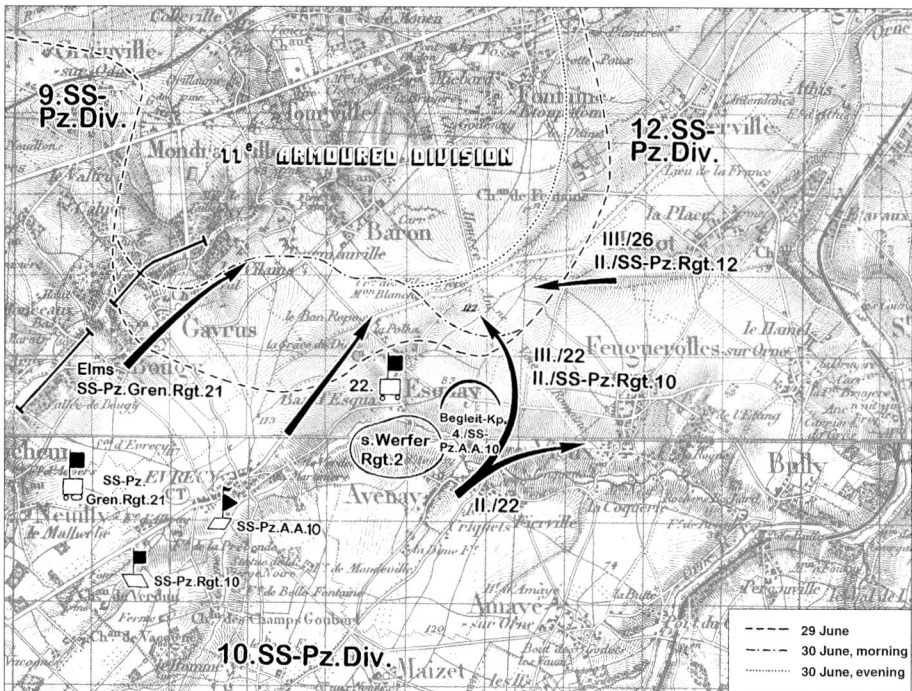

The *Frundsberg* counter-offensive, south of the Odon, on 29 and 30 June 1944. (B.P./Heimdal)

to withdraw, not before it had managed to inflict casualties on a squadron from the 44 RTR with one of its self-propelled guns (StuG), using the woods around Gavrus as cover. At 6.30 pm, the 159 Infantry Brigade reported automatic weapon fire in the woods north of the river, but the situation was under control.

However, in spite of the confusion on both sides, O'Connor took the prudent step of ordering his tank battalions to retreat north of the Odon, leaving behind a few infantry battalions clinging to the bridgehead, as they waited to see how the situation would evolve.

The *Frundsberg*'s night attack

At the end of the day, the only unites that remained south of the Odon were three infantry battalions from the 2 Argyll, 1 Hereford and 4 Shropshire LI, supported by tanks from the 44 RTR. The *Frundsberg* would next re-launch its attack against these elements in the favourable night time conditions. On the division's left wing, SS-Standartenführer Eduard Deisenhofer's SS-Panzergrenadier-Regiment 21 launched an attack which allowed him to reach the southern edge of the hamlet of Les Vilains (1 km north-east of Gavrus, in front of Tourmauville), shortly before 4 am. However, the advance could not be pursued towards Baron due to Allied artillery fire. On the right flank, SS-Oberführer Heinz Harmel launched his other infantry regiment, SS-Panzergrenadier-Regiment 22 (commanded by SS-Sturmbannführer Schulze) against the pivotal objective of Hill 112. This regiment had hitherto been placed in reserve as it awaited its delayed resources. Its first battalion, I./22, arrived from the Evrecy sector and advanced along the road to Caen (passing north of Hill 112). At 1.30 am, it occupied the hamlet of La Polka, near the crossroads located towards the northern exit of Esquay. The companies then positioned themselves north of the road, less than 2 km from Hill 112. The only losses were the result of Allied artillery, as the area had been abandoned by the British. The following morning, the *Frundsberg* would take Hill 112. To the south of the Odon, VIII Corps only held a thin strip of ground in front of Baron, while 2 Argyll constituted a small islet threatened with being surrounded.

German losses are difficult to measure for this day, but they remained steady for the *Hitlerjugend*, which had borne most of the weight of the fighting on Hill 112, as the offensive was essentially devolved to II. SS-Panzerkorps, which attacked in the afternoon. The losses for VIII Corps remained high, amounting to 645 men, of which 88 were killed, 436 wounded and 121 were missing. However, the number of personnel increased to 4,527 officers and 78,732 men.

On 29 June VIII Corps was forced to pull back its tank battalions to the north bank of the Odon following German counter-attacks, thus meaning the failure of Operation Epsom. This photograph by Sergeant Morris, taken on that day, shows General Montgomery sitting on a haystack, with Lieutenant General J.T. Crocker, commander of I Corps, showing him German targets in the area around Caen that were under British artillery fire. This photograph symbolises the end of Epsom. (IWM B 6195)

Rauray, 30 June, 49th Division (1)

The hamlet of Rauray had been recaptured the day before by elements from SS-Panzergrenadier-Regiment 20 (9. SS-Pz.-Div. *Hohenstaufen*) during the counter-attack by II. SS-Panzerkorps. The 49th Division (Polar Bear Division) and tanks from 8th Armoured Brigade were forced to retreat further north. At 3 pm on 30 June, a new attack shook the 49th Division. However, on 3 July, one of the *Hohenstaufen*'s grenadier battalions was forced to retreat after being crushed by the Royal Navy's heavy artillery and that of VIII Corps. Rauray was finally retaken the next day after a final counter-attack by the *Hohenstaufen*, supported by Tiger tanks. During the fighting, 11 DLI lost 200 men and the KG Weidinger also suffered heavy casualties. The following report was made on 30 June by Sergeant Christie.

1. Tanks from HQ Squadron, Nottinghamshire Yeomanry (8th Armoured Brigade). In the foreground is the grave of SS-Obergrenadier Bernhard Zurborg who belonged to III./SS Panzergrenadier-Regiment 26, a HJ battalion which saw action in the area. (IWM B 6218)

2. Formation badge of 49th Division.

3. Formation badge of 8th Armoured Brigade, with a fox's head.

4. Officers consulting a map of the area. In the centre is Lieutenant Colonel Anderson. On the right (in the black uniform) is Lieutenant Colonel Christophenson from the Nottingham Yeomanry (Sherwood Rangers). At the back is Brigadier Crawford, commander of 8th Armoured Brigade, whose insignia can be seen on the shoulder of the officer on the left. (IWM B 6219)

5. Seated on the footboard of a wrecked German car, Private W. Burnett, from Linlithgow (W. Lothian), Scotland, of the 49th Division, writes a letter to his family. On his arm, underneath the 49th Division Formation badge, is the tartan of the Tyneside Scottish, one of 70th Brigade's battalions in this division. (IWM B 6220)

Rauray, 30 June, 49th Division (2)

1. Infantrymen from 49th Infantry Division consolidate their position at the foot of a hedge, protected by Sherman tanks from 8th Armoured Brigade. (IWM B 6225)

2. This Sherman tank crew from 8th Armoured Brigade claimed many panzer victories on 26 June: 2 Tigers tanks, 1 Panther tank and 2 Panzer IVs. From left to right: Sergeant J. Dring, from Grimsby, the tank commander; Trooper Hodkin, from Nottingham; Trooper A. Denton, from Churchill, near Sheffield; Trooper E. Bennett from Fleetwood, Lancashire; L /Corporal S. Gould, from Tamworth in Staffordshire. They are photographed with an armoured vehicle from the Nottingham Yeomanry (Sherwood Rangers), in Rauray, the place of its exploits. (IWM B 6222)

3. Private L. Shaw, from Swinton, near Manchester, was a soldier in the Durham Light Infantry, 49th Division and is seen observing the terrain with a telescope. (IWM B 6227)

2

3

The attack by the *Frundsberg* on Hill 112 is a reminder that elements from the *Hitlerjugend* tank regiment were still in position to the south and east. This interesting photograph, taken on 30 June in the area around Hill 112, shows the crews and officers of II./ 12 who took part in the fighting for Hill 112. 1) Jupp Bieda (H. Walther's driver), 2) Walter Porsch, 3) Herbert Walther, 4) Fritz Freitag, 5) Kommadina. (G.B.)

A close-up image, part of the same report taken on 30 June, shows four sub-lieutenants from II./12. Left to right: SS-Ustuf. Kommadina (battalion communications officer), SS-Ustuf.Porsch (commander of 5./12 following the death of Ostuf Bando), SS-Ustuf. Herbert Walther (battalion aide-de-camp), and SS-Ustuf. Freitag (Engineers, I./12). This picture also shows the diversity of the outfits used: Kommadina wears a jacket cut from Italian camouflaged cloth, Porsch wears a combat jacket for machine-gun crews, while H. Walther wears a leather jacket and Freitag wears the standard camouflaged jacket of the Waffen-SS. All four are wearing *Heer* officer belts. (H. Walther/G. Bernage)

7

The Fifth Day – Friday 30 June

The re-taking of Hill 112

At dawn on 30 June, II./SS-Panzer-Regiment 10 was positioned on its starting line, between Avenay and Vieux. The artillery regiments of the *Frundsberg* and *Hitlerjugend* divisions and the 300 *Werfer* (rocket launchers) from Werfer-Rgt. 2 and 83 (from Werfer-Brigade 8) carried out a powerful artillery attack which crushed Hill 112, where elements of 8 Rifle Brigade were still in their forward positions. Elements of these two German divisions then began their assault on the hill. From Vieux, south-east of the summit, the panzers of II./SS-Panzer-Regiment 10 attacked, along with grenadiers from III./SS-Panzergrenadier-Regiment 22. From Maltot, in the east, panzers from II./SS-Panzer-Regiment 12 and grenadiers from III. (Gep.) / SS-Panzergrenadier-Regiment 26 also moved towards the hill, overrunning the Green Jackets of the 8 RB, who were still dazed by the artillery. B. Zemlitz, a grenadier in III./SS-Panzergrenadier-Regiment. 22 remembers: 'At dawn, the hill was in our hands. There was a lot of loot; the enemy having hastily abandoned the hill following a fierce defence. Our losses were high. We had nine liaison officers at the beginning of the attack; I was the only one left unscathed at the end.' Testimonies from the tank soldiers of the *Hitlerjugend* confirm the speed of the assault, such as that of SS-Unterscharführer Willi Kändler (5./12):

> Very early in the morning, our Werfer rockets screamed over towards the British positions in the 'Kastenwäldchen'. On that morning it was the rockets who determined the success of the attack. It was our fourth assault on Hill 112 and would result in the capture of the small wood and the hill itself. When we arrived, we saw many destroyed vehicles, as well as the wreckages of Sherman tanks.

SS-Oberscharführer Willi Kretzschmar, from the same panzer company, provides a similar testimony:

> The attack moved fast. With no real resistance (unlike the previous attacks), we reached the 'Kastenwäldchen' and Hill 112. We saw ruined tractors, tracked vehicles, anti-tank guns, and Sherman and Churchill tanks. When the situation was clear, I sent our radio operator, Erich Stefan, out to investigate. After exploring the wreckages, he brought back with him boxes of cakes and bars of chocolate and we refuelled ourselves for the next few days of combat.

The summit was taken at 7.30 am, and by noon, the northern slope was in German hands, although they would, in turn, be subjected to Allied artillery.

The alternation of attacks and artillery barrages on Hill 112 meant that it became a veritable 'Norman Verdun', and this course of action would be the general rule in the weeks to come.

Gavrus: the 2 Argyll withdraws

While Hill 112 was retaken by the Germans, pressure continued on the British elements that remained south of the Odon. At 11 am, the 2 Argyll experienced violent mortar fire at Gavrus, particularly D Company, and the battalion's HQ, which was positioned on the approaches to the bridge, north of the Odon, causing heavy casualties for both men and vehicles. The battalion commander, Lieutenant Colonel Tweedie, moved the company to a new position north-east of the bridge, on the plateau above the quarry. However, the mortar fire followed them and it became increasingly difficult to maintain control as they tried to move their men and vehicles. In addition, communications were lost with the other three companies who were in position south of the Odon. Lieutenant Colonel Tweedie reported that:

> My radio linking me to my advanced companies was virtually unusable. The Germans knew our call signs and our frequency waves, interrupting them when we got in touch. D Company and HQ (north of the Odon) had the worst job getting out of the concentrated artillery. At this point, my observation officer and artillery commander, Major Cornwell, was wounded and his radio was destroyed. The equipment we used to keep in

This photograph by Sergeant Laing was taken on 30 June and shows Sherman tanks preparing to attack a German position, sheltered by this large hedge in the Eterville sector (the British term for the area north of Hill 112). These Shermans are from 11th Armoured Division, whose insignia can be seen painted on the rear of one of the tanks. (IWM B 6228)

contact with brigade headquarters was broken as Major Morgan held it in his hands, and was thus rendered unusable. We were then completely out of contact with the brigade.[1]

C Company's fate was no more enviable, to the south of the river. There, after a cold, wet night, followed by a morning with no major concerns, where the main problem was breakfast because there was little food, the battle resumed at 11 am, when mortars were fired against the northern shore. On the previous day, the four 17-pound guns from E Troop, 97th Anti-tank Regiment, which were towed by Crusader tanks and operated by 'blues' with no combat experience, were lost along with two tractors. This happened because C Company's infantry had come under German pressure on the right flank (14 Platoon having been overwhelmed), although 11 Platoon remained at point. By the following day (30 June) C Company's commander, Major McElwee, still had his own 6-pound anti-tanks and held a defensive area south of the Odon, with a company made up of elements from B Company and the remains of C Company (which had partially retreated). At 5 pm, Lieutenant Colonel Tweedie re-established his CP and D Company on the plateau north-east of the double-bridge at Gavrus, but remained exposed to German fire, as we have seen. In light of this situation and the precarious position of those elements that remained to the south of the Odon under Major McElwee, the decision was taken withdraw the men from D Company who had survived the mortar fire, and they retreated to Tourmauville. Two officers who had also escaped the shooting, crossed the river in a chenillette to tell McElwee to withdraw. In his book, the major reports that he refused to withdraw because the officers only had orders from a subordinate tank crew member whom they had met, and he wanted a written order. One of the two officers then replied, 'In God's name, come out of this cursed wood and don't be so pompous.'[2] The last message Major McElwee had received before communications were lost had told him to hold on until reinforcements arrived. He would wait in the Bois de Gavrus for another two hours, before an officer finally gave him the written order he had demanded. McElwee would never consider this retreat as a defeat, but rather as a victory, because 'no one believed that my men and I could come out alive from that wood. And yet, we came out. I retreated in good order with my 203 men and even brought back two anti-tank guns that didn't belong to my company.' The Comtesse de Guitaut and the inhabitants of Gavrus were surprised to find German soldiers after this withdrawal, and the survivors would join the remains of 2 Argyll in Colleville. After four days of combat, the battalion, which had earned the nickname 'bridge sweepers' following its conquering of the bridges at Tourmauville and Gavrus, counted its losses: 33 killed and nearly 160 wounded and missing. The men of 2 Argyll had been the first to cross the Odon, and their withdrawal marked the end of Operation Epsom.

---

1   W. L. McElwee, *History of the Argyll and Sutherland Highlanders, 2nd Battalion* (Reconstituted) (London, 1949).

2   Ibid.

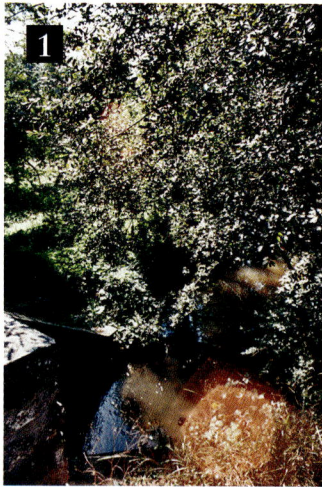

1. The Odon seen from one of the bridges at Gavrus. (G.B.)

2. This photograph was taken by Sergeant Midgeley on 30 June, near Tessel-Brettevillette (west of Rauray) and shows George Couser, from Fernie-Gair (near Hamilton, Lanarkshire), and a small dog that he had found abandoned in Cheux. Gerge Couser was a member of 91 Anti-Tank Regiment, a unit directly attached to VIII Corps, whose insignia can be seen painted on the front of the Jeep. (IWM B 6228)

The *Hohenstaufen* under artillery fire

The end of Operation Epsom was also marked by particularly violent artillery exchanges on both sides. The Green Jackets of the Rifle Brigade had been crushed on Hill 112, just as the Highlanders of 2 Argyll had been in the area around Gavrus. It would be even worse for the *Hohenstaufen* and artillery would now play the leading role in this sector.

At the end of the afternoon on the previous day, III.(gp.)/20 (the third battalion of grenadiers from SS-Panzergrenadier-Regiment 20), mounted on armoured semi-tracked vehicles, and the Panther-Abteilung, (the Panther tank battalion of the tank regiment, 1./9), were gathered in the Bois des Forges ready for an attack on Cheux, when they were crushed by around 100 Lancaster bombers. A gigantic cloud of dust covered the entire area. When it dissipated, the losses among the armoured units proved to be relatively low when considering the intensity of the bombardment. The engines restarted again here and there, and SS-Hauptsturmführer R. Gruber's halftracks managed to extract themselves from the chaos. By the evening, 80 per cent of the halftracks were once more in working order, but the casualties amounted to twenty killed and forty wounded.

The German command also realised that it would not be able to break through. General Geyr von Schweppenburg, commander of *Panzergruppe* West, would only use II. SS-Panzerkorps for limited operations, in order to save time. He considered it essential to keep the panzer divisions in order and to prevent them from being bled dry on the front lines. He even proposed to pull back the units to a defensive line further south, out of reach of the naval artillery, but this was denied by High Command. However, on 30 June, one of the *Hohenstaufen*'s grenadier regiments returned to the attack around 3 pm. On the right was III./19, with II./19 on the left and I./9 in the rear. Third Battalion reached Brettevillette and Queudeville around 4 pm, while 2nd Battalion (with 6th Company) fought in the area 200 meters in front of Rauray. From the start of their attack, the companies came under an artillery barrage and artificial fog that covered a British counter-attack. The battalions retreated. In the area where I./20 were fighting, the artillery killed two and seriously wounded four men. The front line of the *Hohenstaufen* would stop in front of Rauray and in the sector around Grainville, crushed under the field artillery's gun fire, as well as that of the naval guns.

On 29 and 30 June, the *Hitlerjugend* recorded only 56 casualties for both days: 2 wounded on the staff of Regiment 26; 2 wounded in I./26; 3 killed and 1 wounded in II./26; 1 killed and 5 wounded in III./26; 1 killed in the reconnaissance group; 3 killed, 26 wounded and 3 missing in SS-Panzer-Regiment 12; 2 and 8 wounded in the artillery regiment. The total losses for the *Hitlerjugend* Division in both defence and counter-attack throughout Operation Epsom amounted to 1,240 men: 209 killed, 557 wounded and 474 missing. Losses for each day of combat were as follows: 45 killed, 120 wounded, 23 missing on 25 June; 88 killed, 230 wounded, 408 missing on 26 June; 44 killed, 109 wounded and 38 missing on 27 June; 22 killed, 54 wounded, 2 missing on 28 June; 10 killed, 14 wounded, 3 missing on 29 and 30 June. These losses were on average more than three times fewer than those for VIII Corps, which suffered about the same number of casualties for just two days of the offensive and counter-attack.

In contrast, when II. SS-Panzerkorps was attacked on 29 and 30 June, it suffered substantial losses, mainly through artillery fire. Here, the *Frundsberg* Division reported 571 casualties, of which 189 were killed or missing, with the infantry suffering the most, as always. However, SS-Panzer-Regiment 10 suffered the deaths of eight tank crew members, seven of whom died on 29 June. Material losses remain slight, with the same regiment only losing two panzers.

The memorial to the 15th Scottish Division positioned by the road leading to the bridge at Tourmauville. It marks the furthest point reached by the division during Operation Epsom and the 4,042 lives that were lost in the process. (G.B.)

On 29 June, under the blows of the German artillery and II. SS-Panzerkorps, VIII Corps suffered heavy losses: 1,100 men, of which 152 were killed, 706 wounded and 242 were missing. Montgomery's supporters believe that he conceived Operation Epsom to hold the panzer divisions in the Odon and Hill 112 sectors, which, as we have seen, is completely false. He had pushed Operation Epsom after being delayed by the summer storm, while at the same time dreading the arrival of the German reinforcements, including four panzer divisions from II. SS-Panzerkorps, the *Leibstandarte* Division and the *Das Reich* Division. He wanted a race which in two days maximum was to lead him to the Orne and then beyond, through a German front that would have exploded under the pressure. However, a cautious and complex advance, especially by the infantry, would provide time for the *Hitlerjugend* to reorganise and wait for the armoured vehicles of 29th Armoured Brigade on Hill 112, permanently trapping them in an avenue that would become a cul-de-sac, thus allowing the arrival of the German reinforcements. The counter-attack by II. SS-Panzerkorps would also result in a relative failure, since it was only be able to repel VIII Corps, but not destroy it completely. From 26 June to 1 July inclusive, VIII Corps suffered 4,042 casualties, mainly among the infantry, which would later prove costly. The 15th Scottish Division was hit hard by the operation, registering 288 killed, 1,638 wounded and 794 missing. With a total of 2,720 casualties, this represents one quarter of the division's losses suffered during the Second World War. Montgomery would not have infantry numbers needed for Operation Goodwood[3] and would primarily use tanks in this new operation; he would lose half. Operation Epsom was likely to have succeed if it had been launched with energy, according to the principles of Blitzkrieg. Unfortunately, this was not the case, as the British army had not yet embraced these new methods of combat.

---

3   see G. Bernage, *Goodwood*, (Heimdal, 2005)

Stuttgarter Jllustrierte

STADT DER AUSLANDSDEUTSCHEN

1

Das ist V 1

London und Südengland haben seit Wochen erkennen müssen, daß hinter unserer Androhung der Vergeltung Waffen von erheblicher Wirksamkeit stehen. Die erste Vergeltungswaffe ist V 1, die – von Raketen getrieben – schneller als alle gegen sie angesetzten Britenjäger zur Insel fliegt

The retaking of Hill 112

1. The retaking of Hill 112 on 30 June was a symbolic victory for the Germans and allowed them to lock down the Front. 10. SS-Panzer-Division 'Frundsberg' had been engaged in Normandy in the hope of a decisive counter-attack and was finally called to this sector to stop the increasingly critical situation. A war correspondent, SS-KB Apfel, covered the event and his report was published in German newspapers, such as this edition of *Stuttgarter Illustrierte* on 10 August 1944. (B. Jasniak)

2. This article carried the title, 'Attack on Hill 112'. (B. Jasniak)

Sturm auf Höhe 112

2

1 &2. The photographs from this report show grenadiers approaching Hill 112 and looking up at the sky from the roadside ditches, worried by the Allied aerial threat. (Bayeux Memorial Museum)

3. Grenadiers from III./22 (*Frundsberg*) and III./26 (*Hitlerjugend*) approach from the south and south-east to retake Hill 112. The Bois Carré copse, which the Germans called *Kastenwäldchen*, was to the north-east. It would later be called the '*bois des demi arbes*' (half-tree wood) after they were cut down in the incessant artillery fire. At this moment, the terrain appears relatively intact and the grenadiers are seen moving through the wheat. A part of this photograph was published in the *Stuttgarter Illustrierte*.

4. SS-KB Apfel and the grenadiers approach the trees, behind which wounded or frightened infantrymen from the Rifle Brigade are still hiding. The artillery fire from the 300 Werfers were particularly terrifying. The forward artillery fire has ended, as seen by the smoke from behind the trees.

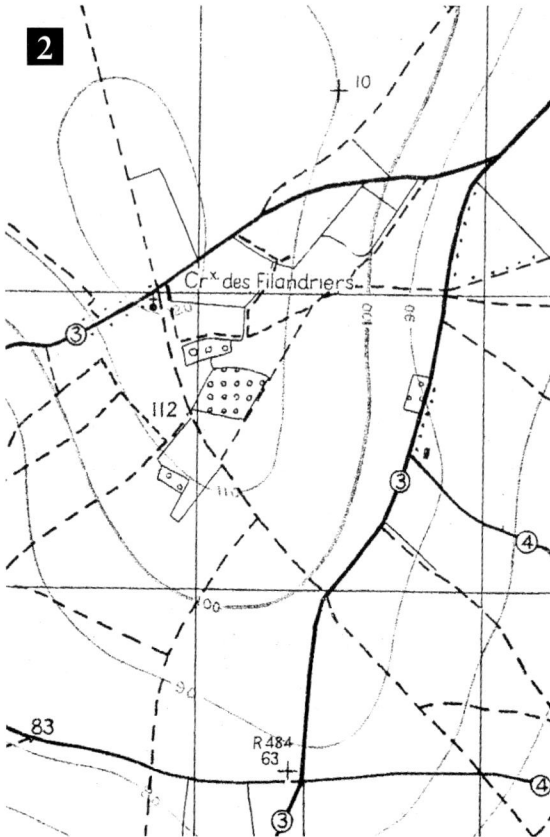

1. The grenadiers rush forward under the protection of the accompanying tanks.

2. This extract from a British staff map shows the location of the Bois Carré and a smaller orchard, north of Hill 112.(B.P.)

3. The grenadiers arrive at the devastated wood and come face to face with a Sherman tank from 3 RTR. (Bayeux Memorial Museum)

4. The report by SS-KB Apfel continues. The grenadiers have reached 8 Rifle Brigade's positions and capture those who have survived the artillery barrage. A Waffen-SS soldier helps a British lieutenant to stand.

1. The grenadiers assemble other prisoners from 8 RB. Here, both the victors and the vanquished are unarmed and the scene looks more like the end of a football match rather than a bloody battle. The fight for this hill would cost the lives of many soldiers, and the adversaries fully respected what each had experienced.

2. A young grenadier, still holding his pistol in his left hand, tries to help another injured British lieutenant.

3. Not everyone had the luxury of being taken prisoner; the numerous corpses providing a testimony to the violence of the artillery fire. (Bayeux Memorial Museum and the Calvados Departmental Archives)

Bibliography

The first French language book to cover the Battle of the Odon in detail was *La Bataille du Calvados*, by Albert Grandais (Editions des Presses de la Cité, 1973). During this time there was an immense wealth of civilian eye-witness accounts available, as well as those of British veterans, which until then had been inaccessible to the French public. In this work, Operations Martlet and Epsom constituted 100 pages of text, but unfortunately, German sources continued to be very meagre, with the exception of Kurt Meyer's book, *Grenadiers*.

In Britain, numerous works devoted to the battalions or divisions involved appeared as early as 1945. These include:

- *The 6th (Border) Battalion, The King's Own Scottish Borderers 1939-1946* by J.R.P. Baggaley (1945)
- *From the Beaches to the Baltic: The Story of G Company, 8th Rifle Brigade* by Noel Bell (1947)
- *The Story of the 23rd Hussars* by G.S.C. Bishop (1946)
- *Borderers in Battle: The War Story of the Kings Own Scottish Borderers* by Hugh Gunning (1948) - - *The Rifle Brigade in the Second World War* by R.H.W.S. Hastings (1950)
- *Operations of Eighth Corps* by G.S. Jackson (1948)

Particularly noteworthy is the *History of the Argyll and Southern Highlanders, 2nd Battalion (Reconstituted)* by W.L. McElwee (1949), whose testimony on the fighting around Gavrus is noteworthy. Other histories were published in later years, but all too often concentrating on a particular unit throughout several operations, with Operation Epsom generally being given a minimal amount of page space. These include:

- *The Fife and Forfar Yeomanry* by R.J.B. Sellar (1960)
- *The Seaforth Highlanders* by J. Sym (1962)
- *The 4th KSLI in Normandy* by Ned Thornburn (1990)

Naturally, there are far too many titles on this particular subject to provide a comprehensive list.

German texts on the subject remained very scarce for a long time, with only Kurt Meyer's *Grenadiers* as the stand out work. The book provided an epic dimension to the role of the '*Hitlerjugend*', but unfortunately gave no indication of losses suffered, which might have led the reader to assume (falsely) that they were high. The testimony of Hans Siegel was quickly circulated, thanks to his success in blocking the centre of the offensive for an entire day with just a handful of panzers. His testimony (of which various versions exist, with slight variations regarding the ending of the engagement) is particularly valuable, both for its detail and clarification of events, but also for his role as the commander of a panzer company. Lastly, the well-illustrated history of 9. SS-Panzer-Division '*Hohenstaufen*' by Herbert Fürbringer (Heimdal, 1984), is a precise and detailed work that formed part of a vast historiography begun by the Germans during the 1970s, often by formers chiefs of staff, who produced highly-documented works based on units that had seen action in Normandy. An example of this is 12. SS-Panzer-Division '*Hitlerjugend*', whose detailed history was written by its former chief of staff, Hubert Meyer, and first published in German in 1982 and then in French in 1991. It is a particularly good source for those studying Operation Epsom. Other books (in French) on German units involved in Operation Epsom include *Panzer-Lehr-Division* and *21 Panzer Division*, by Jean-Claude Perrigault and *10 SS-Panzer-Division* by Jean-Luc Leleu, all published by Editions Heimdal.

Two recent British books offer a detailed study of Operation Epsom, being particularly rich in British sources and testimonies, as well as using extensive German sources. *Operation Epsom* by Tim Saunders (Pen & Sword, 2003) provides a guide to the battlefield in addition to interesting information and maps. Ian Daglish's *Over the Battlefield: Operation Epsom* (Pen & Sword, 2007) is the result of extensive research and fieldwork carried out with British veterans. The use of numerous 1944 aerial reconnaissance maps used by the British Army allows the reader to locate the combat areas precisely. There is little overlap between the two books, with each complementing the other nicely.

For the French reader, the *Bataille du Calvados* remains a useful text. Well-illustrated, the contemporary photographs complement the text, while the modern photographs allow the reader to visualise the locations accurately.

German, Waffen SS and UK Army Ranks

The following table shows equivalent ranks between the German Army, British Army and the Waffen SS. Please note that not all ranks have a direct equivalent. American ranks will be similar to British ones.

German Army	Waffen SS	British Army
Gemeiner, Landser	Schütze	Private
	Oberschütze	
Grenadier	Sturmann	Lance Corporal
Obergrenadier		
Gefreiter	Rottenführer	Corporal
Obergefreiter	Unterscharführer	
Stabsgefreiter		
Unteroffizier	Scahrführer	Sergeant
Unterfeldwebel	Oberscharführer	Colour Sergeant
Feldwebel		
Oberfeldwebel	Hauptscharführer	Sergeant Major
Stabsfeldwebel	Hauptbereitschaftsleiter	
	Sturmscharführer	Warrant Officer
Leutnant	Untersturmführer	Second Lieutenant
Oberleutnant	Obersturmführer	First Lieutenant
Hauptmann	Hauptsturmführer	Captain
Major	Sturmbannführer	Major
Oberstleutnant	Obersturmbannführer	Lieutenant Colonel
Oberst	Standartenführer	Colonel
	Oberführer	Brigadier
Generalmajor	Brigadeführer	Major General
Generalleutnant	Gruppenführer	Lieutenant General
General	Obergruppenführer	General
Generaloberst	Oberstgruppenführer	
Generalfeldmarschall	Reichsführer-SS	Field Marshal